## Praise for *Discover* *in Your Birth Chart*

"Mitchell provides clear, straightforward guidelines and rules for determining the essential character of a person...The fruit of his thorough research is a simple and elegant way to quickly determine fundamental personality traits. The many dozens of example charts bring the ideas to life, and the reader is provided with practical information that can be applied to any chart consultation or reading. Mitchell has done the hard work to sort out how the chart patterns introduced by Marc Edmund Jones actually work in the lives of people, and we are the beneficiaries."

—David Cochrane, founder of Cosmic Patterns Software and cofounder of the Avalon School of Astrology

"Saying that a book 'belongs on every astrologer's bookshelf' has become a painful cliché, but in this case it's not praise, it is actually prophecy—that is where this helpful volume is destined to wind up."

—Steven Forrest, author of *The Inner Sky*

"Whether you are new, inexperienced, advanced, or a pro, this very well-written book is going to be the modern, go-to reference for patterns used in horoscope analysis."

—Basil Fearrington, author of *The New Way to Learn Astrology*

"*Discover the Aspect Pattern in Your Birth Chart* is a fantastic book...Glenn puts chart patterns into easily understandable English...He goes step by step through dozens of these patterns. What I love the most is how he does a very thorough job describing and defining the important focal planets in each pattern...Truly this book is a great asset to all astrologers because it allows the astrologer to see the bigger picture of a natal chart before looking more deeply into the chart itself."

—Alphee Lavoie, NCGR Level IV Certification

"This is a useful book that addresses a vital but neglected skill among many astrologers—recognition of natal chart patterns and their interpretation...The scope of Mitchell's book is such that, between his coverage of shape and aspect theory and a generous number of chart examples, the reader is given everything necessary to develop pattern recognition as a critical skill in the modern astrologer's toolkit."

—Alan Annand, author of *Stellar Astrology*

Discover the

# ASPECT PATTERN

*in Your*

BIRTH CHART

# About the Author

Glenn Mitchell (Tallahassee, FL) is an astrologer with more than thirty years of experience and a PhD researcher in public health policy. He studied with the Faculty for Astrological Studies in London and has been mentored by several renowned astrologers, including David Cochrane, Kathy Rose, and Noel Tyl. He is also a certified expert in Astro*Carto*Graphy by the James Lewis Sladen Foundation (aka the Continuum).

In addition to doing natal consultations, Mitch maintains a blog at www .NewAgeAstrologer and videos at the NewAgeAstrologer YouTube channel. He is in demand as a popular conference speaker and has written articles for multiple astrological journals.

Feel free to reach out to Mitch at gmitchel850@yahoo.com.

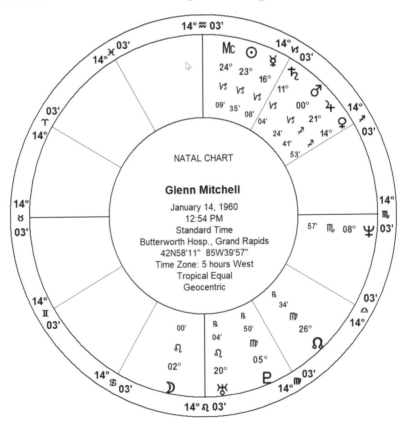

NATAL CHART

**Glenn Mitchell**

January 14, 1960
12:54 PM
Standard Time
Butterworth Hosp., Grand Rapids
42N58'11" 85W39'57"
Time Zone: 5 hours West
Tropical Equal
Geocentric

GLENN MITCHELL

*Discover the*

# ASPECT
# PATTERN

*in Your*

## BIRTH CHART

A Comprehensive Guide

Llewellyn Publications
Woodbury, Minnesota

FIRST EDITION
First Printing, 2020

Cover design by Kevin R. Brown
Interior illustrations by the Llewellyn Art Department
The astrology charts in this book were created using the Kepler Superb Astrology Program, with kind permission from Cosmic Patterns Software, Inc., the manufacturer of the Kepler program (www.astrosoftware.com, kepler@astrosoftware.com).

Llewellyn Publications is a registered trademark of Llewellyn Worldwide Ltd.

**Library of Congress Cataloging-in-Publication Data**
Names: Mitchell, Glenn, author.
Title: Discover the aspect pattern in your birth chart : a comprehensive guide / by Glenn Mitchell.
Description: First edition. | Woodbury, Minnesota : Llewellyn Worldwide, [2020] | Includes bibliographical references and index. | Summary: "This is a basic guide on how to interpret planetary and aspect patterns in a natal astrology chart"—Provided by publisher.
Identifiers: LCCN 2019051219 (print) | LCCN 2019051220 (ebook) | ISBN 9780738762883 (paperback) | ISBN 9780738763316 (ebook)
Subjects: LCSH: Birth charts. | Natal astrology.
Classification: LCC BF1719 .M58 2020 (print) | LCC BF1719 (ebook) | DDC 133.5/4—dc23
LC record available at https://lccn.loc.gov/2019051219
LC ebook record available at https://lccn.loc.gov/2019051220

Llewellyn Worldwide Ltd. does not participate in, endorse, or have any authority or responsibility concerning private business transactions between our authors and the public.

All mail addressed to the author is forwarded but the publisher cannot, unless specifically instructed by the author, give out an address or phone number.

Any internet references contained in this work are current at publication time, but the publisher cannot guarantee that a specific location will continue to be maintained. Please refer to the publisher's website for links to authors' websites and other sources.
Llewellyn Publications
A Division of Llewellyn Worldwide Ltd.
2143 Wooddale Drive
Woodbury, MN 55125-2989
www.llewellyn.com
Printed in the United States of America

*To my wonderful and supportive wife, Lillian.*
*To my mentors, David Cochrane, Kathy Rose, and Noel Tyl.*
*With gratitude to the Faculty of Astrological Studies.*

# Contents

## Chapter 24: Tying It All Together ... 277

# Charts and Figures

## Chapter 9

## Chapter 10

## Chapter 11

## Chapter 12

# Acknowledgments

There are many individuals to whom I am indebted for their insights and assistance. I thank each and every one of you. I feel blessed to have such kind, generous, and understanding friends, family, and colleagues. I will name a few individuals who were there when this book was just an unproven concept. They encouraged me to start and finish the manuscript for this book. Robert Booton, Martina Erskine, Micho Frost, Aria Gmitter, Silvia Pancaro, Eleni Saatsoglou, and Scott Silverman—thank you one and all.

The charts for this book were generated with Sirius 3.0 from Cosmic Patterns Software. Sirius isn't only a great piece of astrology software; it also includes the complete Astro Databank data collection in its database. The one exception is the chart for Dustin Hoffman in chapter 24. That chart was generated with Solar Fire 9 software. Chart searches were also done with Solar Fire 9. Screen captures and the editing on multiple figures were done with Techsmith's Snag-It! 2019 software.

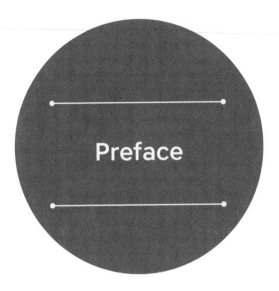

# Preface

Marc Edmund Jones wrote about planetary patterns back in 1941. *The Guide to Horoscope Interpretation* remains the seminal work on the topic. Since it is long out of print and written in a style that some find difficult to read, I've undertaken the task of updating and extending Jones's ideas.

Originally published in 1980 under the title *Perceptions in Astrology*, Bil Tierney's work is equally a classic for the study of aspect patterns. Updated in 1983, it became *Dynamics of Aspect Analysis: New Perceptions in Astrology*.

The two topics—planetary patterns and aspect patterns—intersect and intertwine. The ideal Bucket planetary pattern, for example, contains a Grand Cross aspect pattern.

There's a myth among some astrologers that it takes hours to prepare for a consultation with a client. Those astrologers pride themselves on giving every chart the attention to detail they feel it deserves. Unless we have the good fortune to find celebrity clients willing to retain our services, we need to work more efficiently than that. We need to summarize the information in a natal chart quickly and reliably, in a matter of minutes, not hours. Yes, it can be done that fast and—more important—it can be done well.

I've had the good fortune to be trained by the noted astrologer Noel Tyl. He told me from the first lesson that I was to spend no more than fifteen minutes preparing for a consultation. To get to that point, you have to master the art of chart synthesis. You need to be able to glance at a natal chart and drink in gulps of information.

This book is not a quick reference guide. It's a text for the serious student of astrology. It's aimed at the intermediate to advanced student. Jones felt the need to start with the very basic question "What is a horoscope?" I assume the reader already knows the answer to that question.

When it comes to style, I prefer a more conversational tone than what is found in the average astrology text. Be prepared for plenty of contractions. The occasional sentence fragment, too.

It takes more than a little chutzpah to rework the ideas of someone with the standing of Marc Edmund Jones or Bil Tierney. Rest assured, there is more to this book than a rewording of those classics. Even if you own *The Guide to Horoscope Interpretation* or *Dynamics of Aspect Analysis*, you'll find plenty of new information here.

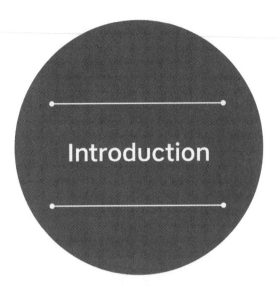

# Introduction

Planetary combinations come in two broad categories: *planetary* patterns and *aspect* patterns. Planetary patterns describe the distribution of planets around the natal chart: how and where they cluster. Examples include the Bowl, the Bucket, and the Splay. They were the focus of Marc Edmund Jones in *The Guide to Horoscope Interpretation*. Aspect patterns describe three or more planets in configurations that result from multiple aspects between the planets. For example, the Grand Trine results from three trine aspects forming an equilateral triangle. Other examples include the T-Square and the Yod. They were the focus of Bil Tierney in *Dynamics of Aspect Analysis*.

The *stellium* is the odd pattern to place. Arguments can be made for placing it under planetary patterns or under aspect patterns. It's a very compact pattern with a profound influence on the client. That's one point for inclusion under planetary patterns: a stellium can be composed of only a few conjunct planets within a single sign or house. A point for including the stellium with aspect patterns is that the other planets could be distributed almost anywhere around the chart. Stelliums appear under aspect patterns in this book. And, yes, I know that technically the plural form should be *stellia*. If and when this book is translated into Latin, that can be corrected.

The division of people and their charts into eight basic planetary patterns might seem insufficient at first. However, astrology does a lot with small taxonomies. Look at all the meanings we derive from just twelve zodiac signs, twelve houses, ten planets, four elements, three modes, etc.

The simple point is this. These eight basic planetary patterns provide beginner and expert alike with a rapid method for entering the natal chart with confidence. The temperaments we've come to associate with each planetary pattern provide us with immediate psychological insights. For sure, there's more to the natal chart than these eight basic planetary patterns. Additional Information that might turn our initial assumptions on their heads is available when we delve deeper into the chart. We use planetary patterns only as a quick introduction, one to begin a meaningful dialogue with the client. For example, we see that the planets are splashed all around the chart. We assume the client might be "scattered" and then we act on that assumption. We proceed to ask the client about those moments of feeling scattered. From there, we have a helpful dialogue: a dialogue where the astrologer can offer strategies to overcome that feeling. When we begin a consultation with an observation that rings true with a client, they immediately begin to relax. We've demonstrated our bona fides.

Jones discussed seven basic patterns. I'm extending that to eight with the Fan shape (sometimes called the Sling pattern). I'm also adding information that simply wasn't available at the time that *The Guide to Horoscope Interpretation* was written. Astrology from a person-centered, psychological approach has advanced since 1941 (or even 1968, the time of the book's reprint). Plus, we now have data based on the thousands of charts of public figures and mundane events in Lois Rodden's Astro Databank (www.astro.com/astro-databank) to answer questions like "How common are these different planetary and aspect patterns?"

I also diverged from Tierney's list of aspect patterns. I noted already the inclusion of stelliums. Another example is Thor's Hammer. In addition, I excluded the Grand Sextile. My search of the Astro Databank turned up only three individuals with a Grand Sextile, making it too idiosyncratic to include.

I've included plenty of examples for each chart pattern. These are all individuals well known to English-speaking audiences. The criterion I used was quite simple: only AA, A, or B Rodden ratings were considered (with a preference for AA ratings). This is a conventional standard for astrological research. "AA" means a birth certificate or birth record from a hospital is in hand. "A" means the birth data came from memory of a parent or someone closely associated with the birth. "B" means the birth details came from a biography. With only one or two prominent exceptions, other birth charts are considered too unreliable to use.

Tierney included retrograde and unaspected planets in his work. I've done the same. These are "bigger bells" that can be seen with a quick glance at the natal chart. I've also included a chapter on planetary imbalances that covers hemispheres, quadrants, elements, and modes. In addition, there are chapters for the most elevated planet, the leading planet, and planets on the Aries Point, each a powerful influence that can be spotted in an instant.

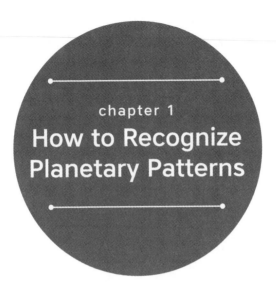

## chapter 1
# How to Recognize Planetary Patterns

A natal chart must be seen as a whole before an intelligent understanding of its parts is possible. Cookbook delineation is always possible using whichever astrology text lies close at hand. The problem with the cookbook approach is the absence of context. The Sun might lie in Aries, for example. The cookbook delineation will report the typical attributes for the Aries Sun, but the expected personality traits for the Aries Sun might not manifest for the individual client before us. Other features in the natal chart might instead be more powerful influences over the individual's psychology.

What is a planetary pattern? It's quite simply any distribution of planets around the birth chart that makes a recognizable shape. We'll be exploring eight basic planetary patterns in this book: the Splash, the Bundle, the Fan, the Bowl, the Bucket, the Locomotive, the Seesaw, and the Splay. These patterns reflect basic psychological drives. They suggest an individual's characteristic response to the world.

In her book *The Art of Chart Interpretation*, Tracy Marks says that not all birth charts have planetary patterns. Fewer still have clearly defined patterns. She goes on to say that when the pattern is not obvious to the eye, the pattern is less likely to be important in the overall interpretation of the natal chart. In her book *Aspect Patterns,* Stephanie Clement disagrees with the statement that the absence of a planetary pattern is quite rare.

Just how common are the eight basic planetary patterns we'll encounter in this book? We can turn to the Astro Databank for an answer. The Astro Databank contains many thousands of natal charts for notable individuals around the world. While generalizing from notables to everyone is perhaps a stretch, there's no reason to believe that notable individuals are any more likely to have a readily discernible planetary pattern than the rest of us. The chart search feature for the Solar Fire 9 astrology software includes the eight basic planetary patterns we'll encounter in this book. The results are tabulated in the following chart.

| Planetary Pattern in Natal Chart | Percentage |
|---|---|
| The Splash | 0.59 |
| The Bundle | 1.54 |
| The Fan | 2.93 |
| The Bowl | 10.42 |
| The Bucket | 7.58 |
| The Locomotive | 31.25 |
| The Seesaw | 13.89 |
| The Splay | 15.63 |

The empirical truth lies between the observations of Marks and those of Clement, as 83.92 percent of all charts in the Astro Databank collection possess one of the chart patterns we'll explore in this book.

In each chapter devoted to a particular pattern in this book, you'll find descriptions that identify the individual planetary pattern. You might find that none of the planetary patterns resemble the natal chart in front of you. That could just mean that particular chart falls in the 16.08 percent of charts that don't match any of these basic planetary patterns. That is, after all, one chart in six (approximately).

Marc Edmund Jones applied very specific criteria to distinguish the different planetary patterns. Still, when we examine actual birth charts, the boundaries between these planetary patterns can become blurred. A practical example is the distinction between the Bowl pattern and the Bundle pattern.

Here we see the natal chart for Al Jardine, an original member of the Beach Boys (figure 1). His chart pushes the boundary for the Bundle shape with Uranus and Mercury forming a partile trine. That keeps all of the planets within the space of a single trine, a requirement of Jones's definition of the Bundle shape.

There's a point where the boundary between the Bowl and the Bundle becomes blurred. What if Al Jardine's Mercury was at 10 Libra 30 instead of 4 Libra 30? If we rigidly applied Jones's definition, we would no longer have a Bundle pattern. Nor would it meet the criteria for the Bowl pattern, since that requires the chart be divided in half by the distribution of planets. Would we then relegate this birth chart to the shapeless category?

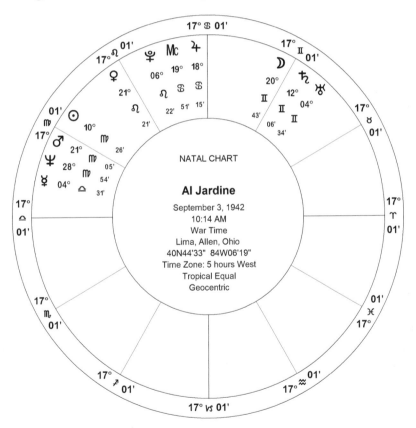

Figure 1: Al Jardine

The situation is analogous to choosing orbs for aspects. There is no absolute right or wrong answer. A few degrees wide of the mark for a particular planetary pattern and most astrologers will conclude it still falls within the same planetary pattern. What if a single planet falls way outside of the Bundle pattern, for example? The astrologer must then rely on practical experience to inform their judgment, not the rigidity of a mathematical specification. When in doubt whether a planetary pattern applies, a few discerning questions posed to the client can help sort it out. Our goal is to fit the proper planetary pattern to the client, rather than the client to the planetary pattern.

Ideal planetary patterns are rare. Flexibility is required to determine when conditions are sufficiently satisfied for a particular planetary pattern. For example, a major condition for the Bowl pattern is a rim opposition. The leading and trailing planets are separated by 180°. (Leading and trailing planets here refer specifically to the planetary pattern and not the conventional definitions of leading and trailing planets from natal interpretation, i.e., the planet that directly precedes the Sun clockwise.) What are we to make of an even distribution of planets that span just 165°, an aspect that Noel Tyl refers to as a quindecile? Do we dismiss the chart as an example of the Bowl pattern? Most astrologers would conclude, "No." Such a planetary pattern resembles the Bowl shape more than any other shape and—more important—better than no shape at all. We would likely assume the psychology associated with the Bowl shape applies and proceed to ask questions of the client to confirm our hunch.

It's important to remember the purpose of planetary patterns: quick and reliable delineation. They serve as a useful guide to chart interpretation because they have broad application and provide immediate, credible insight into a client's basic psychological orientation.

There is the occasional chart that makes us pause and consider. Instead of having the attributes of a single planetary pattern, it instead has attributes from multiple shapes. In that case, we need to fall back on discussion with the client to determine which traits apply.

There will often be aspect patterns present within planetary patterns. Aspect patterns are recognizable shapes that form from multiple aspects. An example is the Grand Trine, which is the product of three individual trine aspects. Aspect patterns are examined in greater depth later in this volume, but they will be noted in context here, too. For example, the ideal shape of the Bucket pattern includes a Grand Cross aspect pattern.

A word of caution before we proceed. Only the ten planets are considered when we talk about planetary patterns. Most astrologers include the North Moon Node (and maybe the South Moon Node as well) in their natal charts. Some include the Part of Fortune. The same is true for asteroids and for planetoids like Chiron. These are all significant chart features, but they play no role in defining planetary patterns.

## High-Focus Planets

Most planetary patterns have one or more high-focus planets. These are generally the planets that the eyes are drawn to when we examine the natal chart.

Several of the planetary patterns include a high-focus planet. Obvious examples include the handles for the Fan and Bucket patterns. Less obvious examples include the leading and trailing planets for the Bowl pattern. We will cover the high-focus planets in detail, as they can come to dominate the chart.

High-focus planets are another way that planetary patterns lead us into the natal chart. Robert Jansky called these planets "high focus" because planetary patterns immediately focus our attention upon these planets, once we become familiar with the pattern. Marc Edmund Jones used the term *focal determinator* for high-focus planets.

Any of the ten planets can be a high-focus planet. Their interpretation is done with customary astrological delineations: we consider the nature of the planet, its mode of expression by sign, and its area of focus by house.

Aspects to a high-focus planet can have added significance. They can offer convenient energy release mechanisms for the high-focus planet. Lance Carter is a noted astrologer on radio, in newspapers, and on the internet. He corresponded with Jones while doing his own research. Carter notes that these "aspects show the special tendencies, habits, unique attitudes, and personal characteristics of the client" (Carter 2010, 21).

The farther that a chart pattern and especially its high-focus planet(s) is from the ideal, the weaker or more diluted the effect will be upon the client.

Salvador Dali possessed a Bowl pattern chart (figure 2). Two planets stand out: the planets that form the rim of the Bowl's shape. In Dali's case, that's Uranus and Neptune.

The high-focus planet(s) is/are the most significant planet(s) in the individual's chart.

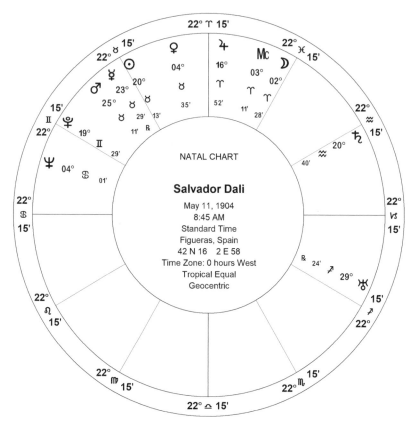

Figure 2: Salvador Dali

Uranus is the leading planet (sometimes called the cutting planet) in the Bowl pattern in Salvador Dali's chart, as it is the first planet to cross the Ascendant as the chart is rotated clockwise. It's the most compelling planet in the chart. Neptune is the trailing planet, as it crosses the Ascendant last. Neptune is also highly significant in the chart. The nature of the leading planet and the trailing planet make a major difference when interpreting the Bowl pattern.

The presence (or absence) of an opposition between the two rim planets strengthens (or weakens) the Bowl pattern's influence.

These rim planets determine the character of the Bowl pattern. The Bundle pattern and the Locomotive pattern also possess rim planets.

A planet alone or separated from the others in a hemisphere is a singleton planet. The handle of the Fan or the Bucket pattern is a singleton planet. The singleton is a natural high-focus planet.

There are secondary factors that guide the astrologer to planets of secondary focal emphasis.

High-focus planets can be subject to hard aspects. When that's the case, extra care is required in the delineation. Hard aspects can be motivating when handled properly.

According to Lance Carter, high-focus planets that are retrograde in the natal chart might demonstrate their influence on the individual in a more personal way. Events might occur prematurely. Things might not go according to plan. Flexibility and personal dedication are required. Even then, the individual might not have great success until later in life.

## The Sun as Focal Planet

The keyword for the Sun as high-focus planet is *assertion*. These individuals possess great confidence. They need to act with purpose, perform acts that fulfill their potential, and use willpower to shape situations to their advantage. When the Sun is in a position of high focus, the individual is in an excellent position to fulfill their goals.

Natural leaders with a regal bearing, these individuals almost always seem to be in charge regardless of the situation. Not lacking in self-confidence, they frequently assume they know what's best for everyone. This can be a delusion.

When the Sun is badly aspected or poorly positioned, the individual can be erratic. When things go wrong, they can become anxious or hot-headed. Exercise and sports can help them blow off steam. Meditation can help center them.

## The Moon as Focal Planet

The keyword for the Moon as high-focus planet is *feeling*. According to Robert Jansky, great intensity of purpose and drive is characteristic of these individuals. Everything they do has a purpose. They bring a great deal of energy to anything they attempt.

Individuals with the Moon in high focus can be too sensitive for their own good. They can be emotionally high-strung, with moods that are easily swayed by events. The mind can be unsettled, shifting quickly from thought to thought. Decisions can depend on how the individual feels at the moment.

They have the ability to relate to almost anyone in an intimate manner. They must guard against a tendency to manipulate people, however. They might have manipulated their parents as a child. Since they are highly sensitive to the emotional environment around them, the Moon as high-focus planet enables them to influence events to bring out the best for everyone.

Some have a deep-seated need to be taken very seriously. This can cause them to demand the complete attention of others.

Reacting on the basis of their emotions is common. They can feel compelled to take a stand without a lot of thought. This can land them in trouble.

### Mercury as Focal Planet

The keyword for Mercury as high-focus planet is *reason*. These individuals feel compelled to act intelligently and to reason their way to solutions. Direct and forthright, their comments can sometimes hurt the feelings of others. They should resist the impulse to say whatever comes to mind.

Effective communication is typical when Mercury is the dominant planet in a natal chart. Their mind is their greatest tool to gain control over life's circumstances.

They can think and act quickly, but they need to guard against acting too rashly. It's fine to learn from mistakes. However, mistakes can be costly when made too often. Sufficient thought needs to go into any decision.

Flexibility is important when Mercury is powerfully placed in a chart. Life's circumstances might change many times during a lifetime, so it's best not to get too attached to any one particular way of thinking, relating, or acting.

Mercury retrograde individuals march to the beat of a different drummer. They are their own person. Their thinking might be on a different level from that of others around them. Misunderstandings, short tempers, and careless actions can be recurring issues in their lives. Accidents can be common, so they need to take great care concerning their environment.

### Venus as Focal Planet

The keyword for Venus as high-focus planet is *relationship*. Venus as the most influential planet inspires the individual to search for a lover, mate, or spouse who can complement them. They need to bond with someone in an intimate way to feel fulfilled. They come on to a potential partner in a very intimate fashion.

Venus as the most influential planet encourages them to act creatively and to enjoy sensual pleasures.

Social standing is a preoccupation. Nice clothing and fine jewelry are prized, since these validate their personal worth. Beautiful things require a profession that provides the necessary resources to buy them.

These individuals require cohesion between the people they care for. They need to belong. Disunity with or among people around them makes them unhappy.

When Venus is direct, self-love leads to love of others. Joanne Wickenburg argues that Venus retrograde reverses the process. Individuals are unable to appreciate their own self-worth until they evaluate their life in relation to others. Self-love results from comparison. Stated differently, their sense of self-worth comes from without rather than from within.

## Mars as Focal Planet

The keyword for Mars as high-focus planet is *initiative*. As Jansky notes, these individuals seem to rise to any challenge and have the ability to persevere in the face of great adversity.

These are individuals who are not afraid to take chances. Their pioneering spirit often places them at the forefront of their profession. They're able to accomplish tasks that others might consider impossible.

They can shock others by their impulsive nature. They can rashly rush into dangerous situations. They need to cultivate caution.

These are individuals who thrive on controversy. They're likely to quarrel until they get their way or until everyone gives up. This can have negative consequences for interpersonal relations. They need to learn there's a place for competition and a place for compromise. If they want to work with others in the long run, they need to look for opportunities to compromise.

Mars retrograde enhances the assertive, combative, "me first" impulses. There can be a tendency to go too far in an attempt to get what they want. This tendency needs to be dialed back for positive, long-term relations to develop. Control issues are common when Mars is retrograde. The individual can become obstinate and unbending in their effort to maintain control. Anger management issues are also common when Mars is retrograde.

## Jupiter as Focal Planet

The keyword for Jupiter as high-focus planet is *enthusiasm*. Life is an adventure for these individuals. They have spontaneous urges to experience all life has to offer.

They're interested in everything. An important life lesson for them is learning to narrow the scope of their attention. Specialization makes them ready for advancement and promotion to greater responsibilities.

A powerfully placed Jupiter can lead to overindulgence. Because things tend to come easily, they can become lazy. They need to learn to tame their desires and maintain a strong work ethic.

These are individuals who know what the right thing is to do. It's not enough to make a significant profit if it's accomplished by questionable means. Prestige is important, too.

Jupiter as a strong planet contributes luck and opportunities. It takes more than luck and opportunities to succeed, however. The individual also needs to know what to do when opportunities arise.

When Jupiter is retrograde, its expansive tendencies begin to exceed realistic limitations. The urge for expansion must be tamed. Jupiter retrograde also suggests that what society considers an opportunity might not be consistent with the individual's inner needs.

Jupiter retrograde urges the individual to reject society's philosophical systems. They will instead want to define their own philosophies, their own sense of morality, their own perspective on religion, etc.

## Saturn as Focal Planet

The keyword for Saturn as high-focus planet is *discipline*. These individuals feel compelled to act responsibly.

Establishing long-range goals is typical when Saturn dominates the natal chart. Marc Edmund Jones characterized these individuals as willing to sacrifice short-term advantage for the achievement of long-range goals.

The establishment of personal reputation and professional standing is a typical Saturn influence. These individuals don't let problems stand in the way.

They confront them head-on and solve them systematically. They might not see immediate results, but they accept that they're in the thick of things for the long haul. They see themselves as survivors who can make it.

These are individuals who don't take the easy way out. They choose difficult tasks as a way to refine their skills and discipline their talents.

These individuals need to develop their competency in specific skills and learn the limits of their talents.

A powerful Saturn retrograde inclines the individual to be strongly influenced by society's rules. Saturn's messages of responsibility and conscientiousness are powerful influences. Strong authority figures are greatly influential.

## Uranus as Focal Planet

The keyword for Uranus as high-focus planet is *independence*. These are individuals who tend to be seekers of new truths, willing to try the new and unproven in order to discover something better or more meaningful.

They'll tend to position themselves at the forefront of change. Uncommon ideas can lead them far afield from more conventional points of view. Their actions might be condemned as wild or radical.

They're self-willed and independent. With Uranus providing the main clue as to why they're sometimes iconoclastic, its location in the chart indicates where those attitudes are likely to be felt.

Uranus retrograde attracts unstable, unexpected, or chaotic experiences. The urge to create change and reform is heightened when Uranus is retrograde.

## Neptune as Focal Planet

The keyword for Neptune as high-focus planet is *imagination*. These individuals tend to be dreamers capable of generating insights and discoveries when they develop the willpower to act and carry out their plans.

They can be extremely idealistic about what they want from life. They can be in love with the whole wide world. Inclined to dream about life, they're not necessarily ready to live an active life. Highly sensitive, they can feel overwhelmed by life's responsibilities and its harsh realities.

There can be a tendency to try to escape from reality by using psychotropic drugs or alcohol.

Neptune retrograde intensifies Neptune's function. The unconscious is stimulated and dream activity is often intensified. Everything that Neptune represents becomes an issue in the individual's life.

### Pluto as Focal Planet

The keyword for Pluto as high-focus planet is *transcendent*. These individuals need to get to the root of social problems. Unlike the revolutionary tendency of Uranus, Pluto works to solve problems a bit at a time through the application of everyday common sense.

With Pluto as a major influence, these individuals might see the worldwide implications of what they do on a personal level. Joining with other like-minded individuals helps them feel they are making a difference.

When Pluto has great authority in a natal chart, the individual will be obsessed with living life to the fullest. They develop a compelling vision of what they want to accomplish and know how they're going to go about doing it. They feel they're fulfilling a destiny.

The flip side of lucid moments of self-actualization is depression over what they can't accomplish and who they can't be.

Pluto's goal is to create global evolution. Individuals with Pluto retrograde see the need for global change more objectively than do those with Pluto direct.

## Classification of Patterns

The eight basic planetary patterns can be organized into two broad groups: the bipolar group and the tripolar group.

The bipolar group includes the Bowl, Bucket, Fan, and Seesaw patterns. The geometry of these patterns allows only for the slight possibility of a Grand Trine. T-Squares and oppositions are frequent in these patterns. The tendency is to form two distinct planetary groups centered about two points of focus or just one solid group in one hemisphere of the natal chart.

The tripolar group includes the Locomotive, Splay, Bundle, and Splash patterns. Their basic geometry is that of the trine (120°). For all except the Bundle pattern, there exists the possibility of a Grand Trine

## The Splash Pattern Preview

The planets are fairly evenly distributed around the chart wheel in the Splash shape. A chart free of planet clusters is rare, however. More common is the sort of pattern we see in Paula Abdul's chart (figure 3). Several of the planets are splashed around the chart, while others cluster together in the same houses.

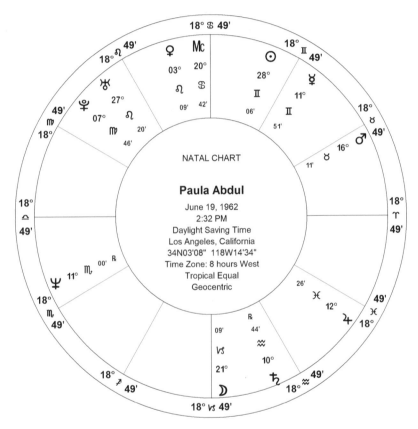

Figure 3: Paula Abdul

Individuals with a Splash shape fall into one of two temperaments: they develop a well-rounded personality with a diverse set of interests or they tend to get spread too thin, too scattered about.

Paula Abdul appears to have fallen into the former category, demonstrating a wide range of creative talents. She's a successful singer, dancer, choreographer, and talent show judge.

## The Bundle Pattern Preview

The planets all lie within the space of a trine in the Bundle shape. It's quite common for a stellium of planets (an aspect pattern discussed in depth in chapter 11) to appear within the Bundle shape.

Individuals with the Bundle shape tend to have a narrow scope of interests. They're noted for their special skills and expertise.

The chart for Olympic downhill skier, and entrepreneur Jean-Claude Killy is a classic example of the Bundle shape pattern, where the planets stretch from 3 Gemini 23 to 3 Libra 03 within the space of a single trine aspect (figure 4).

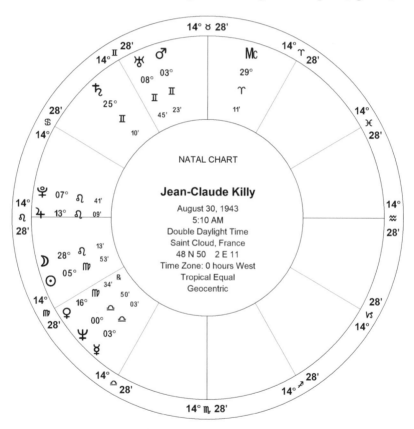

Figure 4: Jean-Claude Killy

## The Fan Pattern Preview

The Fan shape, sometimes called the Sling shape, augments the Bundle shape with a planet opposing the center of the bundle of planets. This opposition serves as a handle and assumes great importance when we interpret the planetary pattern. There is a strong duality between the handle and the cluster of planets.

Richard Branson is an English business magnate, investor, author, and philanthropist (figure 5). His natal chart is typical of the Fan planetary pattern.

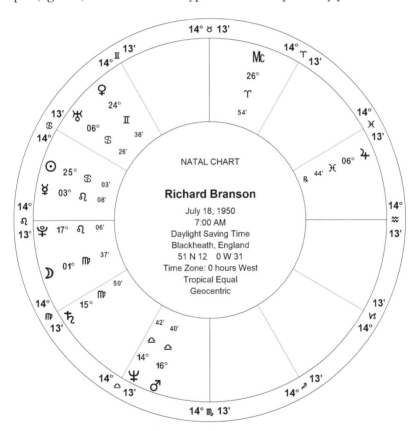

Figure 5: Richard Branson

## The Bowl Pattern Preview

The Bowl shape is among the easiest to identify. It is also among the most common shapes. All of the planets are evenly distributed within a hemisphere of the chart. In the textbook case, the two rim planets form an opposition.

The Bowl individual is a self-contained person. Able to remain calm in the midst of turmoil, they're able to finish tasks they've begun.

The chart for author and poet Elizabeth Barrett Browning has a wide rim opposition between Moon and Venus (figure 6).

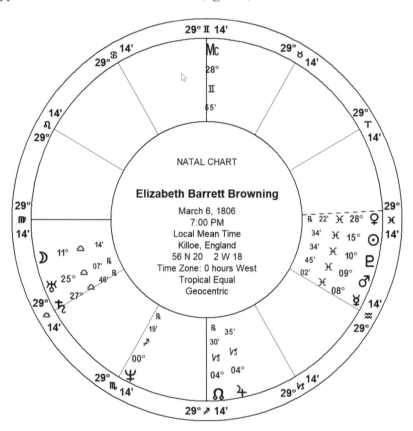

Figure 6: Elizabeth Barrett Browning

## The Bucket Pattern Preview

In the ideal Bucket shape, we start with a Bowl planetary pattern and add an isolated planet that forms an opposition to the center of the Bowl shape. As with the Fan shape, the handle of the Bucket shape assumes great importance. The concentration of energy is high in the Bucket shape.

The presence of a T-Square or Grand Cross in the Bucket shape adds organization and structural strength.

The birth chart of Napoleon I is typical of the Bucket shape (figure 7). While the rim planets don't form an opposition, Uranus in the handle is widely opposed Jupiter.

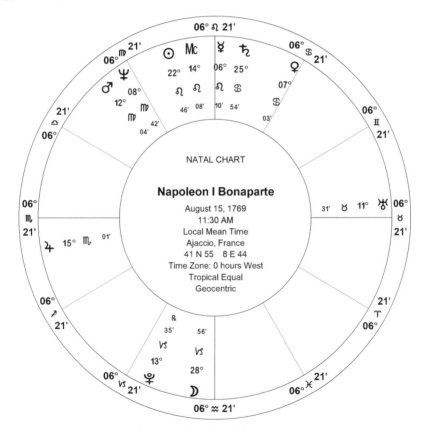

Figure 7: Napoleon I Bonaparte

## The Locomotive Pattern Preview

The Locomotive shape occurs when the planets are evenly distributed around two-thirds of the natal chart. The dynamic imbalance between the occupied portion of the chart and the unoccupied part lends power to this pattern.

These individuals are able to design their own destiny and fulfill it.

Former President Jimmy Carter possesses a Locomotive planetary pattern (figure 8). Eight of the signs are occupied with planets, six between the Jupiter-Pluto quincunx.

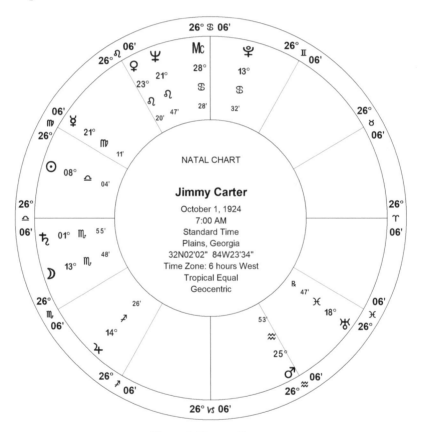

Figure 8: Jimmy Carter

## The Seesaw Pattern Preview

The Seesaw pattern occurs when two groups of planets roughly oppose each other.

Life can be a continual balancing act when the Seesaw shape is present. The individual can expect shifting situations and will need to be flexible about their priorities.

These individuals can be either a team player or the go-it-alone type.

The classic Seesaw shape is evident in the natal chart for playwright Noël Coward (figure 9).

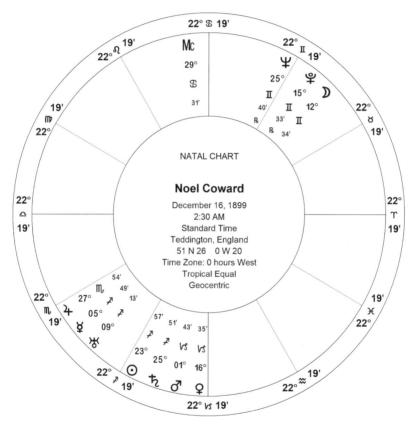

Figure 9: Noël Coward

## The Splay Pattern Preview

The Splay planetary pattern is sometimes called the Tripod shape. The distribution of planets is neither even nor symmetrical. The planets cluster into three distinct groups.

Splay pattern individuals often have an agenda in life that others don't understand.

Lord Byron's natal chart possesses a Splay shape (figure 10).

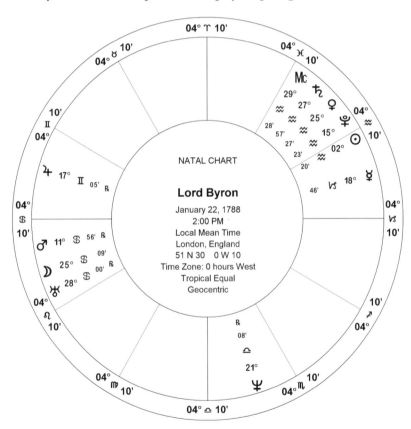

Figure 10: Lord Byron

chapter 2

# The Splash

We will start with the least well-defined planetary pattern: the Splash. When the planets are distributed evenly or "splashed around" the natal chart, we have a Splash pattern.

It is important to note at the outset that the Splash pattern is not some sort of catch-all category. We don't use the Splash pattern just because we can't find a better pattern to classify a chart. It's the rarest of the planetary patterns. As Robert Jansky notes, there are only a few days in a typical year when the Splash pattern is possible. Some years it's not possible at all. You won't find a Splash pattern, for example, in years when a Bundle pattern is possible.

## The Ideal Splash Pattern

The ideal form of the Splash pattern contains five pairs of oppositions, with no two planets in the same sign or house. Two empty houses or signs are also not adjacent to each other. The order of the planets is irrelevant.

The natal chart for songwriter, composer, conductor, and arranger Henry Mancini is a near-ideal example of the Splash pattern (figure 11). Mancini won four Academy Awards, a Golden Globe, and twenty Grammy Awards. Plus, he won a posthumous Lifetime Grammy Award. He was generally known as one of the greatest composers in film.

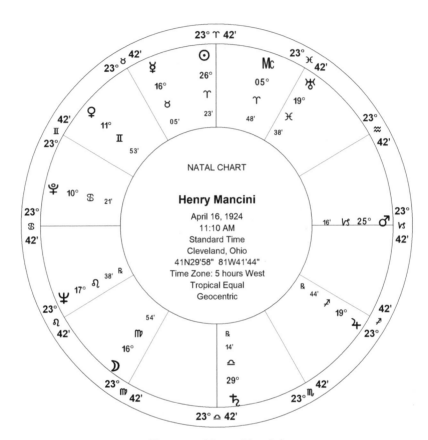

Figure 11: Henry Mancini

With the exception of two planets in the tenth house, each planet in Henry Mancini's chart is found in a different house. Each planet is also in a distinct sign. A Splash pattern like Henry Mancini's that lacks at least one conjunction is rare. Add a second conjunction and it becomes extremely difficult for the chart to form a Splash pattern, since two conjunctions leave us only six more planets to fill out the Splash pattern.

The Splash planetary pattern can blur into three other patterns: the Locomotive, the Seesaw, and the Splay. When you can reasonably choose between the Splash and one of these other patterns, Marc Edmund Jones advised readers to lean against the Splash. The other patterns, he argued, provide more information about the individual to the astrologer.

When approaching a possible Splash pattern, we start with the widest open area between two planets in the chart. We know that if the planets were evenly distributed around the chart, each would be separated by 36°. As the chart begins to differ from that ideal, the planets begin to cluster. If they form a single cluster, the pattern begins to morph into a Locomotive pattern as the open space approaches 120°. Two widely separated clusters and the pattern approaches a Seesaw pattern. Three widely separated clusters and the pattern comes to resemble the Splay pattern.

If you use uneven houses in your natal charts, be careful not to just count the open houses. You need to pay attention to the amount of open space when identifying the Splash pattern. The house cusps can confuse your eyes. A common aspect pattern with the Splash shape is the Grand Trine.

## The Splash Pattern Temperament

What are we to conclude when we see a Splash planetary pattern?

At its best, the Splash pattern can describe an individual who demonstrates a capacity for genuine, universal interest. No other pattern has broader general competency. These individuals are able to do many things well. Jansky said they can be tempted to believe they are especially "gifted" or "fit" for dealing with any kind of situation that comes along.

Don't expect the Splash individual to limit their interest to a single calling or profession. They "splash" their attention and effort in multiple directions. These are the sorts of individuals who make their mark in multiple areas of life.

A wide variety of aspects and aspect patterns are possible in the Splash pattern. An abundance of oppositions, trines, and squares can provide the individual with a multitude of influences and opportunities. Aspect patterns like T-Squares and Grand Crosses can reduce the tendency of Splash individuals to scatter their efforts. So, too, can Grand Trines, especially when they contain the Sun or the Moon.

At its worst, the Splash pattern can mean that the individual is "scattered" in their interests, a Jack of all trades and master of none. This can lead to a general waste of their talents. What's lacking in the Splash pattern is a high-focus planet.

## Counseling the Individual with a Splash Pattern

There have been great achievers with the Splash pattern. What they share is a set of widespread interests and a well-rounded personality.

Individuals with a Splash pattern are especially well suited to management positions. Not only can they draw on their own skills to see their projects through to completion, but they can leverage the talents of a diverse group of individuals as well.

The education that best suits the Splash pattern is one of balance: general enough to provide the individual with a wide range of life experiences and focused enough to provide the necessary skills for a successful career. The Splash individual might change majors in college multiple times as new directions and opportunities arise.

The Splash individual should be encouraged to explore multiple hobbies and pastimes. They will not only provide lifelong satisfaction but will also boost self-confidence.

Focus can be a challenge. It's essential that it be learned if the Splash individual is to make a meaningful contribution in life. Some individuals charge off in all directions at once. They can end up getting nowhere fast. They might know a little about everything, but that knowledge needs to be put to practical use.

If the individual has trouble with focus, then a measure of discipline is required. They need to gather their thoughts and organize them. Meditation can help center the Splash personality.

Too much confidence can cause its own problems. Individuals can feel they can do anything they want at any time. This can cause them to become overextended. The desire to please everyone can cause the Splash individual to become spread too thin. They can accept tasks they can't complete.

The Splash individual needs to learn and accept their limitations. Because they undertake so many projects, they can expect some failures and unfulfilled attempts. They need to avoid deceiving themselves (and others) about their limitations. They need to recognize that their talents have limits. Great achievers accept the challenges they're capable of meeting but don't overstep their abilities.

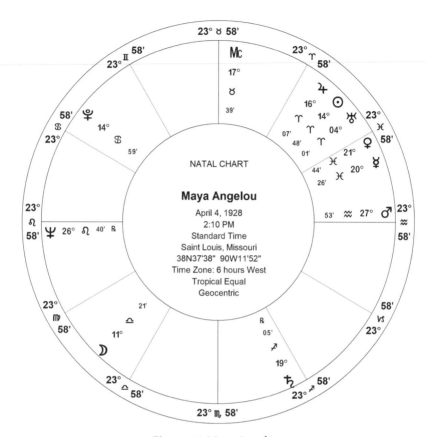

Figure 12: Maya Angelou

Famous writer and poet Maya Angelou has a chart and life that fits the definition of the Splash very well (figure 12). The ten planets occupy eight signs and
seven houses. They're scattered evenly around her chart. Maya Angelou possessed a diverse range of creative talents. She was so much more than a writer
and a poet. She was also a lecturer, an actress, and a dancer.

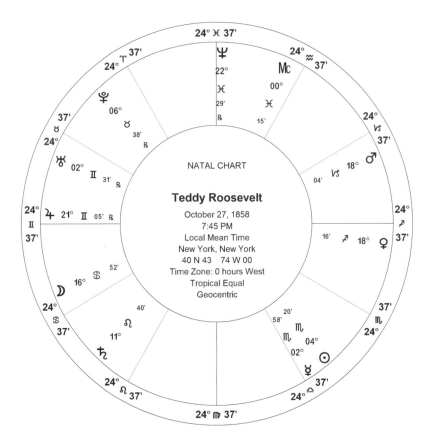

Figure 13: Teddy Roosevelt

The chart of US President Theodore "Teddy" Roosevelt has planets in eight of twelve signs, reflecting his diversity of interests (figure 13). There are also two T-Squares present in the pattern: one between Jupiter opposed Venus with Neptune at the apex and the other between Pluto opposed Sun-Mercury with Saturn more widely at the apex.

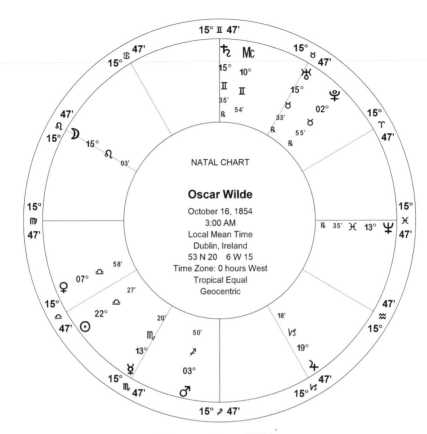

Figure 14: Oscar Wilde

The chart of celebrated author, poet, playwright, and journalist Oscar Wilde also shows a Splash pattern containing a T-Square aspect pattern (figure 14). In his case, the Moon is the apex planet with Mercury-Uranus in opposition. This T-Square goes a long way to explaining the sensitive, eccentric nature of Oscar Wilde. Biquintile aspects are also evident, marking his creative genius.

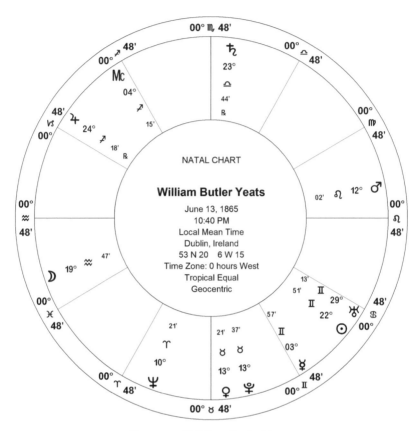

Figure 15: William Butler Yeats

The Splash pattern in the chart of William Butler Yeats could be confused for a Splay pattern, with the wide Moon-Mars opposition forming a Bowl section and then Jupiter and Saturn forming legs of a tripod (figure 15). There is an Air Grand Trine in Yeats's chart involving the Sun, Moon, and Saturn. If we're willing to accept a wider orb, then a second Air Grand Trine is present with the Moon, Saturn, and Uranus.

chapter 3

# The Bundle

Next among the planetary patterns is the Bundle pattern. With the Splash pattern, we looked at the most diffuse pattern. Now we look at the most compact pattern.

Marc Edmund Jones and Robert Jansky both claimed that the Bundle is the rarest planetary pattern. We know from the Astro Databank data that the Splash is the least common planetary pattern, not the Bundle. The Bundle occurs approximately three times as often as the Splash.

Jansky preferred the name Wedge pattern. He argued that all ten planets concentrate their energy to a point, as does a wedge.

Jansky also noted another remarkable quality of the Bundle pattern. He argued it could be called the Magnetic pattern. Bundle-type individuals often have the ability to draw others to them through a kind of personal magnetism. The more tightly bunched the planets, the stronger the personal magnetism. When these individuals become prominent celebrities, they have the ability to draw many fans.

## The Ideal Bundle Pattern

In the ideal Bundle, the planets are distributed within the space of a trine. This often involves a stellium, although the presence of a stellium does not guarantee the Bundle pattern. A stellium can be found within several planetary patterns.

The birth chart of Paul McCartney is a near-ideal Bundle shape (figure 16). The angular separation between Neptune and Venus is a little more than a trine. Paul McCartney certainly possesses the personal magnetism that Jansky described. Neptune is the trailing planet, imparting musical prowess. Venus as the leading planet is preoccupied with beauty and creativity. We'll see with the charts of Igor Stravinsky and Ringo Starr how Neptune tends to be a high-focus planet in the charts of accomplished musicians.

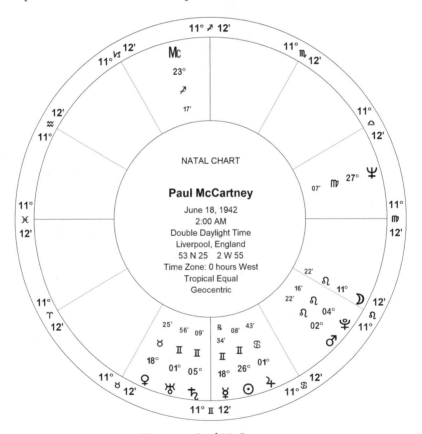

Figure 16: Paul McCartney

Jansky suggests that an allowable orb of 10° is reasonable for the occupied area of a Bundle pattern. Any occupied area wider than 140° falls under the Bowl pattern. Any area narrower than 120° precludes the possibility of a trine. Very few charts with a Bundle pattern lack the defining trine.

The angular separation between the two rim planets determines the strength of the Bundle pattern's influence. The rim planets themselves determine the character of the Bundle pattern.

There's no possibility for any oppositions in the Bundle pattern. The individual must supply their own dynamic drive and direction rather than rely upon the natural disposition that an opposition gives.

The lack of a trine in the Bundle pattern can leave the individual with an inability to handle the challenges of life. What talents they do possess will be reflected in sextile and quintile aspects.

The Bundle pattern for Paul McCartney includes two high-focus planets: Venus and Neptune. These are the two rim planets. Venus is the leading planet, as it is the first planet that crosses the Ascendant as the chart is rotated clockwise. It's the most prominent planet in the pattern. Neptune is the trailing planet, as it crosses the Ascendant last. It's not quite as powerful as the leading planet, but it's still very influential and needs to be considered in the interpretation of the Bundle pattern.

### The Leading Planet

The leading planet is the high-focus planet in the Bundle pattern. These individuals will always bring much of their drive and energy to bear upon it. The energy the planet provides will assume great importance in life. For example, if the Moon is the leading planet, then emotional energy will likely define the Bundle individual. How the energy gets expressed will be dependent upon the sign of the leading planet. Where it gets expressed in the life of the individual will be determined by the house location.

A careful inventory of the aspects to the leading planet is crucial. Each aspect will affect its expression. Look especially for squares to the leading planet. Squares add dynamic drive to the leading planet. Their absence suggests a more passive individual.

The trailing planet is second in importance in the Bundle pattern.

### The Trigger

Because the Bundle precludes a T-Square, Grand Cross, or Grand Trine, the square aspect assumes greater importance. When there is only one square aspect, it automatically qualifies as the trigger. If there is more than one square aspect, the square coming closest to 90° becomes the trigger. By planet, sign, and house, the trigger reflects the individual's drive and motivation. As Jansky notes, when the trigger includes the leading planet, we find a more dynamic and driving individual.

### The Thrust

I noted that the planets in the ideal Bundle pattern occupy a trine aspect. The midpoint between the leading planet and the trailing planet shows the ultimate thrust in life, the long-term objective (or destiny) of the individual (figure 17).

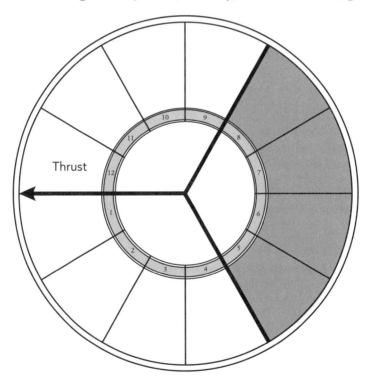

Figure 17: The Thrust of the Bundle Pattern

No planet occupies the point of thrust in the Bundle pattern. This is what distinguishes the Bundle from the Fan pattern: the absence of a handle planet. It was the point of thrust from the tip of the occupied trine that caused Jansky to prefer the name Wedge instead of Bundle for this planetary pattern.

The sign and house of the thrust from the Bundle pattern show how and where the long-term objective will be revealed.

## The Bundle Pattern Temperament

What immediate conclusion do we draw when faced with the Bundle pattern?

We might assume that because the planets are bunched together in the Bundle pattern, the individual will have a narrow focus of interests. This can be the case with this planetary pattern at its worst. More typical is a concentration of attention and energies in pursuit of a handful of interests. The individual is likely to develop special skills and expertise and then organize their time selectively.

The Bundle individual does not depend on external validation from others. As Jansky notes, they tend to be "self-obsessed with their own capacity" (Jansky 1977, 47) and do not seek or require much in the way of feedback. Their willingness to go it alone can give them a pioneering spirit. They might become leaders because they follow their own inner beliefs.

Individuals with the Bundle pattern can appear inhibited. This comes from the value they place on their own life and time. They often develop a well-integrated world about themselves in which they can function with great efficiency. They have the ability to draw and integrate others into their world. Should they gain sufficient prominence and attention, the Bundle type can become a magnetic leader and impose their will upon others. Benito Mussolini is one such egregious example.

Jansky notes that Bundle individuals have a very marked ability to make much from very little. The Bundle will almost certainly contain a number of sextiles, and sextiles represent opportunities. Bundle individuals have the ability to capitalize on each opportunity as it materializes and use it to maximum advantage.

Individuals with the Bundle pattern tend to be self-starters. They require no special supervision or support from others.

Quintiles aspects, which are commonly found in the Bundle pattern, suggest creative bursts of inspiration and creativity.

## Counseling the Individual with a Bundle Pattern

Bundle individuals can develop universal concerns. This can lead to the belief that what's good for them is good for everyone else. They can become self-righteous and develop an autocratic style, like Benito Mussolini (figure 18).

Bundle individuals can earn recognition for their work by perfecting their special talents. They will go further if they limit their efforts to areas that exemplify their special expertise rather than spreading their attention to lots of different interests, as someone with a Splash pattern is wont to do.

Being aware of alternatives gives these individuals the freedom to choose different paths through life. If they allow themselves to be boxed in, they'll miss opportunities. They need to learn to leave themselves options so they can back out of situations that would trap them.

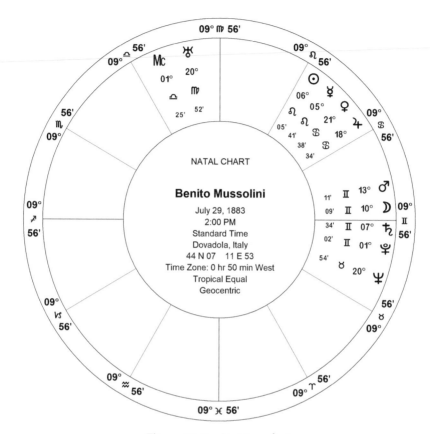

Figure 18: Benito Mussolini

Benito Mussolini's natal chart is frequently used to illustrate the Bundle pattern (figure 18). Neptune as the leading planet forms a near-perfect trine with Uranus as the trailing planet. Mars in a loose square with Uranus forms the trigger for the pattern.

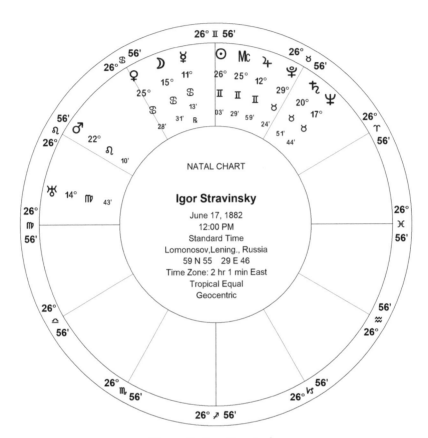

Figure 19: Igor Stravinsky

The chart of Russian composer, pianist, and conductor Igor Stravinsky contains Neptune and Uranus as the rim planets, with Neptune as the leading planet (figure 19). Uranus is also emphasized as the trailing planet. Stravinsky was one of the greatest innovators in music. Some of his work was so innovative that members of the audience walked out of initial performances.

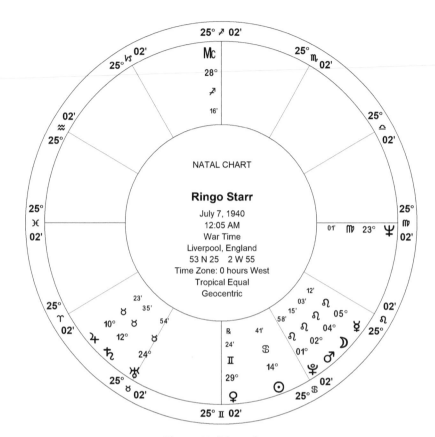

Figure 20: Ringo Starr

The chart for Ringo Starr is a typical example of a Bundle pattern (figure 20). The rim planets are Jupiter and Neptune (music). The angular separation between Jupiter and Uranus is wider than a trine, even slightly wider than Jansky's recommended 10° orb.

Ringo Starr's Bundle pattern possesses a powerful four-planet stellium in Leo in the fifth house, all in the space of just 4°.

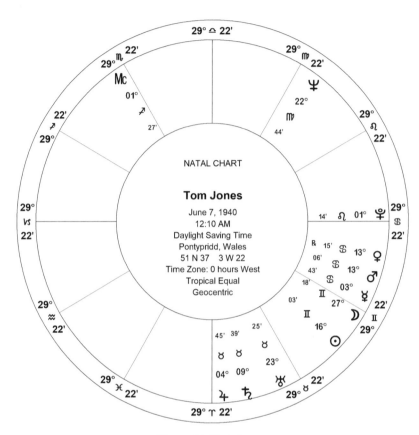

Figure 21: Tom Jones

Tom Jones is another singer with Neptune as the trailing planet and Jupiter as the leading planet (figure 21). Jansky argues that the orb is too wide between the leading and trailing planets in this case. While the orb is 17°59', I would still classify this as a Bundle pattern. It is only the trailing planet that's an outlier. I would start with the assumption of a Bundle personality and ask guided questions of the client to rule the Bundle pattern in or out.

chapter 4

# The Fan

The Fan pattern resembles the Bucket pattern. Both possess a handle planet. The difference between the two is that the Bucket pattern is a Bowl pattern with a handle planet, while the Fan pattern is a Bundle pattern with a handle planet. This modification to the Bundle pattern causes a change in the basic Bundle temperament to the point that it becomes a very distinct pattern.

The Fan pattern was overlooked by Marc Edmund Jones. Robert Jansky also overlooked it in the first edition of *Planetary Patterns* in 1973. His revised edition in 1975 included the pattern.

We might expect the Fan pattern to be rarer than the Bundle, but the opposite is the case, with the Fan pattern occurring almost twice as often as the Bundle pattern.

## The Ideal Fan Pattern

The Fan pattern takes its name from a hand fan with the blade of the fan covering an area of approximately one-third of a circle (120°) It is a Bundle pattern where the handle of the fan extends perpendicular to the center of the blade.

The Fan pattern shares features with both the Bundle and the Bucket pattern.

The two planets on the rim of the Fan pattern ideally will be in trine to one another.

There is no possibility of a rim opposition among the planets in the blade portion of the Fan. There should, however, be a core opposition between the handle planet and an anchor planet located on or close to the midpoint of the blade.

The Kite aspect pattern is possible within the Fan planetary pattern (figure 22). A Kite occurs when the nine planets in the blade form a Grand Trine with a pair of sextiles (60°) at the base of the triangle. The tenth planet forms a core opposition, to form the Fan's handle. As Jansky notes, when a Kite aspect pattern occurs, all ten planets form a tightly knit group "with the energy represented by each planet well integrated into the total makeup of that individual" (Jansky 1977, 70).

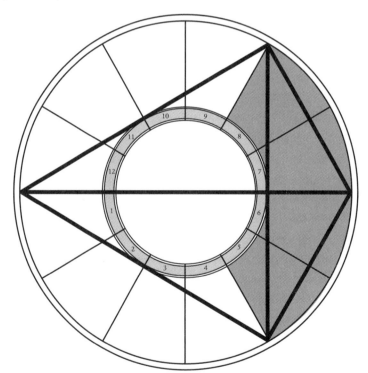

Figure 22: The Kite Aspect Pattern

The ideal Fan pattern is quite rare. The Fan pattern itself, not so rare. As the pattern departs from the ideal, we will no longer find the Kite aspect pattern within.

Jansky classifies the Fan pattern as bipolar, even though a Grand Trine is a possibility. Presumably the reason for excluding the Fan pattern from the tripolar group is the relative unlikelihood of those conditions occurring. As Stephanie Clement argues, the Fan incorporates many features that are tripolar in nature.

When the handle planet is less than a sextile away from one of the rim planets, the natal chart might instead be a Bowl pattern. The closer the orb of the leading planet and the trailing planet to a sextile with the anchor planet, the more effectively they work together.

As the blade narrows, the thrust of the blade planets become psychologically more intense. The greater the deviation of the handle planet, the greater is the frustration in accomplishment felt by the individual. Also, the greater the deviation, the less likely we are to find square aspects. A lack of squares means the frustration experienced by the individual is interpersonal in nature. Frustration comes from the environment and people with whom the Fan individual must deal in their immediate environment.

## The Fan Pattern Temperament

Lance Carter contends that the Fan pattern is a form of the Bucket pattern. He dedicates only two pages to the pattern. Jansky, in comparison, provides an entire chapter. Clement also devotes an entire chapter to the pattern.

The basic psychology of the Fan pattern is to seek out and use the resources of others for personal fulfillment. The leading and trailing planets mark off a 120° section of the natal chart that reveals the limits of the personality and how the outside world perceives the individual. The entire thrust of a Fan planetary pattern is toward the point in the open area of the chart opposite this midpoint, along what Jansky calls the "thrust axis."

It's the handle planet that must be kept foremost in mind. Its energy has great bearing on the character and temperament of the individual. Usually there is some separation between the blade's thrust axis and the handle planet in a Fan pattern. This is particularly significant when the thrust axis and the handle planet are in different signs and/or different houses.

The handle planet is the point of energy input in the Fan pattern. This is the opposite of the handle planet in the Bucket pattern. The handle planet in the Fan pattern is at the center of everything the individual is trying to accomplish. Rather than directing their energy outward through the handle, the Fan individual uses the handle planet as a source of support through which they satisfy their needs.

Individuals with the Fan pattern have a strong sense of directed activity. As Jansky says, they have "a highly directed method of approaching each situation as it occurs in life" (Jansky 1977, 72).

There is an intense sense of lack of those things represented by empty signs and houses.

Fan individuals are pragmatists, ready and willing for new experiences.

## Counseling the Individual with a Fan Pattern

The Fan pattern shares traits with both the Bundle and the Bucket pattern.

Fan individuals can develop deep convictions. They can become self-righteous and develop an autocratic style, as we'll see with Czar Nicholas II and Alabama Governor George Wallace. When they are not boxed in by circumstances, an innate sense of what's practical allows them to turn on a dime.

The occupied section of a Fan pattern shows the types of activities that would be best for the individual to pursue. Carefully check the hemisphere, houses, and signs those planets occupy.

When deprived of desires, these individuals can become unhappy and develop obsessive thoughts to get what they want.

They have strong impulses to love and be loved. This can translate into a strong need to care for and in return be cared for by others.

The Fan person needs constant psychological growth. They desire to become a better person in one way or another. As they grow older, they can be filled with delightful memories of a life well lived or, if unsuccessful, with bitterness and despair.

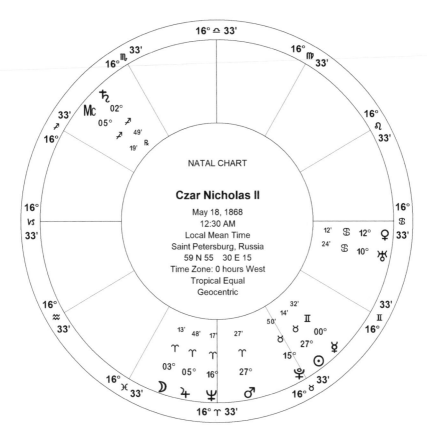

Figure 23: Czar Nicholas II

The natal chart for Czar Nicholas II of Russia shows a near-perfect Fan pattern (figure 23). Saturn at 02 Sagittarius 49' in the handle is opposed to Mercury at 00 Gemini 32. The leading planet and trailing planet are within Jansky's recommended 10° orb for a trine aspect between the rim planets.

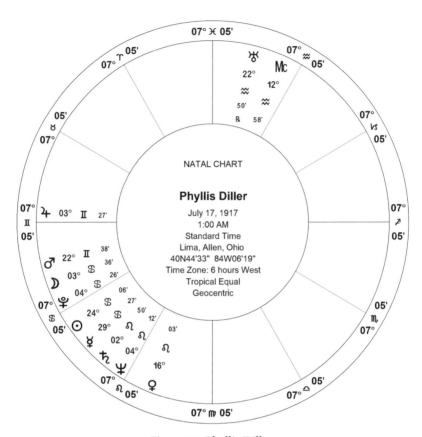

Figure 24: Phyllis Diller

In the case of Phyllis Diller, the handle planet, Uranus, is opposed to the trailing planet, Venus (figure 24). Rather than occupying the space of a trine, the blade occupies approximately 73°, within the orb of a quintile aspect. There was likely tension involving public opinion and what others thought of her performances. The handle planet, Uranus at 22 Aquarius 50, is nowhere near a core opposition. Still, it's so far from the blade of the Fan that most astrologers would judge this to be a Fan pattern.

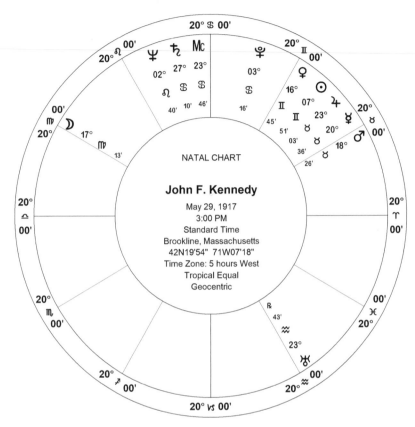

Figure 25: John F. Kennedy

President John F. Kennedy likewise possessed a Fan pattern with a skewed handle planet (figure 25). While Phyllis Diller's handle was two houses away from the axis of thrust in the blade, John F. Kennedy's was skewed by about one sign and one house. Mars-Moon, forming the edge of the blade, are strongly trine.

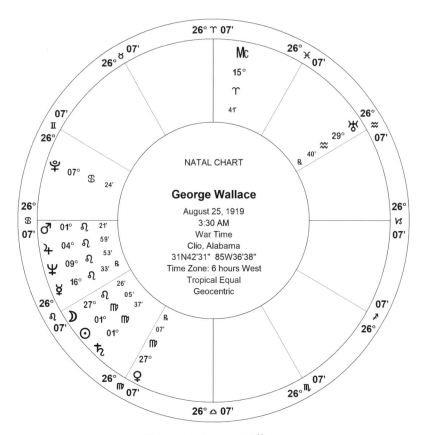

Figure 26: George Wallace

George Wallace's birth chart possesses a near-perfect Fan pattern (figure 26). Three planets are in opposition to the handle, amplifying the power of the blade portion of the pattern. Remembered as a staunch segregationist, Wallace was supported by the NAACP when he ran for governor of Alabama in 1958. A populist and pragmatist, Wallace reversed his segregationist views and included many black leaders in Alabama state government following desegregation in the late 1970s.

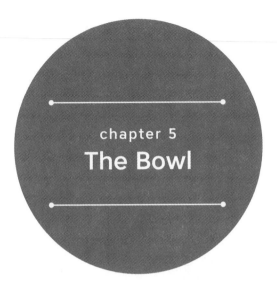

chapter 5

# The Bowl

The Bowl pattern is the most easily recognized planetary pattern we will explore. It does in fact resemble a bowl. The portion of the chart occupied by planets is one-half of the natal chart, give or take. The Bowl pattern is among the more common patterns. Approximately one in ten notable individuals in the Astro Databank possesses a Bowl pattern.

## The Ideal Bowl Pattern

The ideal Bowl pattern has the following geometry:

- All ten planets are found within 180° of the natal chart;

- The two planets at the far edges of the pattern will form a rim opposition of approximately 180°;

- The planets within the Bowl will be roughly spaced in an even distribution, with none separated by more than 60° from the others; and

- The leading planet (the first planet in the pattern to cross the Ascendant) is the high-focus planet.

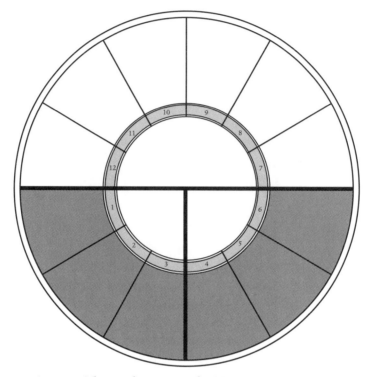

Figure 27: The Bowl Pattern with a T-Square Aspect Pattern

The ideal Bowl is rather rare. Often the rim opposition is lacking because the planets are more tightly grouped together. As long as the rim planets are separated by at least a quincunx aspect of 150° (sometimes called an inconjunct aspect), this provides enough separation to distinguish the Bowl from a Bundle pattern of wide orb. Likewise, when there is a gap of more than 60° within what appears to otherwise be a Bowl, the pattern begins to resemble the Seesaw pattern (see chapter 8). When there is a rim opposition greater than 180°, the pattern remains a Bowl so long as the orb for an opposition is not exceeded. When exceeded, the pattern starts to blur into a Bucket (see chapter 6).

When a rim opposition is present, be sure to check for the presence of a T-Square aspect pattern (figure 27). A T-Square occurs when an opposition is bisected by a perpendicular square aspect. As Robert Jansky notes, the T-Square lends integrative strength and organization to the Bowl pattern. Often the rim planets and the planet at the apex of the T-Square will be in the same mode—a

Cardinal T-Square, for example. The personal characteristics associated with that mode will be of great influence in that case.

The four hemispheres of the natal chart are formed by the cusps of the first, fourth, seventh, and tenth houses. When the Bowl pattern falls entirely within a hemisphere, we have a special sub-pattern called the Hemispheric Bowl. More on this to follow, since Hemispheric Bowls have a more specialized interpretation.

There are cases where the leading planet is conjunct another planet. When that occurs, we treat both planets as leading planets.

### The Leading Planet

The leading planet is the high-focus planet in the Bowl pattern. How much emphasis it exerts depends on the following criteria:

- If the leading planet is the ruling planet of the chart (the ruler of the Ascendant), it is likely the strongest planet in the chart and will have a lot of influence over the individual;

- If the leading planet is the only planet in a particular hemisphere of the natal chart, it becomes what Jansky called a "Singleton in Hemisphere" and gains a lot of influence over the individual; and

- If the leading planet is located in an angular house (especially the tenth house), its influence over the individual is increased.

Pay particular attention to the house of the leading planet. The affairs of life associated with that house will have considerable influence over the individual. As with any house interpretation, it is in this house that the individual will make their greatest impact upon their environment. Generalizations regarding the individual's characteristic manner of self-expression include the following:

*Quadrant I (Houses 1, 2, or 3):* The individual will likely be strongly self-centered and motivated more by what they can accomplish for themselves than for others. They have great faith in their own individual abilities, are not inclined to trust enough to delegate, and are subjective in judgments.

*Quadrant 2 (Houses 4, 5, 6):* The individual will have a tendency to be adaptive, creative, and practical. They seek fulfillment through the development and expression of individual talents and abilities. Rather than initiating actions, the individual is inclined to attempt to incrementally improve upon something they consider to be of importance. They are strongly influenced by the opinions of others.

*Quadrant 3 (Houses 7, 8, 9):* The individual's life and actions tend to be open and exposed to others and are typically matters of public attention and record. They can expect to be called upon repeatedly to give of themselves and their resources. Others can prove to be a constant drain on their energies and resources.

*Quadrant 4 (Houses 10, 11, 12):* The individual tends to be highly self-contained and very much in control of their destiny. Not as self-serving as those with a leading planet in quadrant 1, these individuals are more willing to consider the effects of their actions upon others. Self-fulfillment comes through sharing energies and resources with others. Their sense of self-worth tends to be measured by what others think of them.

### The Trailing Planet

The planet in opposition to the leading planet is the trailing planet. It's next in significance. The trailing planet reveals how the individual balances the influences and inclinations of the leading planet. The trailing planet tries to keep the individual integrated with the world. It helps keep the individual in equilibrium. When the trailing planet is a Singleton in Hemisphere, it can weaken the influence of the leading planet. Any instability between the leading planet and the trailing planet can manifest as psychological instability, conflicting impulses, and the like. This internal dynamic can result in confusion and indecision, or it can cause the individual to assert control over their environment.

### The Hemispheric Bowl

Jansky claims that the occurrence of a Hemispheric Bowl pattern is relatively rare. That's not my experience. It depends on how strict you are about all ten planets being in precisely one hemisphere. If one planet strays a bit, I'm inclined to apply the Hemispheric Bowl delineations. In my experience, they still apply.

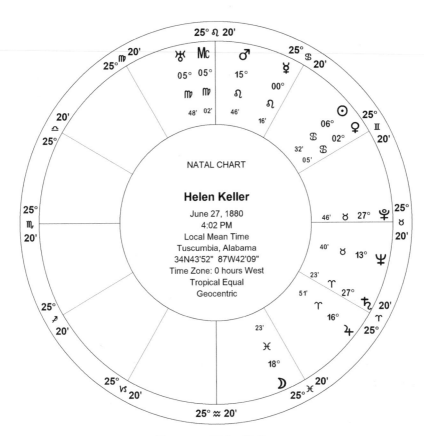

Figure 28: Helen Keller

Helen Keller's natal chart is an example of a Hemispheric Bowl pattern (figure 28). Nine planets are found in the western hemisphere. The tenth planet (Uranus) is in the eastern hemisphere by 10°28'. I would categorize Helen Keller's natal chart as a Western Hemispheric Bowl pattern.

I'm going to offer two interpretations for the Hemispheric Bowl patterns. Those offered by Marc Edmund Jones and Robert Jansky are the more conventional set. Both talked in terms of introversion/extroversion and whether the individual initiates/responds. The interpretations I favor come from noted astrologer Noel Tyl. They are more intensely psychological than the more conventional interpretations. I use Noel Tyl's interpretations routinely as my introduction to every natal chart consultation with a pronounced hemispheric grouping of planets precisely because Tyl's interpretations work so well at establishing an early dialogue with the client.

*All Planets in the Northern Hemisphere (Houses 1–6):* The Bowl is upright and cannot spill its contents. This is the maximum amount of self-containment. The individual is likely an introvert. Jansky also refers to the individual as a "collector." They go about collecting experiences and storing them up. Privacy is a marked characteristic, making it hard to get to know the individual. This can be very isolating as well. Noel Tyl focuses on the meanings of houses 1–6. These are the houses of early development, from the first breath at the Ascendant, to self-worth in the second house, to learning to think and communicate in the third house, to absorbing parental influences in the fourth house, to beginning to give from one's self in terms of love in the fifth house, to cooperating with others in the sixth house. For Noel Tyl, the northern hemisphere represents unfinished business from early childhood development.

*All Planets in the Southern Hemisphere (Houses 7–12):* This is the opposite pattern. The individual will be inclined to be an extrovert. The individual will find it difficult keeping their life private. The Bowl is turned upside down, its contents spilling out. The individual has difficulty retaining the fruits of their efforts for their own benefit. As a result, the individual can feel a constant energy drain. Noel Tyl's interpretation is a sense that the individual has been pushed around, controlled, or victimized by life's experiences. The environment fashions life for the individual.

*All Planets in the Eastern Hemisphere (Houses 10–3):* The Bowl functions as a scoop, with the individual scooping up experiences through the leading planet. The individual is very much an initiator, in control of their own destiny and the cause of most of their own problems. Jansky says to look for a rather controlling person, but one who rarely finishes what they start because their ego gets in the way. For Noel Tyl, a preponderance of planets in the east implies a need for protectionism within the identity. The individual will likely feel urges for ego justification. They will exhibit defensiveness in their personality.

*All Planets in the Western Hemisphere (Houses 4–9):* The Bowl, according to Jansky, is in the "capture" position. The individual is in a position to finish activities initiated by others. They respond to life's circumstances rather than initiate. Major problems will come as a result of the actions of others. The individual is a product of their times and environment. For Noel Tyl, the individual projects their ego onto others. They have a marked tendency to give of themselves so much that they practically give themselves away. The individual tends to turn themselves over to others for direction. They do this rather conspicuously, leaving their self behind.

## The Occupied Bowl Section

For the typical Bowl individual, the occupied signs and houses will occupy their time and attention almost to the exclusion of the unoccupied section of the natal chart. Some individuals feel compelled to explore the areas in the unoccupied section of their chart. It's not uncommon for a Bowl pattern to straddle two hemispheres. The predictable result is an individual who divides their attention between both hemispheres. This can lend creativity to the individual. There's also the possible lack of success that can come from dividing one's time and focus.

## The Unoccupied Bowl Section

The unoccupied signs and houses in the Bowl pattern represent needs that require attention. The individual will attempt to bring their life into balance. They look beyond the limitations of their personal life to find something that compensates for what they lack. They tend to feel that something is missing in their life and feel compelled to find something to fill that void. They might feel they didn't get sufficient opportunities they needed and so feel they must make an extra effort to accomplish something of significance. They might feel they were excluded from their fair share. Some might feel entitled to take what they feel they deserve.

The Bowl pattern represents duality. Bowl individuals tend to wonder whether the cup is half-full or half-empty. The Bowl pattern resembles the Yin-Yang symbol of Eastern philosophy.

# The Bowl Pattern Temperament

The most obvious characteristic of Bowl individuals is a high degree of self-containment. They respond more to external factors than to internal factors as part of their psychological makeup.

The individual's dynamic drives are determined by the relationship between the occupied and unoccupied portions of the natal chart. The positions of the planets in signs and houses in the occupied portion of the chart indicate where the individual feels most secure and self-sufficient, while the unoccupied part of the chart indicates those things for which the individual must strive for self-fulfillment.

The Bowl individual nearly always has some mission in life, the advocacy of some type of cause.

The Bowl pattern is associated with introspective individuals, the sort concerned with finding meaning and purpose in their lives. Self-improvement tends to be a preoccupation of the Bowl individual. Whatever they identify as a worthwhile cause they tend to pursue with steadfast determination.

Generally optimistic, they believe in the basic worthiness of all humankind. This is especially so when the leading planet is in Aquarius and/or the eleventh house.

The Bowl pattern generally bestows an ability to hold steadfast under stress and strain. They perform well in a crisis and can be a steadying influence on others.

Bowl individuals typically require more acceptance and recognition from others. This can cause them to act out for attention, perhaps assuming an air of self-importance.

How much self-containment the Bowl represents depends on the presence or absence of a rim opposition. When a rim opposition is absent, the degree of self-containment diminishes, just as a physical bowl with lower sides can contain less. Bowl individuals strive for balance. The absence of a rim opposition makes balance more difficult to achieve.

How well balanced the individual's personality and character are depends on how evenly distributed the planets are within the Bowl. Look for sextiles, which represent opportunities. Look also for semisquares and squares, as these represent special challenges.

How the individual approaches life's problems are indicated by the quadruplicity of the rim planets:

- *Cardinal Rim Planets:* Attempts to find a solution to a problem and deal with it

- *Fixed Rim Planets:* Attempts to live with the problem

- *Mutable Rim Planets:* The psychology of avoidance: makes believe the problem doesn't even exist

When the rim opposition is missing, look for the closest square aspect between two planets. This "trigger" will be a guide to the basic motivation of the individual.

The Bowl pattern can often produce a singleton planet in a hemisphere of the natal chart. If we look back at Helen Keller's chart (figure 28), for example, Uranus sits alone in the eastern hemisphere. Such a planet can take on an enormous emphasis. If the singleton planet is also the leading planet, its effect is doubly emphasized.

What of the case where, like in Helen Keller's chart, the singleton planet is the trailing planet? In that case, the leading planet and the trailing planet vie for dominance. This is especially true when the two planets are opposed or quincunx.

## Counseling the Individual with a Bowl Pattern

Individuals with a Bowl pattern are likely to report that they feel compelled to achieve. They take the initiative when it's in their best interest. They're individuals with an agenda. Even their hobbies are likely to have a vocational side to them.

I've noted that Bowl individuals tend to be self-contained. Introspective by nature, they often need to find time apart from others to work on their own self-realization.

Clients should be encouraged to have high ideals. At the same time, they need to keep in mind what they can't do or don't wish to become.

There is the danger that Bowl clients will become self-seeking individuals. They can demand that others cater to their needs simply because they have a high impression of themselves. At their worst, they can slip into fantasy and attempt to commandeer what they want because they believe they're on a mission that can't fail, if they only put their mind to the task.

When they feel deprived of the good things in life, Bowl individuals can develop obsessive desires to get what they want.

Clients with a Bowl pattern can be spontaneous and expressive. They're not afraid of new experiences.

Personal efforts by the Bowl individual should bring them comfort and stability. It might even bring power, money, and status. Others might feel jealous as a result.

Bowl pattern individuals tend to be extremely sensitive and can be emotionally vulnerable to the opinions of others.

Compromise can be especially difficult for Bowl people. It's essential that they learn this life skill.

Clients with a Bowl pattern are well advised to determine what's sufficient to meet their economic needs. Then they'll know the minimum they need to earn to meet those needs. In that way, they enhance their self-sufficiency. They can save themselves a lot of frustration and uncertainty when they determine what challenges they can reasonably meet.

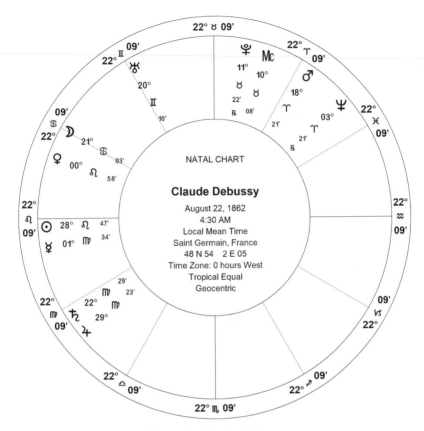

Figure 29: Claude Debussy

The natal chart of French composer and pianist Claude Debussy has Neptune in high focus as the leading planet (figure 29). It's opposed (wide orb) by a Jupiter-Saturn conjunction. Debussy was known for his moody temperament. This is consistent with the self-emptying nature of his Bowl pattern. Debussy possessed an argumentative nature, indicated by Uranus square to Jupiter and Saturn.

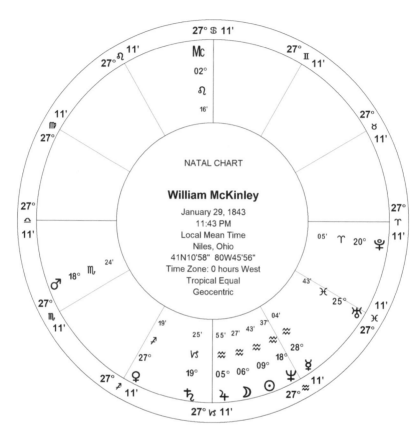

Figure 30: William McKinley

The Bowl pattern of President William McKinley is a northern hemisphere pattern (figure 30). The angular separation between the leading planet (Mars) and the trailing planet (Pluto) is more than a trine, so this can't be a Bundle pattern. The rim aspect is, in fact, a quincunx. There is a stellium in Aquarius, a reflection of President McKinley's utopian ideals.

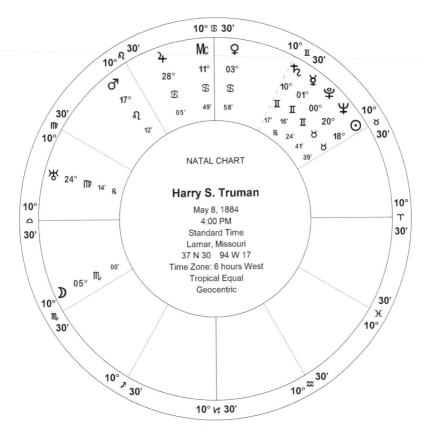

Figure 31: Harry S. Truman

President Truman's Bowl is mostly in the southern hemisphere, spilling its contents onto the rest of his natal chart (figure 31). There's a rim opposition of Sun and Moon. The Sun is the leading planet and is triggered by a square aspect from Mars. In fact, Mars forms a wide T-Square aspect pattern with the Moon. The Sun-Neptune conjunction gave him the moral responsibility to declare, "The buck stops here." Throughout his career, President Truman remained self-contained. He avoided alliances that required underhanded deals.

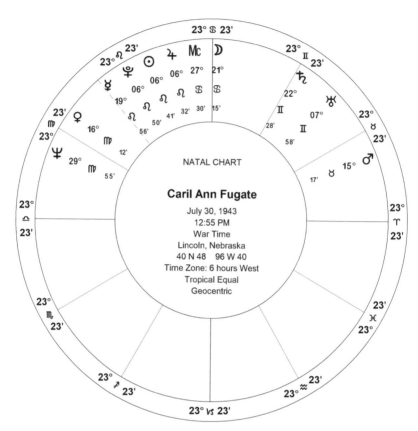

Figure 32: Caril Ann Fugate

Caril Ann Fugate is the youngest female in United States history to date to be tried for first-degree murder (figure 32). She was the adolescent girlfriend and accomplice of spree-killer Charles Starkweather. Her chart possesses a southern Bowl pattern with a tight three-planet conjunction in Leo (all within the space of 18').

chapter 6
# The Bucket

We will now explore the Bucket pattern. It combines a nine-planet bowl with the tenth planet outside the bowl forming a handle. While the Bucket pattern resembles the Bowl pattern, the addition of a handle causes a marked difference in the temperament of the Bucket pattern.

Robert Jansky ranked the Bucket pattern as the second most common pattern, even more common than the Bowl pattern. However, this is not the case when we check the Astro Databank charts. There the Bucket pattern is the fifth most common planetary pattern, coming well behind the Bowl pattern.

## The Ideal Bucket Pattern

The ideal Bucket pattern (figure 33) has the following characteristics:

- The bucket portion of the pattern contains nine planets contained within an angle of $180°$;

- A single handle planet will be found in the open hemisphere;

- A rim opposition will form the edge of the bowl portion of the Bucket, just like in the Bowl pattern;

- There will be a core opposition where one or more planets will form an opposition to the handle planet; and

- The handle planet will make a Grand Cross aspect pattern with the core opposition planet(s) and the rim planets.

The leading planet was the high-focus planet in the Bowl pattern. Not so with the Bucket pattern. It is the handle planet that is the high-focus planet here. It would be a mistake, however, to disregard the leading planet. The rim planets are secondary in their influence.

It is not all that uncommon to find the ideal Bucket shape. Still, there are examples where there is no Grand Cross, rim opposition, or core opposition.

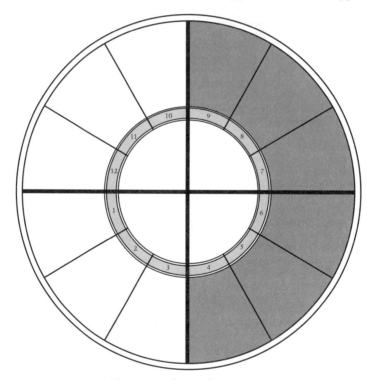

Figure 33: The Bucket Pattern

There are three planetary patterns with which the less-than-ideal Bucket pattern can be confused:

- If any of the bowl-portion planets are separated by 60° or more, then treat it as a Splay pattern.

- If there are two handle planets separated by more than the orb of a conjunction, then treat it as a Seesaw pattern.

- If the potential handle planet is conjunct a rim planet, then treat it as a Bowl pattern.

## The Bucket Pattern Temperament

The personality of a Bucket individual is self-contained, as we would expect from the related Bowl pattern. When we consider the temperament of a Bucket individual, we must keep the nature of the handle planet foremost in mind. Jansky offers the example of Uranus as the handle planet. This individual will place a great deal of emphasis on independence. They will want others to think of them as unique in some way. Refer back to chapter 1 for the basic expression we can expect for each planet as the high-focus planet.

People with Bucket-shaped charts tend to be fixated on goals. They're capable of focusing considerable energy on achieving specific aims with single-minded determination. The sign and house position of the handle planet will show how and in what area of life this effort is likely to be directed.

Where the Bowl pattern personality can compromise, the Bucket pattern individual is generally not so inclined. Resistance to compromise can, as Stephanie Clement notes, be seen as a blessing or a curse. When the Bucket individual sticks to their guns and a positive outcome results, it can be viewed as a positive feature of their character. It's equally likely, however, that this unwillingness to compromise will strain personal relationships, especially when everything becomes a matter of principle to the individual, without any willingness at all to compromise. This can be highly dysfunctional.

The Bucket individual can easily adapt ideas to suit their purpose. Since self-interest runs strong in the Bucket pattern and the individual is motivated toward accomplishment, they can adapt conditions to suit their personal agenda. Again, this is a mixed blessing. The positive outcome is a person who adapts circumstances to meet the needs of others. The negative side is an individual who constantly creates trouble for others by trying to rig the outcome in their own favor.

There are three basic patterns for the handle planet: perpendicular to the bowl-portion, leaning toward the leading planet, and leaning toward the trailing planet. Each affects the basic Bucket temperament differently.

### Handle Planet Perpendicular

The most intense Bucket personalities occur when the handle is near-perpendicular to the rim planets of the bowl portion. Marc Edmund Jones, Robert Jansky, and Stephanie Clement all agreed these individuals have highly directed lives. When the core opposition is absent in the bowl portion, the individuals are no less driven but might lack a strong focus for their energies.

When there is a core opposition to the handle planet and a rim opposition, the result is a Grand Cross aspect pattern (see chapter 13). The aspects that make up this pattern are all characterized as "hard" aspects—oppositions and squares. Individuals born with a Grand Cross experience near-constant crises until they learn to manage those challenging aspects. Once they learn how to manage the Grand Cross, their self-confidence grows. They gain the feeling that they can handle whatever circumstance might arise. Others are amazed at their capabilities.

The perfect Grand Square places all four planets in one mode: cardinal, fixed, or mutable. The thrust of their personality is clearly aimed in the direction of the handle planet with a single mode of action (cardinal, fixed, or mutable).

When in cardinal signs, the Grand Square planets compel the individual to make ambitious efforts. These individuals are characterized by action and energy.

When the Grand Square planets are in fixed signs, the focus becomes more internal. Their own inner values take precedence. Their actions reflect these values. These people are power seekers. They don't like to play by other people's rules.

When the Grand Square planets are in mutable signs, communication is of great importance. Energy flows in both directions, unlike in the Cardinal Grand Square (where energy is directed outward) or the Fixed Grand Square (where energy is focused inward). Individuals with a Mutable Grand Square share equally with others and are born team members.

### Handle Closer to the Leading Planet

When the handle planet lies closer to the leading planet, the individual is likely to be more cautious and self-absorbed. They will think of themselves before making major decisions. They're almost more confident in their endowments and are prone to draw upon their background and life experiences before they commit to any course of action. The handle planet is not so dominant in this position, and the leading planet is more influential.

### Handle Closer to the Trailing Planet

Those with a handle planet that leans closer to the trailing planet are less pre-occupied with themselves and more reactive to external influences. They will tend to be impulsive and overconfident at times. They tend to react to the immediacy of a situation rather than take a long-range view of the matter. They have a tendency to demand attention from others and seek their cooperation. The leading planet's influence is weakest in this position.

## Counseling the Individual with a Bucket Pattern

As with the Bowl pattern, great achievers with the Bucket pattern are self-contained. They can be uncompromising and draw on a deep reservoir of energy and personal resources. It is the nature of the handle planet and the house and sign it occupies that define the quality and direction of the individual's activity.

The Bucket personality feels compelled to explore the area of life defined by the handle planet. The astrologer should help the client figure out how to get the best results from focused activity associated with the handle planet.

Bucket individuals try to gain control over situations and relationships. They can be quite manipulative. The Bucket personality should guard against pushing their own self-interest too far. This can alienate people when their cooperation is needed at a later date. They should be encouraged to work with like-minded individuals. Working together cooperatively with others, they can accomplish more than going it alone.

Bucket people can be incessant worriers. They need to learn to worry only about those things over which they have control. Do something about it or let it go and see what happens is advice they should take to heart.

There is the danger that the Bucket individual will become impatient. This can lead them to become a malcontent and to agitate for change for themselves and others. They need to control their more impetuous and rash impulses. If they rush forward in their zeal for reform while others fear to get involved, they can easily become victim and martyr instead of hero and leader.

The Bucket personality can go on to great achievements when the handle planet and the rim planets form a T-Square. The closer the handle planet (i.e., the apex of the T-Square) is to perpendicular, the better. The missing core opposition means that the rim planets tether the individual to reality.

The addition of a core opposition to the T-Square results in a Grand Cross. This adds strength to all four planets. Constant crisis often accompanies this Grand Cross. Remember, it's the handle planet that focuses and channels the activities of the client. The astrologer should thus focus the client on activities related to the handle planet. The individual can drift without that focus and not get very far in life. The individual is well advised to develop a specialty. Without that, they might get involved in a flurry of different activities and dissipate their energy.

When the handle planet leans closer to the leading planet, the individual might be too cautious and reluctant to take chances. Hesitation can lead to lost opportunities. The client should be advised to rise to the occasion, to go ahead and do what's necessary. When the client is uncertain of their abilities, they should be encouraged to put them to the test occasionally to improve their self-confidence.

When the handle planet leans closer to the trailing planet, the individual needs to learn not to respond to immediate challenges but instead to focus on future possibilities.

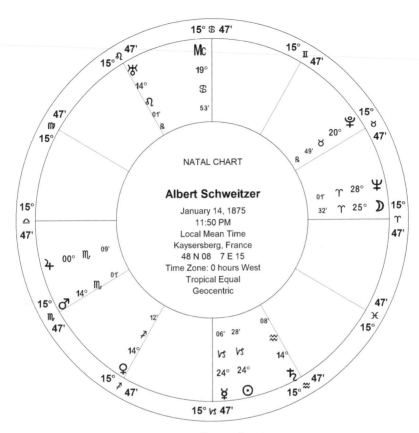

Figure 34: Albert Schweitzer

Albert Schweitzer was a theologian, writer, humanitarian, philosopher, and physician. The Bucket pattern in his birth chart is nearly ideal (figure 34). Jupiter forms a rim opposition to Neptune and the Moon. Uranus in the handle is opposed to Saturn and square to the rim planets. We have a Grand Cross aspect pattern. Only Pluto, outside the bowl portion, mars the pattern. Uranus as the handle planet is consistent with Schweitzer's highly unusual thought and work.

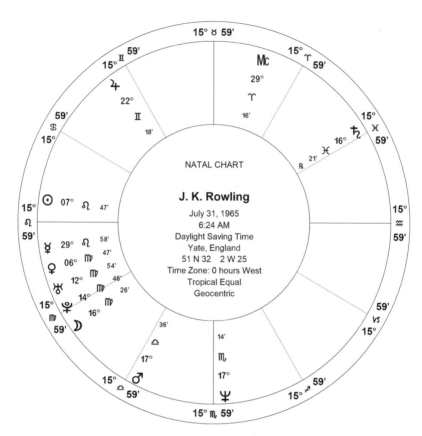

Figure 35: J. K. Rowling

The natal chart for J. K. Rowling contains a core opposition between Saturn and the Moon (figure 35). There is, however, no rim opposition. Instead, Neptune is widely quincunx Jupiter. This places the handle (Saturn) closer to the leading planet, increasing the influence of Jupiter. This suggests that Rowling is a somewhat cautious person, somewhat self-absorbed. We look at the core opposition to determine what drives her life. The Moon reflects the fact that Rowling, like many authors, puts her emotions into her writing.

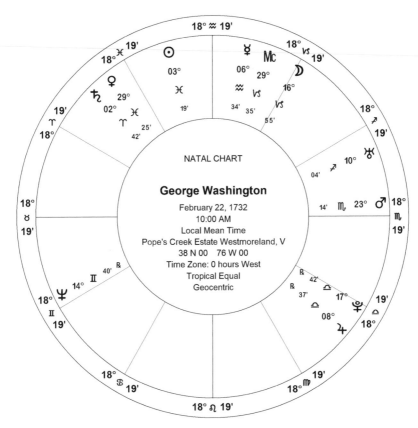

Figure 36: George Washington

President George Washington's natal chart also contains a near-ideal Bucket pattern (figure 36). Saturn and Venus form a rim opposition with Jupiter. There's a core opposition between Neptune in the handle and Uranus at the base of the bowl portion. The handle is not perpendicular. It leans toward the trailing planet. This suggests that President Washington was less internally driven and more reactive to external influences.

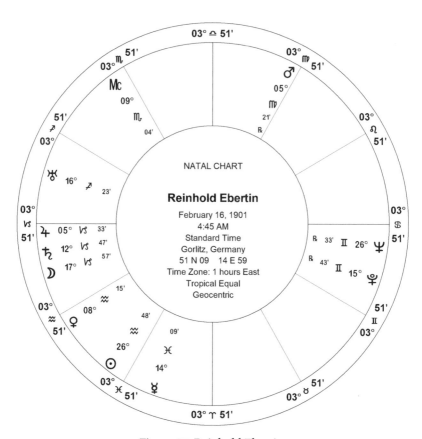

Figure 37: Reinhold Ebertin

The German astrologer Reinhold Ebertin was the founder of the Cosmo-
biology movement (figure 37). His Bucket pattern is an example where the
handle planet leans even more toward the trailing planet. There are no aspects
from Mars, the handle planet, to the rim planets. There is a core opposition
from Mars to Mercury, and Mercury is part of a T-Square involving Uranus and
Pluto.

chapter 7

# The Locomotive

The Locomotive pattern (also called the Wheelbarrow pattern) is the exact opposite of the Bundle pattern. In the Bundle, one-third of the space (120°) is occupied by the ten planets and two-thirds of the space (240°) is empty. This is reversed in the Locomotive pattern, where two-thirds of the natal chart is occupied with planets and one-third of the space is empty.

The Locomotive is the most common planetary pattern in the Astro Databank data.

Robert Jansky says all of the tripolar patterns have "a kind of self-adequacy and sure-footedness of action rooted in their own life's experience" (Jansky 1977, 35). There's a stability to the pattern, based upon the foundation of the trine.

The Locomotive pattern gets its name from the old-fashioned locomotive wheel. Power was applied by a piston. Additional weight was applied at two-thirds of the wheel's circumference to prevent wear and tear on the locomotive engine and the wheels from a side-to-side shimmying.

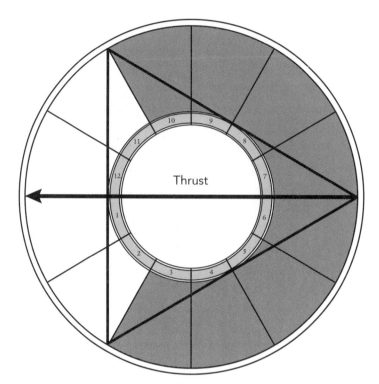

Figure 38: The Locomotive Pattern

Jansky likens the dynamics of a trine to that of "momentum." With momentum, an object in motion tends to stay in motion. An object at rest tends to stay at rest. To get an object from rest to motion, there is an initial inertia to be overcome. Momentum then takes over to keep the object in motion. This describes the dynamics of the trine, especially the Grand Trine.

## The Ideal Locomotive Pattern

In its ideal form, the Locomotive pattern (figure 38) contains the following elements:

- Ten planets are evenly distributed around two-thirds of the circumference of the natal chart, with the remaining one-third empty;

- The two boundary planets (those planets bordering the open one-third of the chart) form a trine aspect within an orb of $10°$;

- The two boundary planets, together with an internal planet, form a Grand Trine; and

- Among the internal planets, there can't be any open space in excess of 60°. One such open space and we have a Seesaw pattern. Two such open spaces and we have a Splay pattern.

The presence of a Grand Trine greatly strengthens the Locomotive pattern. It lends it a strong external thrust and drive directed at the midpoint of the open space. The closer to exact the orbs are for the trines, the stronger the individual's ability to project their personality outward becomes. The house occupied by the midpoint indicates where the individual tries to find accomplishment and fulfillment. The sign of the open midpoint and its ruler indicate the quality of energy that must be mobilized to satisfy the personality.

Noel Tyl refers to the Grand Trine as a closed circuit of self-sufficiency. Inertia is a major problem unless an opposition or square exists to allow the energy of the Grand Trine to escape. Jansky likewise describes this opposition or square as preventing a short circuit.

The presence of a handle planet (an opposition) means we must choose between Locomotive and Bucket. If this handle planet is opposed to the apex of a Grand Trine, then we have a Locomotive pattern. When the handle planet does not participate in a Grand Trine, then preference goes to the Bucket pattern.

The leading planet is the high-focus planet in the Locomotive pattern. It focuses the individual's energy. Stephanie Clement claims, "Life's inspiration comes from the energy reflected by this planet, and all the other planets contribute to the satisfaction of that inspiration." (Clement 2007, loc. 367, Kindle). Just as the engine pulls the entire train, the leading planet in the Locomotive pattern pulls the rest of the planets along with it.

The midpoint of the open space in the chart is a secondary point of energy focus. The house of the midpoint indicates the area of life where the Locomotive-person seeks accomplishment or fulfillment. The sign of the open midpoint and its ruler determine the nature of the energy to be mobilized.

## The Locomotive Pattern Temperament

Locomotive-type individuals tend to have a personality expected of an Aries personality. They can be extremely driven individuals. Inertia is a defining characteristic. When at rest, there is an initial inertia to overcome. Once in motion, they're hard to stop. Their momentum carries everything in their path along with them. The closer the pattern comes to ideal, the stronger the driving force of their personality. When the Grand Trine is absent in the pattern, so is much of the driving energy. As Jansky notes, "They are unable to focus their energy without the 'lens' of the Grand Trine"(Jansky 1977, 38).

That Grand Trine lends them the feeling of self-adequacy. They "know" they've got what it takes to solve a problem. Fact is, sometimes they do, sometimes they don't. It's almost impossible to persuade them otherwise, once they decide to act. They can be very uncompromising in that respect.

Locomotive individuals tend to be very predictable. They have their own peculiar way of approaching a problem. After you get to know them as an individual, you can predict how they will react to a given set of circumstances.

### Hemisphere of the Open Area

The hemisphere where all or most of the open area appears provides valuable information about the inner workings of the Locomotive person's mind.

*Open Area North:* Tends to be a highly extroverted individual who is motivated more by what they can do for themselves than for others.

*Open Area South:* Tends to be a highly introverted individual who seeks public acclaim and recognition for putting the interests of others ahead of their own.

*Open Area East:* Tends to be an individual striving to take control of their own life and destiny. They would prefer to be more in control of the situation than they generally are.

*Open Area West:* Tends to be an individual who finds themselves in a position of leadership or in control of the situation in which they find themselves. They are very much in control of what happens to them.

## Counseling the Individual with a Locomotive Pattern

Individuals with the Locomotive pattern are able to motivate themselves and others. They can take decisive action. They possess an inner drive. They can accomplish what they set their mind to. Power and success are strong drives.

One lesson that the Locomotive type needs to learn is not to run over people with their momentum. Once they get going, they need to be able to apply the brakes when others fail to get out of their way quickly enough. Caution is not the strong suit of the Locomotive pattern. It must be learned to avoid some harsh life lessons.

The Locomotive metaphor fits in another way. Once stopped, it can be difficult to get started again. An example would be the author who writes furiously until writer's block sets in, then cannot put together noun and verb.

The dynamic of the Locomotive pattern is found in the empty one-third of the natal chart. This results in a strong lack or need. The problem to be solved, the task to be achieved, is found here. The client should be advised to look for opportunity and involvement here.

Locomotive types are well advised to get the necessary education to excel in their desired field and then persevere until they're able to position themselves where they want to be. Great achievers are often individualistic and strong-willed, but they also usually start planning for their future early on.

When a Grand Trine is present, the client should be advised to mobilize the element of the Grand Trine (fire, earth, air, or water). Grand Trines that "cross signs" have less momentum, according to Lance Carter, yet are less likely to cause the client's life to "just roll about like a loose cannonball." (Carter 2010, 98).

Locomotive people are moved more by external events and people than by internal dynamics of their character. Just as a train cannot quickly stop or rapidly turn, Locomotive individuals need to be able to anticipate problems and be ready for them if and when they do arrive.

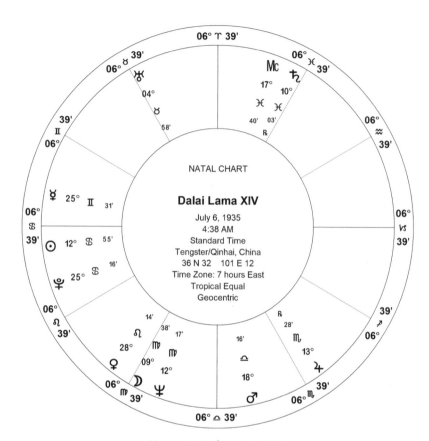

Figure 39: Dalai Lama XIV

The natal Locomotive pattern for Dalai Lama XIV has Saturn as the high-focus, leading planet (figure 39). It makes a trine to Jupiter, the trailing planet. The Sun, Jupiter, and Saturn form a Water Grand Trine for extra momentum. A Mystic Rectangle between Uranus, Saturn, Jupiter, and Moon-Neptune amps up the involved energies. There is also a Kite pattern, with Moon-Neptune at the top of the Kite and Saturn at the bottom. The Kite gives added motivation and potential to the Grand Trine.

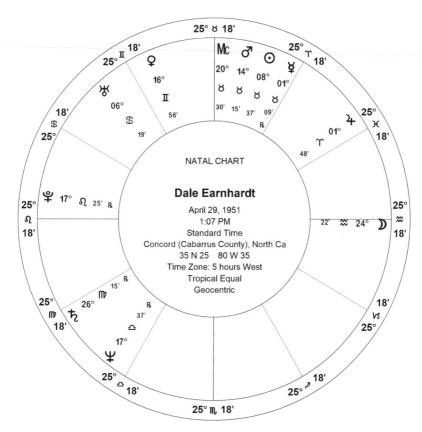

Figure 40: Dale Earnhardt Sr.

Race car driver Dale Earnhardt Sr., known as "the Intimidator," possessed a natal Locomotive pattern with the Moon as the high-focus, leading planet (figure 40). The Moon, Neptune, and Venus form an Air Grand Trine for added momentum. There are five planets in fixed signs, including a Moon-Pluto opposition. Uranus is at the apex of an out-of-sign T-Square involving Jupiter, Uranus, and Saturn. Mars is at the apex of another T-Square, this one in fixed planets between Moon, Mars, and Pluto.

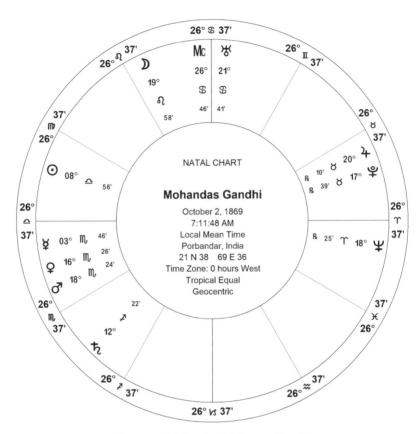

Figure 41: Mohandas Mahatma Gandhi

Neptune, the planet of compassion, is the leading planet in the Locomotive pattern for Mohandas "Mahatma" Gandhi (figure 41). Saturn is the trailing planet. The Moon and Neptune form a trine, but Saturn is barely out of orb to complete a Fire Grand Trine. The Moon is at the apex of Fixed T-Squares involving the Jupiter-Pluto conjunction and the Mars-Venus conjunction.

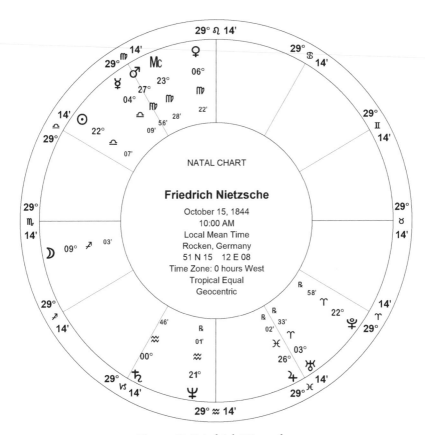

Figure 42: Friedrich Nietzsche

The Locomotive pattern in the natal chart for philosopher Friedrich Nietzsche contains a sesquiquadrate rather than a trine between Venus as leading planet and Pluto as trailing planet (figure 42). Pluto and the Sun form the opposition in a T-Square with Saturn at the apex.

chapter 8

# The Seesaw

One way of distinguishing planetary patterns is to identify an irregular versus a regular distribution of planets around the natal chart. In the Seesaw pattern, there are two groups opposing each other. In the Bucket pattern, we have a single handle planet opposing the other nine planets. In the Seesaw pattern, we have two or more planets opposing the others. There are two unoccupied areas opposing each other as well. Robert Jansky refers to this as the Hourglass pattern.

## The Ideal Seesaw Pattern

The ideal Seesaw pattern (figure 43) has the following geometry:

- The planets group themselves into two groups or clusters around the ends of an imaginary central axis;

- The planets can be in an 8:2, 7:3, 6:4, or 5:5 distribution, with at least two planets in each group;

- There are three oppositions—a core opposition lying along the central axis and two boundary oppositions defining the boundaries of the Seesaw shape;

- There is a Grand Square, the four planets equidistant from each other around the chart, forming four square aspects and oppositions,

- There is at least 90° of open area on either side of the two groups to clearly mark off where the two groups are located; and

- All ten planets are located within the boundary oppositions.

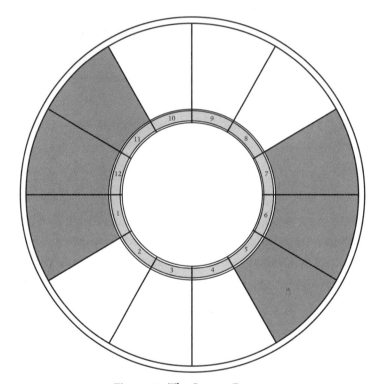

Figure 43: The Seesaw Pattern

The leading planet for each group has less significance than in other patterns. The leading planets should not, however, be overlooked. Their house and sign locations work like they do in the Bowl and Bucket patterns. They are points of contact between the individual and the environment.

There are instances where the Seesaw pattern is skewed to one side of the central axis. As long as there is at least one opposition and preferably two oppositions within orb, the Seesaw pattern is possible.

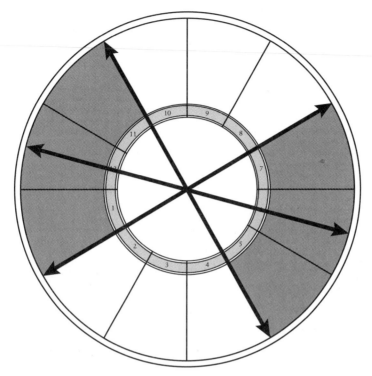

Figure 44: Seesaw Pattern Oppositions

## The Seesaw Pattern Temperament

The most telling trait of the Seesaw pattern is the nature of the opposition(s). There is a basic polarity so that the individual tends to swing from one general point of view to the other (figure 44). There must be at least one opposition present. Oppositions always indicate that contrary forces are present. Jansky recommends viewing the Seesaw as one giant opposition, pulling the individual in two different directions. These individuals tend to show a duality of interests and tend to oscillate back and forth.

Seesaw individuals show either a tentativeness through constant alternation or an open-mindedness that they express in creative ways. Jansky likens the Seesaw person to the archetypal Libran. They go through life trying to achieve a degree of harmony and balance.

Planets in opposition are generally in the same mode: cardinal, fixed, or mutable. They're also usually found in compatible signs: fire/earth or air/water.

The opposition(s) manifest as interpersonal challenges. These individuals seek balance between themselves and others in their immediate environment through compromise. They have a genuine interest in others at a personal and humanistic level.

The Seesaw pattern is inherently mutable. These individuals have a ready capacity for adjustment to the reality of any situation. They are able to reconcile opposing viewpoints and conflicting forces. They naturally bridge differences. Fixity frustrates the Seesaw individual. They prefer fluid situations.

What is being balanced comes from the sign and house of the planets at the center of each group. Compromise and balance flow easily when the central planets are in opposition. It is possible that there will be no core opposition, nor even a central planet in one or both groups. The concern of each group will still focus on the sign and house at the center of each group. The absence of a core opposition means the individual will have greater difficulty in achieving or maintaining balance.

The preponderance of planets determines which group has the greater significance. With a 5:5 ratio, the groups will be roughly equal in influence. This contrasts with an 8:2 ratio, where the group of eight planets will carry more weight.

When all of the personal planets are on one side of the Seesaw, the individual tends to become fully immersed in personal issues. There is less focus on societal and transpersonal issues.

It is possible for a "stray" planet to be placed outside the two groups of planets in the Seesaw pattern. When this happens, the stray is a high-focus planet. According to Jansky, this planet represents a special capacity or gift.

## Counseling the Individual with a Seesaw Pattern

The strength of the Seesaw pattern lies in the linkage of contrasting planetary energies. The result is a balancing dynamic. The merger of contrasting potentials can create a type of tension that results in a reactive personality.

Great achievers with the Seesaw pattern can successfully handle various and simultaneous relationships, projects, and commitments. They are able to achieve their goals through balancing opposing points of view. They're capable of working with others on different levels, and when emergency strikes, they're capable of taking charge and doing what needs to be done.

Seesaw people are sometimes seen as fickle. They alternately go this way or that, as their mood dictates. What some see as fickle, others see as versatile. These individuals are not afraid to change their mind when circumstances require. Sometimes they hedge their bets by playing both sides of a situation.

Seesaw individuals are best advised to develop lots of interests. An education that allows them to go into more than one line of work suits them best.

Versatility gives them the ability to choose the type of life they'll live. They should balance themselves by coordinating their time and talents. They need the courage to be themselves and fight for their beliefs when necessary but at the same time remain open to compromise when the situation needs unity and cooperation. That way, they can fulfill career obligations and lifelong ambitions.

Seesaw individuals should develop their ability to analyze problems and situations and learn to make snap decisions that are correct. That way, they can avoid becoming immobilized due to a lack of decisiveness.

It is common for Seesaw individuals to have different experiences and people pulling first this way and then that way throughout their lives. They need to use their balancing abilities to remain centered under those circumstances.

They need to learn that not every stated opinion requires an immediate reaction. Until they do, they can be easily manipulated.

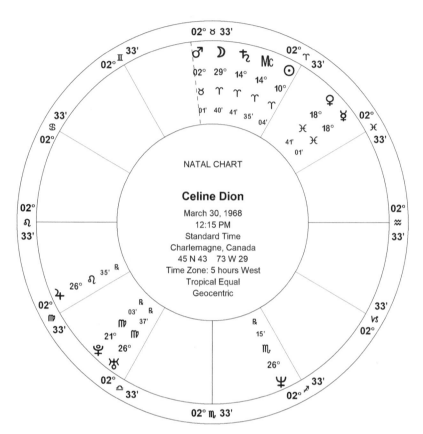

Figure 45: Celine Dion

Celine Dion's chart is an excellent example of a Seesaw pattern that has wide gaps between the bundles of planets, with gaps of 114° and 112° (figure 45). None of the oppositions are crisscrossing boundary oppositions. There is a very wide core opposition between the Sun and Uranus. There are four oppositions all together involving Mercury, Venus, Uranus, and Pluto. The Sun is at the midpoint of one of the bundles, with the empty point opposing the Sun at the midpoint of the other bundle.

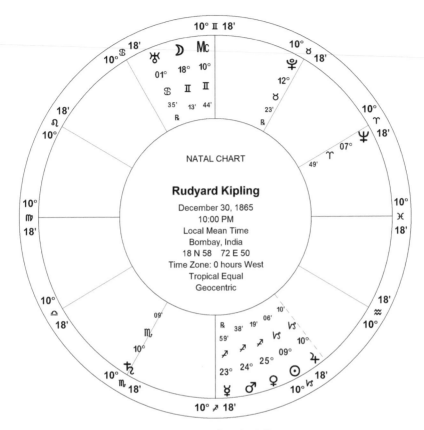

Figure 46: Rudyard Kipling

The natal Seesaw pattern of Rudyard Kipling contains two opposing groups of planets in a 6:4 ratio (figure 46). There is a core opposition between the Moon and the conjunction of Mercury, Mars, and Venus. There is a wide boundary opposition between Uranus and the conjunction of Sun and Jupiter. Neptune is powerfully placed at the apex of a T-Square involving Uranus (widely) and the Sun-Jupiter conjunction.

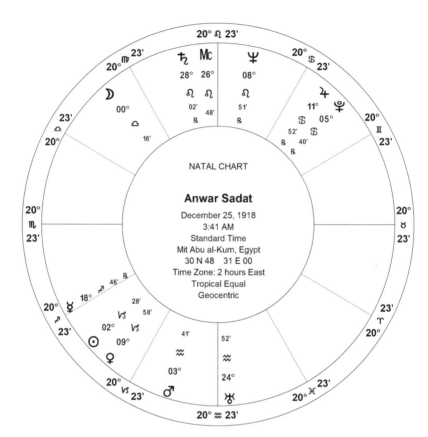

Figure 47: Anwar Sadat

Anwar Sadat, the third president of Egypt, met with Israeli Prime Minister Menachem Begin and US President Jimmy Carter at Camp David. The See-saw pattern in Sadat's natal chart shows the Moon straying from the otherwise tight groupings of planets (figure 47). The Moon sits right on the Libra Aries Point (at 00 Libra 16). There is a boundary opposition between Saturn and Uranus. Mars and Neptune form a core opposition. Additional oppositions include Sun-Pluto, Venus-Pluto, and Venus-Jupiter.

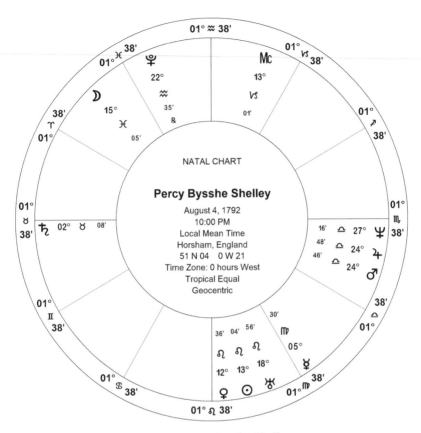

Figure 48: Percy Bysshe Shelley

The natal Seesaw pattern of lyric poet Percy Bysshe Shelley has three planets in one grouping that spans a sextile opposed by seven planets in the space of a quintile (figure 48). The Moon and Mercury form a core opposition. Saturn forms a boundary opposition with the Mars-Jupiter-Neptune conjunction. The second boundary opposition is between Pluto and the Sun-Venus-Uranus conjunction.

chapter 9

# The Splay

We now come to the second most common planetary pattern (according to the Astro Databank): the Splay pattern. Robert Jansky preferred the more descriptive title the Tripod pattern. The Splay pattern results when three clusters of planets are uniformly distributed around the natal chart. The planets in each cluster typically form multiple conjunctions.

The Splay is the most difficult planetary pattern to identify. There are natal charts that defy categorization. They do not fit any of the seven planetary patterns discussed previously. They are too spread out, are too irregularly spread out, or lack defining features and focal points. The Splay pattern offers a possibility for those natal charts that don't fit any other planetary pattern.

## The Ideal Splay Pattern

Marc Edmund Jones and Jansky disagreed on the ideal characteristics for the Splay pattern. Jones argued that the Splay is a residual pattern, a classification for anything that doesn't fit the other planetary patterns. He described it as neither even nor symmetrical in the distribution of planets. Jansky gave much more rigor to the definition of the Splay pattern. According to him, the ideal Splay (figure 49) has the following characteristics:

- It MUST contain a Grand Trine;

- The pattern MUST NOT contain any oppositions, except when the orb does not exceed 10°; and

- The spread of each spoke (or ray) MUST NOT exceed 60° (the width of a sextile).

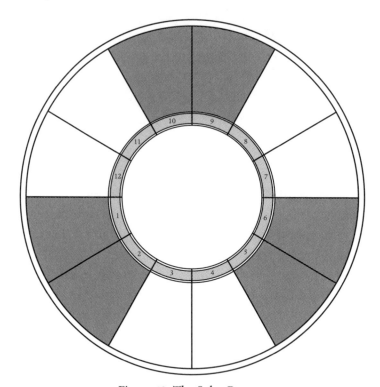

Figure 49: The Splay Pattern

The logic behind Jansky's narrower definition of the ideal pattern is to make the Splay pattern easily visible.

The Splay will typically contain at least one stellium by sign or house (or both).

## The Splay Pattern Temperament

Stephanie Clement notes, "The personality of the Splay person might be easier to identify than the pattern itself. Here you find a person who has wide and varied interests, yet also has areas where profound attention is concentrated and directed" (Clement 2007, loc. 1045, Kindle).

The lack of oppositions in the Splay pattern results in individuals who are "free-wheeling," according to Jansky. Operating from a sturdy base, they are difficult to upset or overturn. The requirement of a Grand Trine means they operate from a center of self-sufficiency.

Jansky refers to the Splay as the "pattern of genius." Some individuals with a natal Splay pattern do demonstrate some sort of natural genius. The fact that the world does not contain a large surplus of geniuses is another reason that Jansky limits the definition of the ideal Splay pattern.

Once a Splay person overcomes the inertia associated with a Grand Trine, it can be hard to keep up with them.

Splay individuals tend to hold a rather narrow view of life. They tend to regard their way as the best way. They can't see (and would never admit) that the solutions of anyone else are as good or better than theirs.

The sure-footedness of the Splay pattern can lend a heightened sense of self-worth to these individuals. They tend to have greater self-confidence and a stronger personality drive than other planetary pattern types.

## Counseling the Individual with a Splay Pattern

Individuals with a natal Splay pattern tend to live life on their own terms. They have no problem being labeled "different." When it suits their purposes, they are capable of conformity.

Great achievers with the Splay pattern tend to be rugged individualists who can stand apart from others and yet influence them. They can be a powerful influence through sheer force of personality.

Fixity of purpose is typical of Splay people. They're unlikely to change their mind, unless it is beneficial to do so. Compromise is a life lesson that Splay individuals need to work on. Otherwise they can expect personal relationships to suffer.

Splay pattern people are well advised to focus their education on one specialty but with the possibility of pursuing several avocational studies that will become captivating ways to pass time in the future.

Splay individuals can diffuse their energies by engaging in too many projects at the same time. If they can avoid overcommitment and time their efforts right, then everything should work out okay.

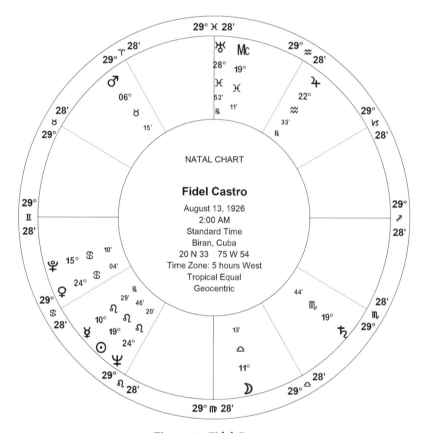

Figure 50: Fidel Castro

If we include the possibility of the Ascendant or Midheaven serving as one of the legs in a Grand Trine, then the natal Splay pattern of Fidel Castro—communist revolutionary and former president of Cuba—includes a Water Grand Trine (figure 50).

Jansky used a noon chart for Fidel Castro. The Astro Databank reports a birth time of 2:00 a.m., with a Rodden rating of DD, indicating there are conflicting, unverified times of birth. Curiously, both the 12:00 noon and the 2:00 a.m. birth time result in a Splay pattern. There is also a pair of oppositions in both birth times. In the chart shown here, Jupiter is opposed to both the Sun and Neptune.

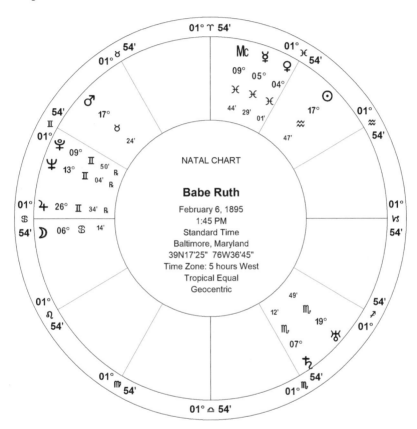

Figure 51: Babe Ruth

Jansky included the natal chart for Babe Ruth as an example of the Splay pattern even though it includes an opposition between Mars and the Saturn-Uranus conjunction (figure 51). Certainly, the Babe's athletic genius was beyond question. A Water Grand Trine draws on the Moon, Venus, and Saturn. Although the Seesaw pattern is also a possibility for Babe Ruth's chart, the Splay better fits his psychological drives and leadership.

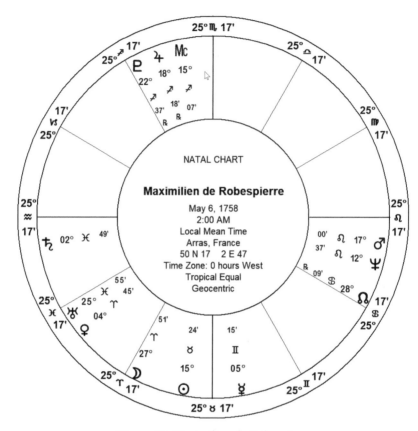

Figure 52: Maximilien de Robespierre

The natal Splay pattern in the chart of Maximilien de Robespierre is near-ideal (figure 52). It features a wide Fire Grand Trine between the Moon, Mars, and Jupiter-Pluto. There are no oppositions. However, the spread of one of the spokes is a trine, much wider than a sextile.

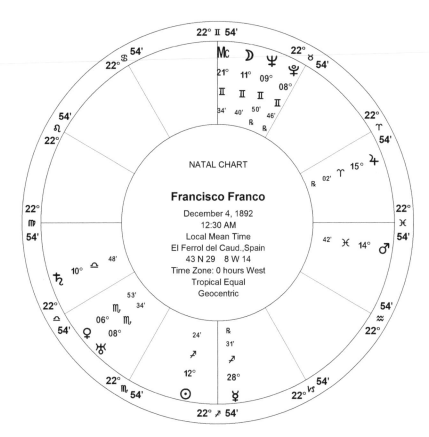

Figure 53: Francisco Franco

Several planetary pattern candidates exist for the natal chart of Generalis-simo Francisco Franco (figure 53). A case for the Seesaw pattern can be made by pointing to two opposing groups, one with an open space corresponding to a trine and the other being less than a square. A Locomotive pattern is possible, with Saturn as the leading planet. Mars is the apex of a Mutable T-Square with a Sun-Moon opposition. I favor the Splay pattern with the Moon, Neptune, and Pluto forming one group, the Mars-Jupiter semisextile forming a second group, and the remaining planets forming the third group.

chapter 10
# How to Recognize Aspect Patterns

A proper analysis of aspects is critical to the interpretation of a natal chart. Aspect patterns are another quick path to chart interpretation. The experienced eye can see the major aspect patterns at a glance and understand motivations from the central core of the chart.

Aspect patterns are built from the basic aspects in a natal chart: conjunctions, oppositions, trines, squares, quincunxes, etc.

The chart search feature for the Solar Fire 9 astrology software includes the twelve basic aspect patterns we'll encounter in this book. The results from the Astro Databank are tabulated as follows.

| Aspect Pattern in Natal Chart | Percentage |
| --- | --- |
| Three-Planet Stellium | 41.67 |
| Four-Planet Stellium | 7.11 |
| Five-Planet Stellium | 0.72 |
| The T-Square | 62.50 |
| The Grand Cross | 5.81 |

*(continued)*

| Aspect Pattern in Natal Chart | Percentage |
|---|---|
| The Mystic Rectangle | 5.47 |
| Hard Rectangle | 0.91 |
| Grand Trine | 31.25 |
| The Kite | 10.87 |
| The Yod | 15.63 |
| Thor's Hammer | 16.67 |

Each individual chart has a single planetary pattern. While there can some-times be uncertainty as to which planetary pattern applies to a chart, we pick just one at most. One in six charts doesn't fit any of the planetary patterns in the first part of this book.

Aspect patterns are not limited to one per chart. A chart can possess—and usually does possess—several aspect patterns.

More traditional forms of astrology focus on planets, and interpret them in terms of signs, houses, and rulerships. Less emphasis is placed on the relation-ships between planets via aspects.

Astrological psychology has been the dominant paradigm in the West since Dane Rudhyar's *The Astrology of Personality* back in 1936. The focus of astro-logical psychology is on interrelationships in the birth chart and how those are indicators of basic drives and motivations. Rather than playing ring-around-the-rosy with planets, signs, and houses, the contemporary astrologer is more likely to find their way into the natal chart through planetary patterns, aspect patterns, unaspected planets, and retrograde planets. These are features of a chart that can be analyzed in just a few minutes, and they're rich in meaning.

Any natal chart is loaded with information. So much information, it can overwhelm the less experienced astrologer. Their insecurity over missing something critical often leads them to spend too much time on a client's chart prior to a consultation. Consultations usually last an hour to ninety minutes, depending on the astrologer and how much detail they try to convey to the client. Time with the client typically includes a brief period of introductions to help the client relax, the analysis of the natal chart, a brief forecast for the coming six months to a year, and questions from the client. There is simply no time to go into great detail about all of the facets of the client's chart. We have to focus on what astrologer Kathy Rose calls the "bigger bells." Planetary patterns are among those bigger bells. We now add aspect patterns to our gulps of chart synthesis.

I'm not arguing that planets in signs and houses and associated rulerships have no place in natal interpretation. They do. The experienced eye can quickly appreciate, for example, the chain of dispositors in a chart. A complete synthesis of a natal chart includes such detail. But we have to start somewhere. Planetary patterns and aspect patterns allow us to start with the forest before we move on to examine the individual trees. They provide the keys to a holistic interpretation of the horoscope.

You'll find that planetary patterns and aspect patterns resonate with your clients. These patterns tap into motivations and energies that are often unconscious. When a client validates the challenge(s) of an aspect pattern, it's a good way to begin a consultation. It always helps when the client sees themselves in our astrological interpretations. They see for themselves that astrology works. It has meaning for their life.

Some astrologers do readings. They tell the client at the outset not to interrupt the interpretation and that there will be time at the end for questions. I prefer consultations, with full dialogue and no jargon. I find that aspect patterns stimulate conversation. They get the discussion off to a good start.

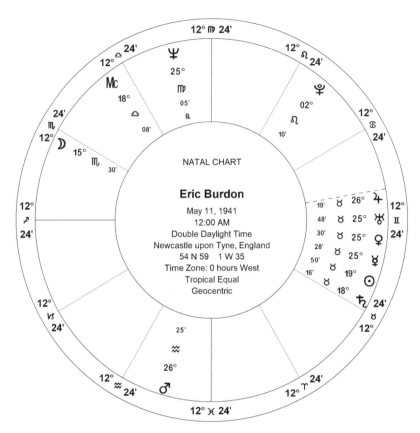

Figure 54: Eric Burdon

## The Stellium Preview

There is debate about the composition of a stellium. Some astrologers hold that it must contain four or more planets in a sign or house within the orb of a conjunction. Others, like me, argue that there need be only a triple conjunction in a sign or house to qualify. No one would doubt that the natal chart of Eric Burdon, singer of the rock band the Animals, contains a stellium (figure 54), with six planets, all within the space of 8°, in the sixth house. Don't let the 12:00 noon birth time fool you. It has an AA Rodden rating, meaning it's from a birth certificate or hospital birth record.

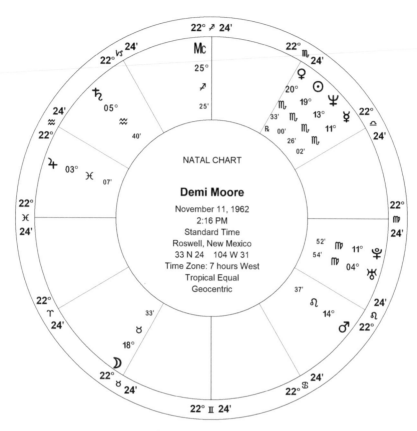

Figure 55: Demi Moore

## The T-Square Preview

A T-Square (or T-Cross) occurs when two planets are in opposition aspect to each other and both make a square aspect to a third planet. The pattern resembles the letter "T" when viewed in the chart. In the case of Demi Moore, the opposition is between the Moon and the Sun-Venus conjunction (figure 55). There are squares between the Moon and Mars and between the Sun-Venus conjunction and Mars.

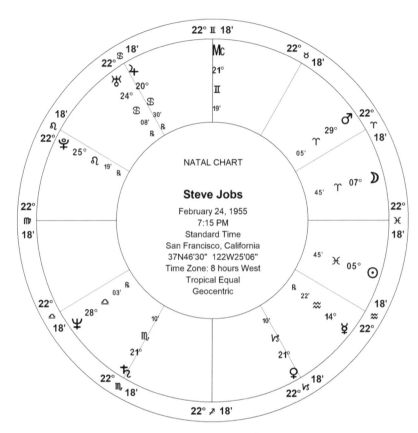

Figure 56: Steve Jobs

## The Grand Cross Preview

The Grand Cross pattern is a configuration of very intense aspects. Two pairs of oppositions are connected by four interlocking squares. The natal chart for Steve Jobs contains a Cardinal Grand Cross (figure 56). Mars and Neptune form one opposition. Venus and Jupiter-Uranus form the other opposition. Mars squares Jupiter-Uranus and also Venus. Neptune squares Jupiter-Uranus and also Venus. Steve Jobs's Grand Cross is just a little wide in orb.

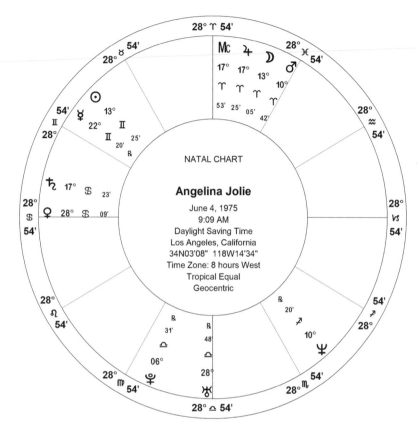

Figure 57: Angelina Jolie

## The Mystic Rectangle Preview

The Mystic Rectangle is composed of two opposition aspects connected by two trine and two sextile aspects. The harmonious trine and sextile aspects can be considered release points for the tension of the oppositions. In the case of Angelina Jolie, Pluto opposes Mars and Neptune opposes the Sun (figure 57). The Sun and Mars are sextile, as are Neptune and Pluto. Mars is trine Neptune, and the Sun is widely trine Pluto.

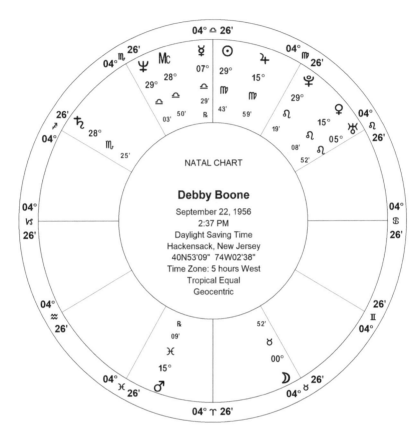

Figure 58: Debby Boone

## The Hard Rectangle Preview

The Hard Rectangle contains two sets of oppositions whose ends are in semi-square and sesquiquadrate aspects to each other The individual is pressed to solve the tension applied in the two oppositions by indirect means. Debby Boone's natal chart contains a Hard Square with Mars opposed to Jupiter and the Moon opposed to Neptune (figure 58). The Moon and Mars are semisquare, as are Jupiter and Neptune.

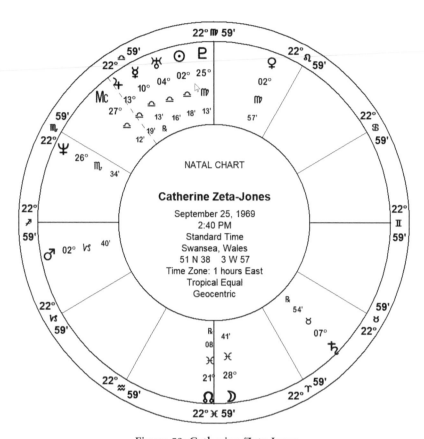

Figure 59: Catherine Zeta-Jones

## The Grand Trine Preview

The Grand Trine is formed from three individual trine aspects. Typically, the planets will share the same element. The natal chart for Catherine Zeta-Jones has an Earth Grand Trine (figure 59). Venus is trine to Mars, Mars is widely trine to Saturn, and Saturn is widely trine to Venus.

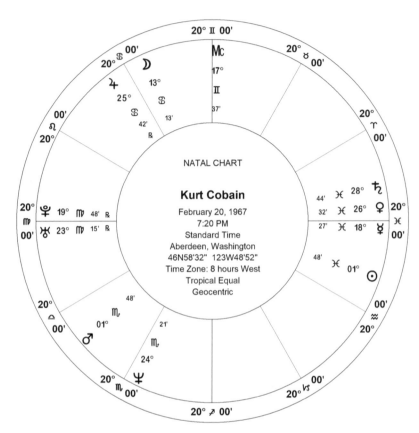

Figure 60: Kurt Cobain

## The Kite Preview

The Kite pattern is an extension of the Grand Trine pattern. What's different? A planet is in opposition to one of the "points" of the Grand Trine. In the case of Kurt Cobain, a Water Grand Trine includes an opposition between Uranus and Mercury (figure 60).

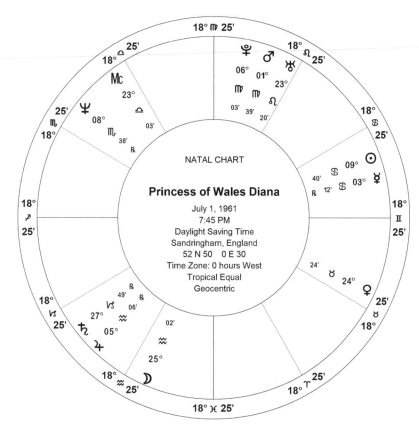

Figure 61: Diana, Princess of Wales

## The Yod Preview

The Yod, also called the Finger of God or Finger of Fate, is a triangular pattern formed from two quincunxes and a sextile. In the case of Diana, Princess of Wales, Mars and Mercury form quincunxes to Jupiter (figure 61). Mars and Mercury are also separated by a sextile.

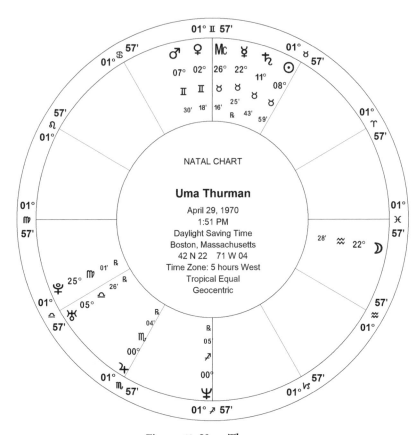

Figure 62: Uma Thurman

## The Thor's Hammer Preview

Thor's Hammer is an aspect pattern consisting of a square and two sesqui-quadrate interconnecting aspects. In the case of Uma Thurman, the square is between the Moon and Mercury (figure 62). Uranus is at the apex.

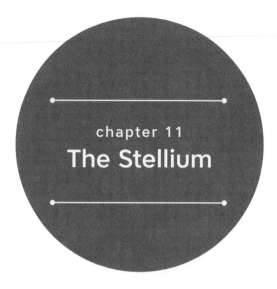

## chapter 11

# The Stellium

A stellium is a bundle of planets all within the orb of a single conjunction. They combine together to work as a single "super planet." The stellium is at its strongest when the planets all share the same sign and the same house. A stellium packs a strong punch.

A stellium is a highly charged zone of your birth chart. You favor these energies. Others sense them. If it's powerful enough, a stellium can eclipse your Sun, Moon, and Ascendant sign as the most outstanding combination of impulses in your natal chart.

## The Ideal Stellium Pattern

There are differing interpretations among astrologers regarding the definition of the ideal stellium pattern.

Donna Cunningham made a distinction between the stellium and the three-planet conjunction. She argued that the stellium requires four planets or more within the orb of a single conjunction. Then she turned around and treated the three-planet conjunction just like it was a stellium.

There's another classic rule that some astrologers observe: a stellium must have two or more planets that are not the Sun, Mercury, or Venus. Why those three in particular? Because Mercury and Venus never travel very far from the

Sun. At any given time, Mercury is at most 28° from the Sun, and Venus is at most 47° away. It's too easy to make a three-planet conjunction from just the Sun, Mercury, and Venus. They're often in the same sign together.

There are two kinds of stelliums that everyone agrees upon: a stellium by house, when the planets all occupy the same astrological house, and a stellium by sign, when all the planets occupy the same astrological sign. The stellium is stronger when all the planets are in the same house and sign. Some astrologers also recognize the dissociate stellium. That's a stellium where the planets cross boundaries for both house and sign.

There's also the delicate matter of orb, especially for those of us who use a tight orb of, say, 7–8° for a conjunction. That's a narrow space in which to fit five or six planets. Most astrologers will stretch the orb a bit for a stellium. How far? That's a matter of experience. Of course, the closer the orb, the more intense the experiences and energy of the stellium.

So we're left with this ideal definition of the stellium pattern: the stellium pattern is composed of four or more planets within orb of a conjunction in the same astrological sign or house and two of which must not be the Sun, Mercury, or Venus.

That's the ideal. The working definition I use includes the three-planet conjunction and the dissociate stellium. I retain the need for two planets to be other than the Sun, Mercury, and Venus. Why? Because there are just too many days of the year when the Sun, Mercury, and Venus fall in the same sign.

## The Stellium Pattern Temperament

The most potent stelliums, as Donna Cunningham notes, occur with the slower-moving planets: Saturn, Uranus, Neptune, and Pluto. They represent major social, political, and economic changes that affect entire generations. They have a profound effect on those born under them. Conjunctions among the slower-moving planets occur infrequently, as shown in the following chart.

| Stellium | Frequency in Years |
|----------------|--------------------|
| Saturn-Uranus | 45 |
| Saturn-Neptune | 35–37 |
| Saturn-Pluto | 33 |

*(continued)*

| Stellium | Frequency in Years |
|----------|--------------------|
| Uranus-Neptune | 172–173 |
| Uranus-Pluto | 111–143 |
| Neptune-Pluto | ~500 |

There was a "super conjunction" in Capricorn during half of 1988 and all of 1989 involving Saturn, Uranus, and Neptune. Everyone born on the planet during that time had a three-planet conjunction. Many born during the winter months also had the Sun, Mercury, and/or Venus in Capricorn as well. So many millions of people were born with a stellium during those months.

There are pluses and minuses involved with the stellium pattern. Here are some reasons stelliums can be a great asset:

• Stelliums can provide a strong sense of mission or purpose;

• They can make life quite an adventure, a meaningful journey;

• They offer an intense focus on one house and sign of your chart, through which you can grow;

• Over the course of a lifetime, the individual can accumulate considerable experience related to their mission; and

• Several different kinds of energy are brought to bear on the matters of the stellium's house(s), which allows for the development of a unique range of useful skills.

Here are some reasons stelliums can make you vulnerable:

• Stelliums can be too much of a good thing—too many eggs in one basket;

• The individual might become so focused on one area that they lack a healthy mental, emotional, and physical balance;

• When things go wrong, the sense of loss can be devastating; and

• Transits that affect the planets in the stellium can have a domino effect when not managed well.

The house(s) of the chart that the stellium occupies reveals the areas of life the individual is most invested in and where they're most vulnerable. The behaviors and actions that can create difficulty for the individual are further shown by the qualities of the sign and planets involved in the stellium.

Not everyone born with a particular combination of planets in a stellium will have the same experiences and challenges. Stelliums work like any other chart feature. There's the individual's background to consider. Their level of social, economic, and psychological development has an impact. Plus, there's free will to contend with.

Factors that strengthen a stellium's impact include the following:

• The more planets involved in the stellium, the stronger the impact;

• The closer the planets in the stellium, the stronger the impact;

• When all the planets in the stellium are in the same sign AND house, the impact is stronger;

• When the planets in the stellium are split into two houses or two signs, the impact is weaker;

• When the planets in the stellium are within 10° of the Sun, Moon, Ascendant, or Midheaven, the impact is stronger;

• When one or more outer planets are present, the impact is stronger;

• When planets in the stellium are also part of a major configuration like a T-Square, Grand Trine, or Yod, the impact is stronger; and

• When the ruler of the house or sign of the stellium is part of the stellium, the impact is stronger.

When a single house holds several planets, it becomes a major focus for an individual's efforts. There's often a sense of being driven, of pursuing a destiny they must fulfill. They feel they have a calling in life. The areas of life described by the house(s) where a stellium is placed provide important clues to the mission. Each planet involved in a stellium has an important role to play in the mission.

## The Stellium in Aries

People with Aries strongly featured in their chart—and this includes Aries stelliums—are symbolic of the fighting spirit. That can make them fierce protectors and strong champions of the people and causes they adopt. Their energy tends to focus on independent initiative and action, and on individualistic expression. They have an abundance of leadership qualities. They tend to be pioneers in their field of interest. On the less positive side, they can be overbearing in getting what they want and ignore the wishes and feelings of those around them. Rash and impetuous, they can rush into action without considering the long-term consequences. Positive polarity lends an outgoing expression to the sign. Cardinality provides initiatory and self-starting energy. The element of fire tends toward dramatic, lively, and confident expression.

### The Stellium in Taurus

People with Taurus strongly featured in their chart—and this includes Taurus stelliums—crave a sense of security and stability. Unlike the Aries love of the game, the typical Taurus personality loves the rewards of the game. They're peaceful and easygoing. They're extremely sensual in nature, in love with life's earthly pleasures. Dogged and stubborn in their allegiance, they are some of the most dedicated people. Averse to change, they can be extremely stubborn and fixed in approach. They're not afraid to take their time in order to get the job done properly. Somewhat on the introverted side, they tend to build intimate relationships that last for a long time. Reluctant when it comes to conflict and aggression, they tend to shut down in the presence of loud and aggressive individuals. Their slow pace can be irritating to fire and air signs.

### The Stellium in Gemini

People with Gemini strongly featured in their chart—and this includes Gemini stelliums—typically have a quick mind and an eagerness to learn. That helps them keep up with today's constantly evolving technologies. They pick up new skills and information easily. They're not afraid to speak up for what they believe in. They can be charming individuals due to a gift of gab, a good sense of humor, and a flattering interest in other people. Gemini is a prominent air sign. Like air, these individuals are ever changing. Like the other mutable signs (Virgo, Sagittarius, and Pisces), Gemini might seem to scatter their interests in many different directions, and might even be considered a dilettante. When the stellium is in one of the vocational houses (second, sixth, or tenth) or forms an angle to the career-related Midheaven, this might take the form of changing jobs or even careers several times.

### The Stellium in Cancer

People with Cancer strongly featured in their chart—and this includes Cancer stelliums—typically have deep attachments to family. This could even be a family of their own choosing, for example, coworkers if the stellium is placed in the sixth house. They're extremely intuitive and sentimental. They'll go out of their way to help others. They'll do anything possible to avoid conflicts. They're quiet and very reserved about their feelings. Their traits include a strong sense of domesticity, femininity, and sensitivity. Chief among their traits is an inherent need to serve as a caregiver. They're strongly prone to codependent relationships, in which they overindulge or enable those they care for in ways that keep them from growing into independence. Like the other water signs, Scorpio and Pisces, Cancer individuals are extremely sensitive to their surroundings and to people.

### The Stellium in Leo

People with Leo strongly featured in their chart—and this includes Leo stelliums—typically are fun, adventurous, genuine, generous, and highly charismatic. They're confident and full of vigor and energy. They're happiest when they're surrounded by people. They love to entertain lavishly. Some might be too caught up in themselves and be very self-centered, but they're never too self-absorbed to help anyone who needs it. They don't hold a grudge and they're very forgiving. They have respect for and an understanding of people's differences. They love the new and extraordinary and despise dull, regular routines. If this is what they are faced with, they'll simply create their own drama and excitement. They want only the best, which can lead to lavish, excessive spending habits. Public image is very important to them.

### The Stellium in Virgo

People with Virgo strongly featured in their chart—and this includes Virgo stelliums—typically have many practical skills and are willing and eager to be useful. Very independent, they're able to put their intelligence to use and get things done for themselves. Analytical and observant, they have a keen eye for detail. They can also be fussy, perfectionistic, and overly critical, never letting up on themselves and others. Their narrow-mindedness can cause their creativity to suffer. They might dwell too much on the past and overcomplicate things. Dedicated and unselfish, they can sacrifice their own needs to an unhealthy degree, even becoming martyrs. Before a Virgo plunges into anything, they need to analyze all the facts and know all the details to make a decision. This can make them seem indecisive and slow.

### The Stellium in Libra

People with Libra strongly featured in their chart—and this includes Libra stelliums—are typically peaceful and fair and hate being alone. Partnership is very important to them. They're diplomatic, romantic, highly aesthetic, and a little indulgent. They're cooperative team players. They can be wonderful assets because of their people skills. They strive for justice and fairness. Difficult traits include indulgence, indecisiveness, laziness, and excessiveness. Their decisions are never taken lightly because they take so many factors into consideration. This includes everyone else's opinions. They have good critical faculties and are able to stand back and look impartially at matters. They tend to be idealistic and peaceful people who are easygoing and rarely feel that fighting or arguing is the best solution to a problem.

### The Stellium in Scorpio

People with Scorpio strongly featured in their chart—and this includes Scorpio stelliums—typically have intense and sustained passions. Scorpio is a fixed water sign, and water symbolizes emotions. With emotionality so pronounced, some hold on to a grievance for years, brooding on how to get even. They rarely, if ever, forgive and forget. Likewise, they will always remember a kind gesture and repay it. Determined and decisive, they will research until they find out the truth. Fiercely independent, they can accomplish anything they put their mind to, and they won't give up. Scorpios are all about control. They need to be in control at all times. To be out of control is very threatening, even dangerous, to the Scorpio's psyche. When they control, they feel safe. Negative emotions of jealousy and resentment are common.

### The Stellium in Sagittarius

People with Sagittarius strongly featured in their chart—and this includes Sagittarius stelliums—typically are outgoing and outspoken. They possess an enviable sense of optimism about life. These are people who love to travel and are most in their element when exploring new places or meeting new people. Given the choice between freedom and security, these people will choose freedom each and every time. They love knowledge almost as much as they love travel and adventure. They can be extremely egocentric and generally want to impose their views on others. These people are confident, but sometimes to the point of being arrogant. Their optimism can make them oblivious to the fact they could be at fault at times. They are immune to criticism.

### The Stellium in Capricorn

People with Capricorn strongly featured in their chart—and this includes Capricorn stelliums—typically prefer to plan and rehearse everything in advance. As a result, they typically excel at anything they turn their mind to. They tend to be highly practical people who like structure, organization, tradition, and stability. They possess an inner state of independence that enables them to make significant progress in their personal and professional lives. Belonging to the element of earth, they are noted for their practicality and grounding. Not only do they focus on the material world, but they also have the ability to make the most of it. Unfortunately, this element also makes them stiff and sometimes too stubborn to move from one perspective in a relationship. They can have a hard time accepting the differences of other people.

### The Stellium in Aquarius

People with Aquarius strongly featured in their chart—and this includes Aquarius stelliums—typically are avant-garde in their ideas. They're also highly adaptive and sociable, yet detached and practical in their own way. Like all air-sign individuals, they have the traits of being naturally social, friendly, and people-oriented. They possess a strong desire to leave the world a better place than they found it. They have an inherent need to make sure life is as fair as possible for everyone. They possess an incredibly high energy level. Most can't stand the idea of being bored and seek out constant interaction with the world around them. They can be sensitive and even vulnerable. As far as careers go, they're better off self-employed or in a position where they work independently. When told what to do, they can be quite contrary.

### The Stellium in Pisces

People with Pisces strongly featured in their chart—and this includes Pisces stelliums—typically are spiritual and creative and have a gift for detecting someone's true feelings. According to Donna Cunningham, "Neptune-ruled Pisces is one of the more challenging signs for a stellium because it might encompass the highest highs and lowest lows of human existence. In a single lifetime, the Neptunian type can go from pinnacle to bottom and back again" (Cunningham 2013, 49). People with Pisces stelliums are more intuitive than others, and artistic talent is common. Pisces are the dreamers of the zodiac. Caring and sympathetic, they typically enjoy helping others and intensely dislike confrontation. They react strongly to the moods of others, often assuming those same moods themselves. They're the sign that is most prone to depression, dependency, and escapism.

### The Stellium in the First House

Several planets in the first house—and this includes first-house stelliums—typically determine the personality of an individual and how they present themselves to the world. The signs and planets in this house affect the development of the self and give an indication of how the person will develop as an individual. Behaviors depicted by the first house generally grow out of roles defined by family dynamics in childhood or the early environment. They become an automatic response to social situations. If you have a first-house stellium that includes one of the outermost planets (Saturn, Uranus, Neptune, or Pluto), that planet colors the impression you make on the outside world, especially when it's conjunct the Ascendant. You might come across to others as the sign that outer planet rules, rather than the sign that is actually on your Ascendant.

### The Stellium in the Second House

Several planets in the second house—and this includes second-house stelliums—typically have a lot to do with a person's own self-worth, how they feel about themselves. If a person doesn't think highly of themselves, then they're likely to have a hard time with a stellium in the second house. What they do with their money and the things they own can reveal a lot about the second-house personality. The second house gives an in-depth understanding of what an individual does to make themselves feel stable and secure. Having outer planets as part of a stellium in the second house suggests that money can become an issue that consumes a great deal of their energy and thought. Some astrologers downplay the lessons related to money handling in the second house, but this does a disservice to clients since personal finance and money handling can be important life skill issues for clients.

### The Stellium in the Third House

Several planets in the third house—and this includes third-house stelliums—typically evidence a very active mind. It suggests a number of strong interests. A constant search for knowledge is common. Topics of interest are described by the signs and planets in the third house. Individuals with a third-house stellium need to talk. Talking helps them feel better. Often they're great conversationalists. Siblings can have an especially profound effect on them. Relationships with siblings can be the strongest bonds, stronger even than the bond with their spouse. The Sun, Moon, Mercury, or Venus in the stellium can show supportive siblings. Mars can suggest competition and conflict. With Saturn, an older sibling who has accomplished a great deal might dwarf them. With Uranus, siblings might be mavericks. With Pluto, there's often a power struggle. A sibling might even have been abusive.

### The Stellium in the Fourth House

Several planets in the fourth house—and this includes fourth-house stelliums—typically place an emphasis on home. Everything can come back to home and family. This stellium also brings a focus to family roots, heredity, the nurturing parent, and the senior years. Scorpio, Neptune, or Pluto can reflect family secrets. This could indicate that the early family life was a focus of emotional intensity and battles for power and control. The individual might carry over some childhood patterns into their adult home life. A powerful connection with the nurturing parent is suggested by a fourth-house stellium. Prone to nostalgia, these individuals can become emotionally stuck in the past.

### The Stellium in the Fifth House

Several planets in the fifth house—and this includes fifth-house stelliums—typically show huge potential in theatrics or art, particularly if the ruler of the Midheaven is part of the stellium. These people are the life of the party, and a life of enjoyment and recreation, a connection with the inner child, and a genuine interest in creativity are common. In one way or another, children are likely to have a big place in the life of an individual with a fifth-house stellium, with children of their own or working in a professional capacity with children. The sign and planets in the stellium might give clues to the types of art or performance the individual is gifted at. Subject to intense romantic attachments, they have a lot of love to give.

### The Stellium in the Sixth House

Several planets in the sixth house—and this includes sixth-house stelliums—typically suggest a workaholic personality. Much of their energy is bound up in the workplace. Health is a twin concern. Health and work are interrelated in our attempts to find work that is deeply fulfilling. As Donna Cunningham noted, "When people whose 6th is strong (especially when the Sun is there) feel happy and satisfied in their daily work, they tend to stay well, feel good about themselves, and generally enjoy life. For a person whose 6th hosts a stellium, unhappiness in work often takes a toll on health" (Cunningham 2013, 62). When the Sun is part of a stellium in the sixth, self-esteem is bound up in the quality of work. Many Virgo traits show up with a stellium in the sixth house, even when there are no Virgo planets.

### The Stellium in the Seventh House

Several planets in the seventh house—and this includes seventh-house stelliums—typically describe how we function in committed relationships such as marriage and in business partnerships—both the actual individuals and the type of connection between them. Libran traits tend to manifest in relationships, specifically indecision when dealing with others. Those with a seventh-house stellium have many wants and needs in partnerships and thus might have many mates before finding the right one. They might work with their life partner.

A constant need to be around people is typical. They tend to feel incomplete when alone. The mix of planets can make it more difficult to maintain harmony within the relationship. There is a tendency to deny the qualities seventh-house planets describe and project them onto the partner. Mars in the seventh might say something like, "I'm not temperamental, but the people I get involved with always are."

## The Stellium in the Eighth House

Several planets in the eighth house—and this includes eighth-house stelliums—typically describe our experiences and approach to sexuality, birth, death, rebirth, healing, regeneration, transformation, taxes, and debt. That's a lot of meaning for one house, and individuals with an eighth-house stellium can spend considerable time and energy learning to integrate all those concerns. Many are largely beyond our control, and knowing when to make control an issue and when to release tends to be an important life lesson. Obsessions with the uncontrollable can greatly complicate life. Another major concern is how we deal with the finances and resources of others we're close to. A really important issue with an eighth-house stellium is the topic of sex. The nature of the planets and signs involved affect attitudes toward sex and any difficulties with it.

## The Stellium in the Ninth House

Several planets in the ninth house—and this includes ninth-house stelliums—typically share Sagittarius's focus on higher education and the search for answers to life's bigger questions. The eternal student but also a teacher at heart, these individuals are likely to wind up teaching some of what they master. There is a danger that they can live too much in their head and not deal with the practical realities of life. The Moon in a ninth-house stellium often indicates a mother who placed a high value on education and pushed hard for her children to get one—the tiger mom. With Uranus, the education could be interrupted. This could be due to unconventional beliefs and interests as well as rebellion against traditional academic authorities. Saturn in a ninth-house stellium could also symbolize delays or difficulties due to financial hardship or family responsibilities.

### The Stellium in the Tenth House

Several planets in the tenth house—and this includes tenth-house stelliums—typically represent a preoccupation with career, long-term goals, lifetime achievements, and our status in the world. Individuals with a strong tenth-house emphasis tend to be very career-oriented, rather than necessarily focused on money (second house) or on work for its own sake (sixth house). When money is important to them, it tends to be more for the status it confers. With a stellium in the tenth house, there are sometimes issues with the choice of profession and dealing with authority figures. This is a take-charge stellium. These people want to be the leader. They tend to be extremely ambitious, with a flair for business. The career track will seldom be traditional when the tenth house features the outer planets (especially Uranus, Neptune, or Pluto) or the signs these planets rule (Aquarius, Pisces, and Scorpio). Donna Cunningham notes that many individuals with outer planets conjunct the Midheaven "grew up in dysfunctional homes, with difficult or inconsistent experiences of parental authority" (Cunningham 2013, 65).

### The Stellium in the Eleventh House

Several planets in the eleventh house—and this includes eleventh-house stelliums—typically suggest a concern with social causes. Peers, group and organization membership, networking, and social action can be critically important. Involvements with groups, associations, and organizations can swallow up the individual so that they lose themselves in the group cause. They might find they become part of the herd in terms of collective values when in any group, so it might be better if they work with small, creative groups in which they feel a sense of control and stability. Friendship can be a great source of support. However, friends can also enable their bad habits and behavior patterns. Watch out when an eleventh-house stellium is transited by aspects from one of the slower-moving planets (Saturn, Uranus, Neptune, or Pluto), as it can indicate a crisis period in one or several important friendships.

### The Stellium in the Twelfth House

Several planets in the twelfth house—and this includes twelfth-house stelliums—typically need to get outside of themselves and involve themselves in service to others. Without that individual release, they can become quite neurotic! They have to be careful not to fall into the snare of rescuing behavior and codependency. These individuals tend to have great natural psychic ability. A person with a twelfth-house stellium is focused in their own, hidden world and can find it difficult to go out and face reality. They generally don't do well in the limelight and might even prefer to work alone. Highly imaginative individuals, they can become easily confused and unable to focus. As Cunningham writes about twelfth-house stelliums, "As challenging as it is, 12th house placements can bring you great joy and inner fulfillment" (Cunningham 2013, 81).

### The Dissociate Stellium

There are two general categories of stelliums: the stellium by sign and the stellium by house. Both can, however, have a dissociate form. The stellium by sign can cross a house cusp, thereby occupying two houses. The stellium by house can likewise cross a zodiac sign boundary and thereby occupy two zodiac signs.

When either dissociate stellium pattern occurs, there is a blurring or blending of interpretations involved.

When a stellium occupies two houses, then the signs and planets involved in the stellium will make themselves felt in two different areas of life. The individual might alternate between the two concerns or manage to find a creative way to blend the affairs of the two houses.

When the stellium occupies two signs, there will be two different ways the individual approaches the tasks and concerns of a house. For the individual to feel whole rather than torn and confused, those different approaches need to be reconciled in some way. This can be a challenge because the two signs will involve different polarities—yin and yang—making the task of their successful blending all the more difficult. Stelliums can be challenging for individuals. Nobody said living with a stellium was easy.

## Counseling the Individual with a Stellium Pattern

For the individual with a stellium, understanding this aspect pattern is likely the single most important set of insights astrology has to offer them.

While planets in a stellium can show great promise, it depends on how the individual uses them. The abilities can be misused or wasted. It depends on the character of the individual.

Awareness of the strengths and weaknesses of each piece of a stellium is the primary tool for mastering it. The individual needs to appreciate the house and sign involved for each planet in the pattern.

Individuals who can't accept the qualities of the stellium's sign—both the good and the bad traits—are less likely to develop the stellium's promise to its fullest.

The key factor with a stellium is not to become consumed with that one area in life. Individuals with a stellium might discover that they are devoting too much time and energy to activities associated with the stellium. The best way to determine whether the individual is making effective use of their stellium is to look at the opposing sign and assess whether that area of their life is receiving equal attention. If the needs of that section of their natal chart is also being met, then the individual is likely finding the correct balance in life.

Alienation is a feeling that many with stelliums share. Individuals can become intently focused on their mission. Some missions are so unusual that other people can find the stellium person hard to understand. Individuals with Uranus, Neptune, or Pluto in their stellium are especially prone to alienation.

Though individuals might be preoccupied with their real passion—the calling the stellium represents—it's important that they also work consciously at preserving important relationships. The stellium's work can crowd out many other concerns, leaving the partner, family, and friends feeling neglected and unloved. It might even cause them to withdraw. Spending quality time together can keep love alive and create a happier, healthier balance in the individual's life.

Clients with a strong sixth house or a Virgo stellium should be counseled to seriously look for a vocation that meets their deep need to be productive and useful, so they can stay healthy. They might need to make sacrifices to train for fulfilling work.

When an individual has several planets in one sign, there's also a strong potential for expressing even the best traits to the point that they get in the way of the person's physical and emotional well-being. When you do an inventory of the positive potentials of a stellium's sign with a client, think also about ways the client might be overdoing them and throwing their life out of balance.

You will very likely encounter the client who claims the sign of the stellium doesn't fit them. There are many reasons this might occur, including the following two:

- The house(s) of the stellium might dominate the sign(s); and

- The planets involved in the stellium might be a stronger influence than the sign(s).

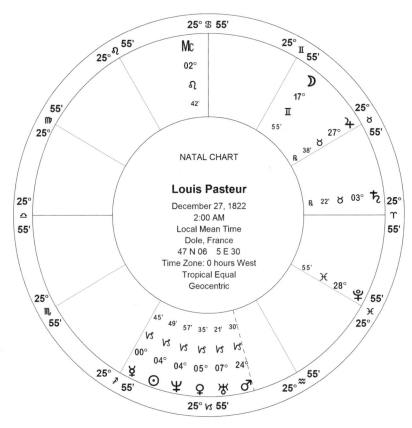

Figure 63: Louis Pasteur

Scientist Louis Pasteur has a five-planet stellium in Capricorn in the third house (figure 63). This is a stellium by sign and by house. There are six planets in Capricorn in the third, but Mars is too widely separated from the other five planets. An orb of 17°9' is too wide for a conjunction. It's true that most astrologers broaden the orb for a conjunction within a stellium, but Mars would be too distant for most astrologers. Communication is emphasized by six planets in the third house and especially by Mercury on the Aries Point (00 Capricorn 45).

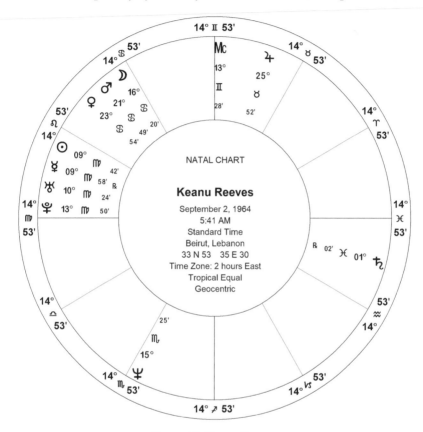

Figure 64: Keanu Reeves

The natal chart for actor Keanu Reeves is very interesting (figure 64). It has two stelliums: a three-planet stellium in Cancer in the eleventh house and a four-planet stellium in Virgo in the twelfth house. An argument can also be made that the chart is a Fan planetary pattern with Saturn in the handle. One could also treat Jupiter and Neptune as a rim opposition for a Bucket pattern with (again, with Saturn in the handle). Stelliums are common in Fan and Bundle patterns because of the concentration of planets in such a compact space.

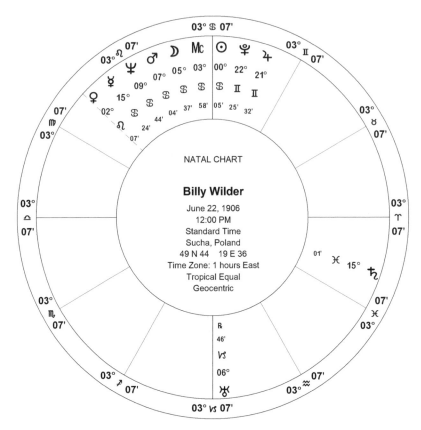

Figure 65: Billy Wilder

A strong case can be made for a five-planet stellium by sign for playwright and screenwriter Billy Wilder (figure 65). Five planets in Cancer span an orb of 15°19'. This is somewhat wider than most astrologers would allow for a single conjunction, but most would find it acceptable for a stellium. The Sun is also spot on an Aries Point at 00 Cancer 05'. This represents the potential for public projection, to become well known. Making his living from writing and publishing is also suggested by two conjunct planets in Gemini in the ninth house. The stellium is dissociate, since it crosses the cusp of the tenth house.

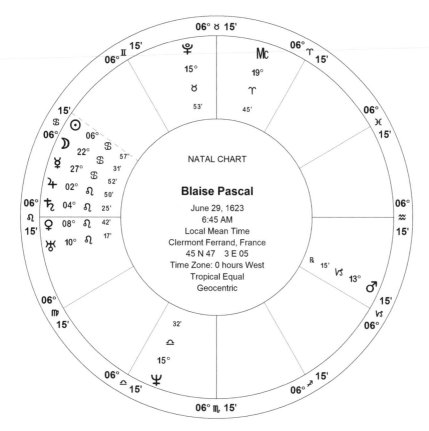

Figure 66: Blaise Pascal

The natal chart for French philosopher Blaise Pascal also presents some interesting synthesis challenges (figure 66). The absence of a rim opposition makes the argument for a Bucket pattern less persuasive than that for a Fan pattern. We have another dissociate stellium. The distance from the Sun to the Moon is a little under 16°, too far for my taste, even for a stellium. How to handle the Moon is tricky. If we accept it as part of the stellium, then the entire sweep of the stellium would be almost 18°. I would argue the stellium runs between Uranus and Mercury, an orb a little wider than 12°.

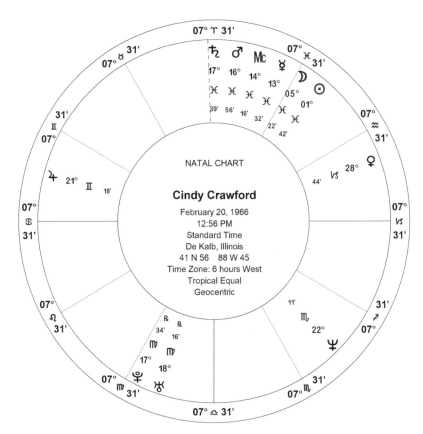

Figure 67: Cindy Crawford

The argument for a five-planet stellium is stronger for American actress and model Cindy Crawford (figure 67). Though the stellium is dissociate (crossing the cusp of the ninth house), all of the planets are in Pisces. The orb of the stellium is just a hair over 16°. If that orb is too wide for your taste, then drop the Sun at 01 Pisces 42 from the stellium. Then the orb drops to approximately 12°.

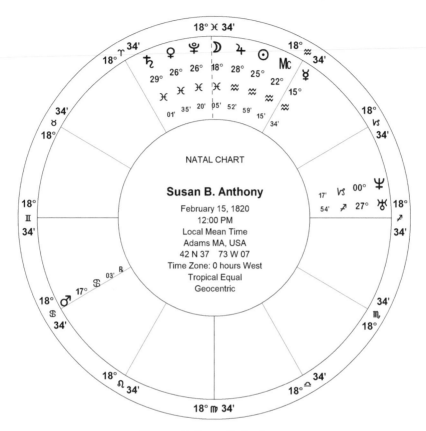

Figure 68: Susan B. Anthony

Susan B. Anthony was an American social reformer and women's rights activist who played a pivotal role in the women's suffrage movement. Her natal chart possesses a pair of dissociate stelliums, each with four planets/points, both directly abutting each other (figure 68). The four-point stellium in Aquarius crosses the ninth-house cusp. The four-planet stellium in Pisces crosses the tenth-house cusp. Both stelliums are consistent with her commitment to humanitarian social reform.

chapter 12
# The T-Square

When two planets in opposition are both squared by a third planet, we call this aspect pattern a T-Square. This aspect pattern in ideal form looks like a large "T" formation. Bil Tierney quotes Tracy Marks's *How to Handle Your T-Square* (subsequently expanded and revised as *Planetary Aspects: An Astrological Guide to Managing Your T-Square*) as claiming that at least 40 percent of natal charts contain a T-Square. We already know from the Astro Databank that the number is closer to 62 percent, or nearly two-thirds of charts of notable individuals contain a T-Square.

A T-Square suggests simultaneously pronounced strength and overemphasis *and* imbalance or deficiency. The two squares create frustration and tension. The third planet seems pulled simultaneously in two directions from the opposition. The attempts of this focal planet to restore its balance and escape the pressure of the opposition can result in a powerful release of energy—negative or positive—depending on the psychological maturity of the individual.

While nearly two-thirds of all charts contain a natal T-Square, everyone experiences multiple T-Squares throughout their lifetime. This is the result of transits, secondary progressions, solar arcs, and the like. If you were to study just one aspect pattern, the T-Square is that pattern. It's that important.

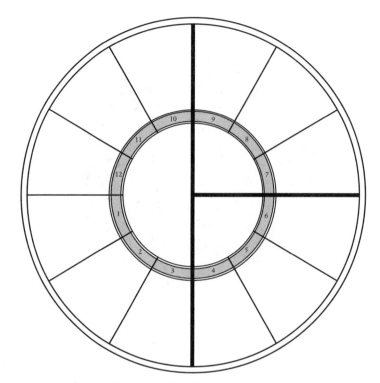

Figure 69: The T-Square Pattern

## The Ideal T-Square Pattern

The ideal T-Square pattern is diagrammed in figure 69. It consists of an opposition between two planets, with a third planet forming a square to each of the opposition planets. The planet forming the squares is called the focal planet (or the apex planet). The empty space across from the focal planet is also a sensitive area in the natal chart. Simple, right? Well, that's the ideal form! In practice, the opposition might be wide and/or the squares not quite so exact. There can also be conjunctions at either end of the opposition or with the focal planet.

According to Tracy Marks, a T-Square is strong under the following conditions:

- All of the planets are within a tight orb (3°);

- The T-Square contains one or more exact aspects (1°);

• The T-Square is angular; or

• The focal planet is at the midpoint of two other planets.

A T-Square is weak under the following conditions:

• One planet is in a sign of a different mode from the other two planets;

• The orbs are wide (over 6°); or

• A planet is within the sign opposite the focal planet and nearly squares or opposes one of the planets in the T-Square.

## The T-Square Pattern Temperament

Frank Clifford claims T-Squares "in particular reveal the major life challenges and themes—the areas in love and work that we get obsessed with and that take up much time and focus" (Clifford 2012, 19). That's a lot of influence for just one aspect pattern!

The T-Square is often found embedded in planetary patterns, such as the Bowl or the Bucket.

The T-Square symbolizes a lot of tension and conflict in one's life, but it also sparks action and the necessary drive to achieve resolution. As Tracy Marks notes, "The t-square indicates not only the primary conflicts a person experiences, but also the talents and personal characteristics which he or she is motivated to develop, and which can lead to considerable achievement and satisfaction if expressed constructively" (Tracy Marks 2014, loc. 12, Kindle).

Stated differently, a T-Square is an aspect that can pose extreme challenge but also bestow great benefit. It all depends on how the individual handles the T-Square's impulses.

The focal planet of a T-Square is the point of greatest overcompensation and activation. It's where the energy of the opposition is condensed and expressed. It's also where the individual seeks to resolve the conflict.

Subconscious impulses focus on the unoccupied area opposite the focal planet. (If this point is occupied, then we have a Grand Cross and not a T-Square.) Any moon phase or planet transiting this sensitive point will highlight the areas of life where the person feels emptiness, that something is missing, or where they overcompensate for the attention they give to the focal planet.

Square and opposition aspects are supposed to be stressful aspects. The T-Square contains both. That's not a cause for panic! It's true that living with the demands of a T-Square can be very challenging. But it's equally true that when the energy of this configuration is well directed by a psychologically mature individual, it often leads to significant accomplishments. This is a frequent aspect pattern among the most successful people. Oprah Winfrey has a T-Square. So does Martha Stewart. The list of notable individuals in the Astro Databank with T-Squares is long and impressive. It's a frequent pattern in the charts of CEOs, political leaders, celebrities, and creative people. It can be argued that because of the challenges these people experienced from their T-Squares, it makes them all the more successful since so much focus is brought about by the T-Square itself.

### The Aspects Involved in a T-Square

Getting to a T-Square's meaning for an individual can be a challenge.

First, there's an opposition involved in a T-Square. Oppositions are considered "hard" aspects that cause friction. Unless the opposition is dissociate (i.e., out of sign), the planets in opposition will be the same polarity. An example would be Cancer and Capricorn. Oppositions tend to be confrontational and divisive. One of the planets involved is active at any given moment, though rarely both planets. There's a push-pull effect, a kind of tug-of-war. In addition to sharing the same polarity—yin or yang—the two planets also share the same modality, unless the opposition is dissociate. So if one planet is cardinal, we expect the other in the opposition to be cardinal as well. Often a person identifies with one side of the opposition and sees the other side as being out there in the world. They project it and find it in another person because they don't acknowledge it as being part of themselves. When oppositions are resolved, growth takes place. Instead of using the opposing energy to breed conflict, the mature individual with a T-Square uses the opposing energy to balance.

Second, there's a pair of square aspects involved in a T-Square. Squares are tenser and more provoking than oppositions. Like oppositions, squares share the same modality: cardinal, fixed, or mutable. Squares reveal conflicting parts of our nature that will have to be resolved through self-reflection, discipline, and personal growth. Tension is necessary to stimulate action, though too much tension results in stress. The planets involved in a square act at cross purposes. Squares can be motivating. They force us out of complacency. Squares are often more difficult to handle when we're young. They force us to grow and learn important life lessons.

## Tearing the T-Square Apart

There's always a lot going on in any T-Square. So the next step is to break it apart and consider common links between the planets, signs, elements, modes, and houses involved. Any recurring themes will help our assessment. Let's consider for a moment the Dissociate T-Square for science fiction writer Philip K. Dick, whose chart is shown later in this chapter. There is a nice tight square between Mars and Uranus in cardinal signs. It's the Sun that's in opposition from a mutable sign. The dominant thrust of this cardinal T-Square is very impatient but also enterprising. Cardinal signs blend with the persevering yet also stubborn and unyielding Sun in the mutable sign of Sagittarius.

The focal planet is often the most dominant planet in the natal chart. The secret to using a T-Square effectively is to learn to use its energy wisely and purposefully rather than compulsively and obsessively.

When interpreting the T-Square, the following considerations apply:

- *The mode (quadruplicity) of the T-Square:* Is it cardinal, fixed, or mutable? Is it dissociate?

- *The focal planet:* Is it direct or retrograde? What is its placement by sign and house? What house(s) does it rule in the chart?

- *The opposition:* Are the planets involved direct or retrograde? What is their placement by sign and house? What houses do they rule in the chart?

- *The empty space of the T-Square:* What is its degree, sign, and house? What is the sign and house of its ruler?

- *Other aspects:* Are there trines and sextiles between planets in the T-Square and planets outside the T-Square? Are there other favorable minor aspects, such as quintiles or noviles?

## The Cardinal T-Square

Cardinal T-Squares are the most dynamic and active. They can bestow vitality, drive, and self-assertion. Individuals with a Cardinal T-Square are inclined to rash actions relating to personal activities, home and family life, long-term relationships, and career commitments. They thrive on excitement and challenge, so much so that they can be in a perpetual frenzy and attempt to overdo in their desire to do too much too soon. The Cardinal T-Square is typically the most extroverted of the different T-Square configurations. As Bil Tierney notes, "Life for those with this driving configuration can seem like one circumstantial crisis after another" (Tierney 2015, 98).

Individuals with a Cardinal T-Square need to learn not to leap into new activities without giving them full and careful deliberation. As Tracy Marks says, "They need to cultivate the positive Libran qualities—balance, moderation, awareness of other people, perspective, and the ability to evaluate and compromise" (Tracy Marks 2014, loc. 207, Kindle).

### The Fixed T-Square

Fixed T-Squares are the most determined and self-willed. These individuals can feel compelled to or be obsessed with satisfying their own desires. Unlike with the Cardinal T-Square, individuals with a Fixed T-Square build up their energy slowly and then release it with powerful force. Their own fixated needs often block those of others when they refuse any attempt at compromise. A natural ability to hold firm to their own principles in the face of opposition can leave them almost immune to outside influences. Rarely as energetic as those with a Cardinal T-Square, individuals with a Fixed T-Square have such a reserve of power and emotional stamina that they seldom buckle under setbacks and pressure, persisting until their goal is achieved.

Individuals with a Fixed T-Square need to find suitable outlets for their pent-up emotions and frustrated desires. They need to learn to periodically vent their feelings in a constructive manner. They also need to learn to become more sensitive to the needs of others. Acceptance of and respect for the values of others is an important life lesson for individuals with a Fixed T-Square.

### The Mutable T-Square

Mutable T-Squares are the most restless and changeable of the different T-Square configurations. They typically feel compelled to take life as it comes, moment to moment. Thus, they are unlikely to plan ahead or be goal-oriented, like the Fixed T-Square. Those with a Mutable T-Square can overtax their nervous system due to overstimulation. They can best work out their nervous stress through intellectual pursuits that require intensive study. Their natural inclination, however, will be to dabble in many different interests. Because they're so adaptable, they can appear vacillating or even weak-willed.

Individuals with a Mutable T-Square need to learn to face challenges head-on, with more determination. They need to discover a mission or purpose, one that can keep them centered and restrict their tendency to spread themselves too thin.

### The Dissociate T-Square

When one of the planets in a T-Square falls into a different mode than the other two, the result is a Dissociate T-Square. Any of the three planets can be out of sign. The most significant pattern is when the focal planet is dissociate. Undertones to the trine and the sextile can occur. While this can ease internal pressure, it can also leave the individual less motivated to overcome the obstacles associated with the T-Square. A lot depends on the nature of the focal planet. Saturn as the focal planet, for example, will bestow a drive to overcome obstacles, offering the individual great strength and patience.

### The Angular T-Square

When two planets combine with the Ascendant or Midheaven, the result is still a perfectly valid T-Square.

When the Ascendant is involved in a T-Square, the tension in the aspect pattern is directed toward the individual's personal identity and self-image. T-Squares with the Ascendant are generally indicative of an identity crisis. This is especially likely to be the case when the Ascendant is in the position of the focal planet. Once the individual learns to skillfully coordinate the opposition challenges, they might display less insecurity, uncertainty, and defensiveness. When the Ascendant is the focal planet, the Descendant occupies the empty space in the T-Square. This enables the individual to apply the lessons learned about self-awareness to relationships with others.

When the Midheaven is part of the T-Square, the life lessons shift from self-identity to social identity. The challenge is to find some way to make a meaningful mark on society. The individual is compelled to accomplish and achieve. What others think of their efforts matters enormously to them.

### The Missing Leg

According to Tierney, the sign and house positions opposite the focal planet (sometimes referred to as the "missing leg" of the T-Square) indicate where the tension is most acutely felt. "It seems to play a very central role in directing the individual as to how to best work out the dilemma indicated by the T-Square" (Tierney 2015, 96). The sign shows the typical attitudes and the house indicates the life situations for the ideal resolution of the T-Square's inherent tensions.

## The Focal Planet in a T-Square

Frank Clifford writes, "A t-square is like a pressure cooker of energy, edginess, and stress. It symbolizes facets of ourselves which are at odds with one another" (Clifford 2012, 80). The focal planet is the dynamic point of release and resolution. It's where the pent-up tension finds its release. The sign and house placements of the focal planet can be expressed so vividly and repeatedly in the individual's life story to the point where the nature of the opposition is ignored. Because the tension of the T-Square finds its release primarily through how the focal planet's energy is handled, we need to consider the nature of different focal planets.

### Focal Planet—Sun

When the Sun is the focal planet in a T-Square, it suggests an ingrained urge to accomplish important things in an independent manner. Pride and ego can be important life lessons for the individual. The individual needs to learn to become less demanding and self-centered. Productively channeled, this T-Square can reflect significant leadership ability. Great achievement is possible once the T-Square is harnessed. Until the energy of the T-Square is successfully channeled, the individual tends to be preoccupied with achievement and recognition in a manner that can be too self-seeking and overpowering for the taste of others who see it as arrogance and self-glorification. Independence and willfulness attract power struggles. When the tension of the Sun as focal planet is worked out, the individual can stand out as someone truly special—highly admired and regarded because of their desire to make relevant contributions to community, society, or the world at large.

When the Sun is the focal planet in a Cardinal T-Square, we expect an uncooperative streak. Undue self-confidence and bossiness are common traits, too.

The "me first" persona is obvious to others. This can antagonize people. When channeled positively, there is a lot of vitality. The individual can be wholeheartedly driven toward accomplishment.

When the Sun is the focal planet in a Fixed T-Square, we expect a highly obstinate individual, the sort who is impervious to most influences. With a tendency to steamroll opposition, power struggles are inevitable until the Sun as focal planet is positively channeled.

When the Sun is the focal planet in a Mutable T-Square, nervous strain and physical exhaustion are common results of these individuals pushing themselves too hard to learn as much as possible. Mutability means the individual is less likely to follow a consistent life path. The objectives are prone to periodic modifications as the person's attention shifts. These individuals can be intellectually headstrong.

## Focal Planet—Moon

When the Moon is the focal planet in a T-Square, it suggests an easily triggered emotional nature. Until the tension of the Moon as focal planet is resolved, the individual will tend to strike a highly defensive posture. A sense of security is critical. They can easily feel threatened. There can be a marked tendency to overreact to stressful situations. Mood swings are a frequent occurrence. This can adversely affect close personal relationships. The stress reactions are likely to continue until the individual learns to reprogram negative subconscious programming from their youth. The challenge is to become less attached to others, less vulnerable, and less defensive.

When the Moon is the focal planet in a Cardinal T-Square, hair-trigger emotionality is expected. Their hypersensitivity means these individuals can easily take offense, even when no offense was intended. The Moon as the focal planet in a Cardinal T-Square tends to be spontaneous and impulsive. Greater discipline and self-control are required to positively channel the Moon as focal planet in a Cardinal T-Square.

When the Moon is the focal planet in a Fixed T-Square, it suggests inflexible emotional needs—instinctive habits of reaction that are impervious to change. These individuals can easily get stuck in the past, ruminating on conditions that no longer exist in the present. To positively channel the Moon focal planet in a Fixed T-Square, the individual needs to learn to drop inner defenses that operate contrary to expressed feelings (like overeating as a stress reaction).

When the Moon is the focal planet in a Mutable T-Square, it suggests a high degree of emotional changeability. Restlessness is common. So is a need for new and varied stimuli. The individual might be inclined to over-rationalize their emotional reactions. Emotional commitments can be a challenge. There is a marked tendency to vacillate and waver or even contradict. Picking up on social cues can be another challenge. In order to constructively channel the Moon as focal planet in a Mutable T-Square, the individual must learn to absorb and assimilate the feelings of others rather than downplay their importance.

## Focal Planet—Mercury

When Mercury is the focal planet in a T-Square, it strongly suggests a desire to share acquired knowledge, skills, and abilities expressively with others. The individual is likely to focus much attention on higher education and scholarship. There is a tendency toward nervous exhaustion from so much mental and verbal energy. The mind is seldom at rest. Individuals with Mercury as focal planet seek out mental challenges. Logic and reason are the mainspring of their motivations. They need to remain in touch with their instincts and intuitions if they are to live more fully.

When Mercury is the focal planet in a Cardinal T-Square, it greatly accelerates the individual's thinking process and the ability to draw connections and associations. The individual is a quick learner. There can be an impulse to rashly apply what is learned. This impulse can extend to jumping to conclusions before all of the evidence is available. To positively channel Mercury as focal planet in a Cardinal T-Square, the individual needs to slow down and organize their thoughts before speaking.

When Mercury is the focal planet in a Fixed T-Square, it suggests that the individual does not calmly tolerate challenges to their thoughts from others. They're hard to influence because of the fixity of their ideas. These individuals tend to overvalue their own opinions and downplay those of others. Mercury as focal planet in a Fixed T-Square can be subject to a one-track mind. They can be so preoccupied with advancing their ideas that they're unaffected by feedback from others.

When Mercury is the focal planet in a Mutable T-Square, it tends to signify mental vacillation, resulting in nervous exhaustion and a lack of concentration. These individuals can spread their attention so thin that minor matters distract from what's truly important. They feel compelled to know a little bit about everything that piques their interest. A lack of focus can make them nervous and irritable. To channel the energy of Mercury as focal planet in a Mutable T-Square, the individual must learn to discipline their mind and focus on the subject of interest until they obtain a thorough understanding of the matter.

### Focal Planet—Venus

When Venus is the focal planet in a T-Square, the individual tends to exhibit a strong social drive. The tension in the T-Square can manifest as a feeling of being unloved and unappreciated. As Tierney notes, "Usually, he has values that are not compatible with those he attracts, creating emotional tension and a feeling of inequality" (Tierney 2015, 117). The individual wants peace and harmony in their social relationships. Similar to a Grand Trine, the individual expects what they desire to come easily and without struggle. They can become lazy and complacent and can have difficulty with self-starting.

When Venus is the focal planet in a Cardinal T-Square, it suggests that the individual tries too hard to gain the approval or acceptance of others. When soliciting help from others, they can appear to be an opportunist. They might jump in and make quick commitments they later regret. To positively channel Venus as focal planet in a Cardinal T-Square, they need to learn to share and cooperate patiently.

When Venus is the focal planet in a Fixed T-Square, it suggests that the individual will have set, inflexible values that inhibit social relationships. Their unwillingness to compromise can result in conflict and resentment. Fixed focal planet Venus is the least sociable and easygoing of all Venus focal planet individuals. They struggle to maintain their independence and autonomy. It can take a long time and a lot of testing for them to forge friendships.

When Venus is the focal planet in a Mutable T-Square, the result can be an individual who is fickle in love and reluctant about forming long-term relationships. They can be especially restless in relationships that do not give them sufficient space to emotionally decompress. These individuals tend to be social butterflies and appear to be pleasant, agreeable, and congenial. When the tension of the T-Square is successfully resolved, the individual is better able to forge long-term relationships. They might find themselves making contributions in the fine arts, cultural interests, and social affairs.

### Focal Planet—Mars

When Mars is the focal planet in a T-Square, we expect a strong-willed individual who prizes independence. These individuals often have headstrong urges. The result can be an aggressive, assertive temperament. As a result, the individual can find themselves constantly embroiled in heated controversy. There can be a strong strain of resistance to authority in favor of following their own independent way. They're very capable initiating projects. It's the follow-through to completion that can be lacking.

When Mars is the focal planet in a Cardinal T-Square, the individual reacts to opposition with an extreme tendency toward confrontation. Immediate desires tend to be met with impulsive and even disruptive conduct. The individual is likely to view their behavior as brave and principled. Self-assertion is rarely a problem. Quite the opposite—there can be explosive confrontations until the individual learns to positively channel the T-Square.

When Mars is the focal planet in a Fixed T-Square, the most notable trait is a headstrong obstinacy. Their huge reserve of energy enables them to persevere through all setbacks and hardships. Once a plan is made, external pressure has little chance to dissuade the individual. Their strength of conviction tends to intimidate any who stand in their way.

When Mars is the focal planet in a Mutable T-Square, the individual will tend to scatter their attention and activity. Focus is a life lesson that must be mastered to overcome the T-Square. They need to be able to see a task all the way to completion before their attention drags them off to a new project. Boredom, distraction, and intermittent attention are common problems for these individuals.

### Focal Planet—Jupiter

When Jupiter is the focal planet in a T-Square, the individual tends to be preoccupied with the search for greater meaning in life. They naturally approach practical affairs from a philosophical point of view. These individuals are likely to challenge current views on social morality, religious orthodoxy, and political theory. The T-Square encourages the individual to learn the lessons of benevolence, tolerance, acceptance, and charity. Another tension associated with this T-Square is a tendency to moralize or proselytize. The individual needs to learn how to share their personal faith in an acceptable fashion.

When Jupiter is the focal planet in a Cardinal T-Square, the individual tends to pursue their search for greater meaning in life in a vigorous, energetic manner. They can be headstrong and aggressive in pursuing their search for meaning. They tend to be highly impatient with social restrictions and resist such limitations. The initiating drive of cardinal planets can propel the individual into roles of social leadership.

When Jupiter is the focal planet in a Fixed T-Square, the individual lacks the crusading zeal of the Cardinal T-Square. Their life philosophy tends to be opinionated and dogmatic. The life lesson for a more positive channeling of this T-Square is to be more open-minded, flexible, and eclectic. Absent that, Jupiter's sense of self-righteousness could manifest as bigotry and prejudice.

When Jupiter is the focal planet in a Mutable T-Square, it can suggest someone who is very eclectic when it comes to life philosophy. They can restlessly move from one philosophy to another. A problem similar to that of the Grand Trine is associated with focal planet Jupiter in a Mutable T-Square: there's often a desire for instant enlightenment without any effort to earn it.

### Focal Planet—Saturn

When Saturn is the focal planet in a T-Square, we expect a serious individual who takes a practical, realistic approach toward long-term goals. They tend to experience delays and setbacks in their early years. Recognition, social prominence, and professional respect tend to come later in life. Important life lessons include patience, planning, timing, and maturity. Strong ambitions are characteristic of Saturn as focal planet. Self-doubt and discouragement are typical until the positive aspects of the T-Square are channeled, when the individual gains discipline and self-control.

When Saturn is the focal planet in a Cardinal T-Square, it suggests an individual who often experiences anxiety, frustration, and apprehension. This comes about from resistance whenever they push too hard for immediate achievement. In their early years, they tend to encounter discouragement. The energy within the Cardinal T-Square reinforces their ambition, enabling them to meet and overcome difficult challenges. Executive ability is a typical trait, but along with that comes an impatience from the cardinal planets. Individuals need to resist the impulse toward a domineering attitude.

When Saturn is the focal planet in a Fixed T-Square, the individual can be rigid and resistant. Control can be an important issue. They can seek to overpower and manipulate any issue that comes under their authority. This person can be quite obstinate and uncompromising when it comes to security and safety. Tierney writes, "He can endure all struggles and persistently hang on until his well-defined aims are achieved" (Tierney 2015, 129). If the individual is to positively channel this T-Square, they must be less defensive, less absolute, and less dictatorial.

When Saturn is the focal planet in a Mutable T-Square, it can be beneficial. Saturn adds discipline and focus to the individual's mental energy. The individual often experiences difficulty in communication until the T-Square is positively channeled. The life lessons that need to be learned include focus and ridding themselves of negative, pessimistic attitudes. These individuals can be overly rational skeptics. They have a drive for higher education and the credentials it confers because they fear appearing inept in matters that are important to them. When the tension of this T-Square is channeled positively, the individual can assume executive authority without resorting to power plays and control tactics.

### Focal Planet—Uranus

When Uranus is the focal planet in a T-Square, it suggests an individual who can act as a catalyst for social reform. These individuals often feel a strong impulse for radical disruption of the status quo. The energies associated with this T-Square often encourage them to behave in too extreme a fashion. Uranus as the focal planet is associated with a high-strung temperament. This can be lessened through a variety of mental stimulations. The urge to break down whatever impedes the individual from implementing their unique ideals needs to be controlled if the T-Square is to be positively channeled. When this T-Square is not positively channeled, the individual can be a social misfit, one who is out of tune with the status quo. Used constructively, this T-Square can result in an individual who is a visionary with the necessary charisma to alter mass consciousness.

When Uranus is the focal planet in a Cardinal T-Square, the individual relishes the role of social activist. They tend to try and implement their views of progress in all of their social relationships. This can alienate or intimidate others. When this T-Square is negatively channeled, the result can be lawlessness and social defiance. This impulse can be intensified when Mars or Pluto is also involved in the T-Square. When this T-Square is channeled positively, the individual is less of a firebrand and more of a social innovator, the kind of person who can initiate sweeping social reforms.

When Uranus is the focal planet in a Fixed T-Square, the individual can be a law unto themselves. They often ignore the views of others, instead pursuing their own personal values. Not as prone to question authority as those with the focal planet in a cardinal sign, these individuals are inclined to ignore existing rules and regulations in favor of their own personal values. As Tierney writes, "On an interpersonal level, he demands to have the privilege to constantly express freedom the way he desires" (Tierney 2015, 133). The life lesson when Uranus is the focal planet in a Fixed T-Square is the understanding that their vision of the truth is not universal.

When Uranus is the focal planet in a Mutable T-Square, the result can be a highly original thinker, one who defies the existing body of knowledge. As a result, these individuals can be perceived as an intellectual misfit or idiosyncratic eccentric who espouses what others consider to be subversive ideas. They can flit from one ideal to another without warning or explanation. When these individuals learn to positively channel this T-Square, they can become a progressive agent for social change.

### Focal Planet—Neptune

When Neptune is the focal planet in a T-Square, the individual can be especially sensitive to all sensory stimuli. They are usually able to experience nearly any form of emotional state of consciousness. They can be especially likely to be deeply inspired on a feeling level. Their delicately balanced inner nature can lack the ego structure to cope with the mundane requirements of daily life. Such activities might seem too demanding and unfulfilling. The presence of two squares from Neptune can leave this individual prone to self-deception and escapism. As Tierney notes, "Although impressible to a fault, he will be forced to learn how to become more discriminating and selective about what he absorbs from the environment. Vulnerability only increases when he avoids the disciplines of self-analysis and discernment" (Tierney 2015, 135–136).

When Neptune is the focal planet in a Cardinal T-Square, the individual is susceptible to taking impractical and poorly organized action. The tendency is to jump impulsively into poorly defined activities with blinders on. These individuals often feel compulsively pulled toward ambitions that are very idealistic. What they can miss is attention to the finer details, even being unaware that there are finer details. The life lesson they need to learn is to slow down and organize their affairs with careful planning and attention to detail. They can be vulnerable to disillusionment and even depression until they learn to squarely face mundane life. Patience and concentration are needed to bring their idealistic vision into being.

When Neptune is the focal planet in a Fixed T-Square, the individual is prone to deep emotional desires that are difficult to satisfy on a practical level. Fixity tends to set habits of mind in granite, so any illusions they have about themselves or others will tend to resist change, even when the facts are presented. They are able to delude themselves for a long time as a result. Once they come to the realization that their emotions have provided false messages and the object of their devotion is a sham, they can become so disillusioned that substance abuse can become a release. These individuals can instead channel this T-Square positively by focusing on activities that release their deep well of compassion through a willingness to serve others.

When Neptune is the focal planet in a Mutable T-Square, the individual can be too impatient to allow their inner dreams and beautiful ideals to manifest. They can withdraw from projects when too much responsibility is involved. They tend to couple a lack of endurance with a highly active imagination, which tempts them to take shortcuts and make shaky plans. They can easily become mentally confused when under stress. This type of individual tends to miss social cues. Tierney notes, "The urge to remove oneself from the everyday pressures of life by escaping into his head is very strong." (Tierney 2015, 138). The Mutable T-Square couples a lack of willpower with a tendency to give in rather than face obstacles. When the tension from this T-Square is resolved, the individual is better able to use their abundant inspirational energies.

## *Focal Planet—Pluto*

When Pluto is the focal planet in a T-Square, the individual attacks life with an almost ferocious intensity. They have ample strength of focus and psychological stamina. They can be heedlessly one-track when pursuing their aims. Pluto confers an obsessiveness, a compulsiveness, that can sap their emotional energy when the inner source of it is not understood. Tierney argues that Pluto as the focal planet is perhaps the most challenging type of T-Square because it forces the individual to undergo a complete metamorphosis in order to positively channel its energy. There can be a bipolarity as the individual swings between the use of force, manipulation, and subversion and the attempt to overcome those temptations in favor of a genuine desire to avoid the abuse of power.

When Pluto is the focal planet in a Cardinal T-Square, the individual is so individualistic in orientation that they are often loners who do not integrate well with others. Control can be an important issue, so much so that they can spurn genuine offers of assistance for fear that offer is really a ruse to wrest control. When they feel challenged or threatened, their immediate reaction can be to confront and overwhelm. This can make cooperation with others almost impossible at times. It is incredibly difficult for them to share power. When required to relinquish power, they can seethe with resentment. The life lessons the individual can expect to learn can involve some explosive power struggles before they can be expected to cooperate well with others.

When Pluto is the focal planet in a Fixed T-Square, the individual can be obsessive or even compulsive about achieving their desires. They can endure a lot in terms of emotional strength. Once their mind is set on a course of action, they can be incredibly determined, regardless of the obstacles to be confronted. Along with persistence, an intense strength of conviction tends to go along with Pluto as focal planet in a Fixed T-Square. To positively channel this T-Square, the individual needs to learn that others are not always set on their personal or professional destruction.

When Pluto is the focal planet in a Mutable T-Square, it suggests the sort of individual who can have revolutionary impulses. Not satisfied to just understand the surface detail, they're drawn to the underlying fundamentals. They have to know how things work at their core. They tend to be quite stimulated with any investigation or research into relevant but obscure data. These individuals can be effective social propagandists and radical thinkers. It can be difficult for them to turn off their mental processes, which can lead to periodic nervous exhaustion. When the Mutable T-Square is positively channeled, the individual can tap into deep reserves of creative energy. There will still be a tendency to encounter social resistance. Personal transformation, after all, does not mean that the social environment changes. They can eventually be accepted as individuals and even praised for their efforts to uncover some important social truth.

## Counseling the Individual with a T-Square Pattern

Eventually, a series of crises, tests, and challenges will help the individual perfect the skills necessary to overcome the obstacles, frustrations, and conflicts from the squares and opposition inherent in the T-Square. The honing of necessary life skills will be necessary. This includes learning to relate to others at the emotional level. With the right life experiences, great achievements and success are possible through the T-Square.

When diagnosing a T-Square for a client, where do we start to look for the problem?

We begin with a look at the unoccupied sensitive point in the chart across from the focal planet. Look at that particular house to see what the house focus is. Then focus on house rulership(s) for the answers to any problems.

It's important to look for aspects that can "harmonize" the opposition or squares in a T-Square. Check to see if there are any trines or sextiles to one end of the opposition or to the focal planet.

The area opposite the focal planet is critical. This area of the chart (its sign and house) indicates the gaps or deficiencies in personal development that need to be addressed in order to bring stability to the life of the individual.

There is the danger that the individual overcompensates and expresses too much of the qualities of the empty area of the chart. This can create overwhelming problems of its own. Perhaps the individual oscillates back and forth between the open space and the focal planet. This continual swinging back and forth can also be problematic. What the individual requires for the proper expression of the T-Square is balance between the open area and the focal planet.

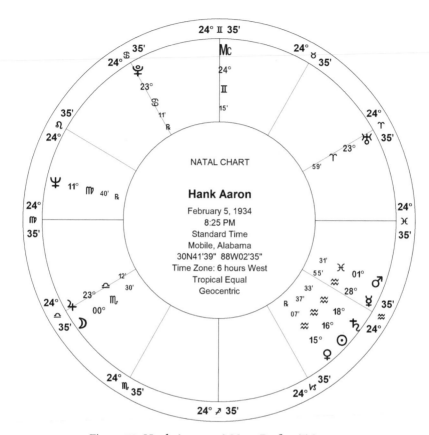

Figure 70: Hank Aaron—A Near-Perfect T-Square

Baseball Hall of Famer Hank Aaron has a near-perfect T-Square in his natal chart (figure 70). The opposition between Jupiter and Uranus has an orb of just 47', and the squares to Pluto are equally as tight. All of the planets involved in the T-Square are in cardinal signs: Aries, Cancer, and Libra.

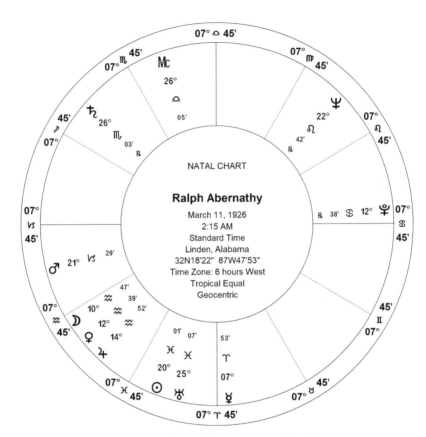

Figure 71: Ralph Abernathy—A Less Perfect T-Square

Contrast the T-Square for Hank Aaron with that of US civil rights activist
Ralph Abernathy (figure 71). The opposition between Neptune and Jupiter has
an orb of nearly 8°. The square between Saturn and Neptune is nice and tight,
but the square between Saturn and Jupiter is extremely wide, roughly 11°. At
least the planets are all in the same modality. All are in fixed signs: Leo, Scorpio, and Aquarius.

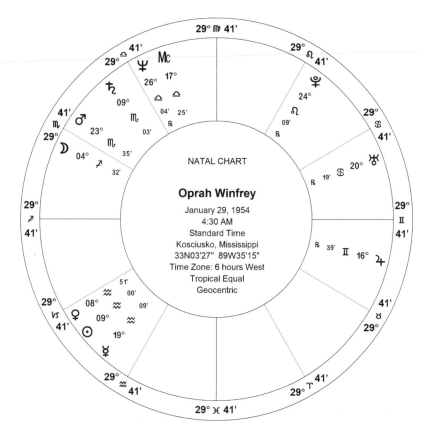

Figure 72: Oprah Winfrey—A Typical Example of a T-Square

The T-Square for Oprah Winfrey occupies fixed signs: Pluto in Leo, Mars in Scorpio, and Mercury in Aquarius (figure 72). The orb between Pluto and Mars is good and tight, and the orbs involving Mercury are reasonable. This is a very typical example of a T-Square aspect pattern.

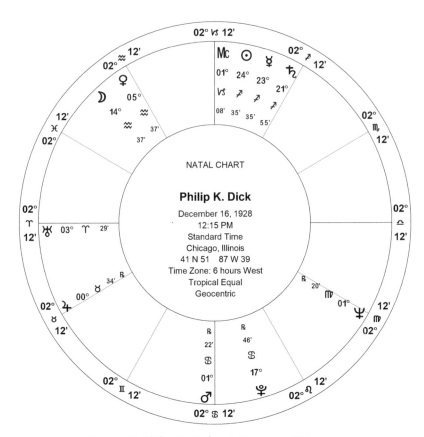

Figure 73: Philip K. Dick—A Dissociate T-Square

When one of the planets falls in a different modality than the other two, we call the result a Dissociate T-Square. This is most significant when it's the apex planet that's out of sign. In the case of science fiction writer Philip K. Dick, it's one of the opposition planets that is out of sign. There is a nice tight square between Mars and Uranus in cardinal signs: Cancer and Aries. It is the Sun at 24 Sagittarius 35 that is in a mutable sign.

chapter 13
# The Grand Cross

A Grand Cross occurs when four planets are all separated from each other by square aspects. Also called a Grand Square, a Grand Cross can also be viewed as two oppositions separated from each other by squares. It's really four interlocking squares. There's one planet in each element (fire, earth, air, water), but they're all in only one mode (cardinal, fixed, mutable). There's no focal planet to contend with.

Since all of the aspects in a Grand Cross are considered challenging aspects, the Grand Cross is seen as a series of crises, where aspects of the personality are working at cross-purposes that serve to nullify each other. This pulls the individual in several simultaneous directions, ultimately leading to indecisiveness and even an inability to produce concrete achievements. It can take extraordinary effort to overcome the conflicts in a Grand Cross.

Obstacles can come from within (attitudes) or from external circumstances. Rarely will a person with this combination choose the path of least resistance. They instead tend to seek out challenges.

## The Ideal Grand Cross Pattern
The ideal Grand Cross is formed by the intersection of two oppositions. More specifically, those two oppositions square each other, creating a cross (or

square) in the chart. The ideal Grand Cross (figure 74) also has all four planets in the same mode (cardinal, fixed, mutable). It's a complete fourth harmonic syndrome.

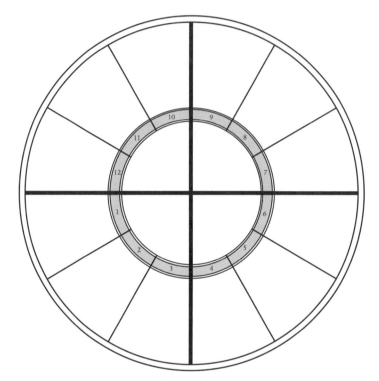

Figure 74: The Grand Cross Pattern

Bil Tierney claims the Grand Cross isn't a typical aspect pattern to encounter in natal charts, but data from the Astro Databank suggests otherwise. Almost 6 percent of the charts of notable individuals contain a Grand Cross. That's a little more than one out of twenty charts.

It sometimes occurs that one or more planets are in a different mode from the rest. This is a Dissociate Grand Cross.

## The Grand Cross Pattern Temperament

Many astrologers consider the Grand Cross to be an unfortunate aspect pattern, a burden for life. Other descriptions include hemmed in or trapped by circumstances, a stubborn and inflexible personality, or a lifetime of multiple conflicts, with each crisis triggering the next. Tierney gives important insight when he writes that a Grand Cross "can be especially restrictive and self-limiting for the individual who shows little capacity for self-discipline and moderation in life" (Tierney 2015, 85).

This important language from Tierney references self-discipline and moderation, since some highly successful individuals have a Grand Cross in their natal chart. If individuals handle the Grand Cross badly, they might experience inner disharmony and tension. The four squares in the ideal Grand Cross can generate an inner sense of friction, strain, and pressure. These disharmonies and tensions can trigger stressful situations in the external environment. This is particularly true for personal relationships, where antagonism and discord can result.

Not all is doom and gloom with the Grand Cross. The pair of oppositions can also result in perspective and balance. The natal Grand Cross can give the individual the ability to focus intently on one goal. These individuals can be relentless. Success eventually comes their way and rewards them for their perseverance and diligence. The Grand Cross can also empower them to live a purposeful life.

Whether the impact of the Grand Cross on the individual is negative or positive, some effect is almost certain and depends upon the free will of the person. Those born with a Grand Cross in their natal chart might find themselves constantly pulled in dueling directions.

Each Grand Cross mode has its own unique expression and interpretation.

### The Cardinal Grand Cross

The Cardinal Grand Cross is typically focused on the question of self and identity. The Cardinal Grand Cross can express as an identity crisis. Cardinal signs also encourage action, initiation, and impulsiveness. There also can be an overdose of push, drive, and aggression. This can result in painful confrontations. The individual can feel compelled to initiate poorly planned projects and yet lack the perseverance to complete what was rashly started. Cooperation and consideration of others can be a recurring challenge for individuals with a Cardinal Grand Cross.

## The Fixed Grand Cross

The Fixed Grand Cross is concerned with security, resources, and self-worth. Fixed signs can also contribute inertia. That means it can be difficult to get these individuals to move, to change. Once on the move, however, they can be difficult to stop. The Fixed Grand Cross is associated with emotional crises emerging from inner frustrations. As Tierney notes, "The four squares intensify the willfulness and unyielding fixity of this quality" (Tierney 2015, 87). There can be a very marked tendency for individuals to internalize their feelings. The result can be enduring blockages. Emotional flexibility is required if the Fixed Grand Cross is to be positively channeled.

## The Mutable Grand Cross

The Mutable Grand Cross is concerned with healing, reasoning, and communication. These individuals need to display balance and dignity in the way they communicate with others and take everyone's needs into consideration when calling for change. The Mutable Grand Cross can result in being able to see all sides, which can lead to indecisiveness, a lack of concentration, and diffusion of energy. It often manifests as a great deal of nervous energy and restlessness. The major challenge these individuals are likely to face is spreading their interests over too wide a range—too many irons in the fire. To avoid running in circles, they need to learn to discipline their mind.

## The Dissociate Grand Cross

When one planet of the Grand Square falls in a different mode, the Dissociate Grand Cross results. This means that at least one planet is not in a natural square and its opposition is not a natural polar opposite. The opposition will move in the direction of a quindecile aspect (165°). The quindecile aspect denotes disruption and upheaval. This adds to the imbalance inherent in a Grand Cross. Other aspects shift as well. The out-of-sign planet approaches a trine in one direction and a sextile in the other. That can help ease the tension and prompt a more flexible attitude on the part of the individual.

## The Angular Grand Cross

An identity crisis is a frequent manifestation when a Grand Cross involves three planets and the Ascendant. The major crises that tend to accompany the Grand

Cross might pressure the individual to confront and adjust their self-image. The tensions are less internalized when an angle is part of the Grand Cross. They're more likely to be felt by others, for better or worse.

When the Midheaven is one of the four points of the Grand Cross, the result tends to be an individual with powerful potential for professional involvement, social status, and public ambitions. The individual can be too aggressive, manipulative, or domineering. Regardless, when the Midheaven figures in a Grand Cross, the individual will likely channel its energies into the social realm.

## Counseling the Individual with a Grand Cross Pattern

The individual who has this pattern of planets in their natal chart has the potential to feel blocked, directionless, and pulled in many directions.

Having a Grand Cross in a birth chart might bring burden to a person, especially at those times when challenges arise together at the same time. These simultaneous challenges affect different areas of the person's life, which can make them very difficult to cope with.

The individual needs to remain adaptable and flexible and apply more common sense. One way to use the Grand Square in a positive manner is for them to focus their attention on a planet that forms a positive aspect to one or more of the planets involved in the Grand Cross. This would be a planet that trines (or sextiles) two of the planets involved. Positive aspects can be a beneficial source of relief and help harness the powerful energy of that square to their advantage.

Finding the right point of balance to be able to take advantage of a Grand Square can be a challenge. The key to positive channeling comes from developing balance between the two oppositions. When those oppositions are balanced, they create a solid foundation. When the oppositions are out of balance (i.e., too much attention being directed to one influence over the other), the squares (tension and frustration) become powerful.

The test for any Grand Cross comes whenever there's a transiting aspect to it. All four of the Grand Cross's energies try to spring into action simultaneously, and each in its own manner. The individual can feel overwhelmed or pulled apart. The key to dealing with a Grand Cross is to be alert to the stressors and how to handle them.

The Grand Cross individual can also typically benefit from the suggestion to slow down and tackle one major objective at a time. They should work on developing composure and steadiness.

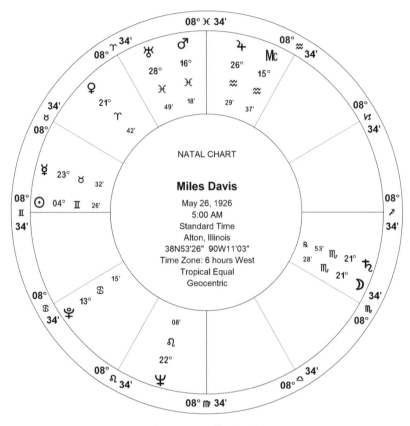

**Figure 75: Miles Davis**

World-famous jazz trumpet player Miles Davis has a Grand Cross that includes Mercury opposed to a-Moon-Saturn conjunction. Jupiter and Neptune are also opposed (figure 75). Davis was known for his highly volatile outbursts with record producers, other performers, and audience members. The fixed nature of the Grand Cross is associated with highly charged emotional reactions.

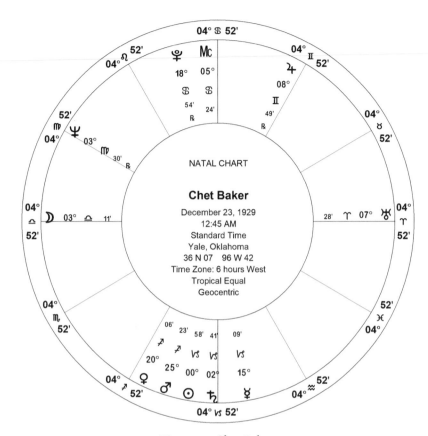

Figure 76: Chet Baker

Another famous trumpet player and vocalist, Chet Baker, has an Angular Grand Cross (figure 76). Moon, Uranus, and Saturn are all in cardinal signs. The Midheaven at 05 Cancer 24 completes the Grand Cross. Baker earned a lot of attention and critical praise throughout the 1950s, particularly for albums featuring his vocals. Drug addiction plagued him from the early 1950s until his death in 1988.

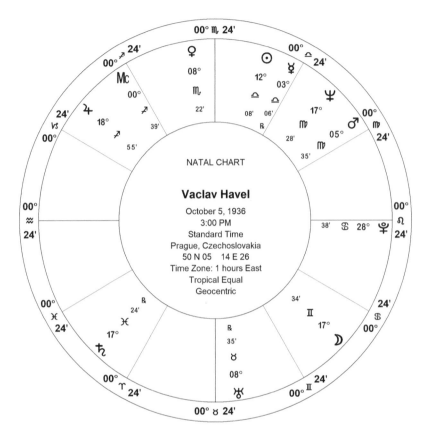

Figure 77: Vaclav Havel

Vaclav Havel was a Czech statesman, writer, and former dissident. He served as the last president of Czechoslovakia from 1989 until the dissolution of Czechoslovakia in 1992 and then as the first president of the Czech Republic from 1993 to 2003. He possesses an extremely tight Mutable Grand Cross between Moon, Jupiter, Saturn, and Neptune (figure 77).

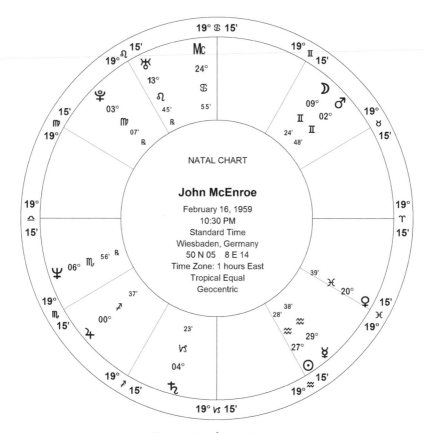

Figure 78: John McEnroe

Known for his fiery outbursts on the tennis court, John McEnroe has a natal chart that includes a Dissociate Grand Cross with three planets (Mars, Jupiter, and Pluto) in mutable signs and Mercury in fixed sign Aquarius (figure 78). Although Mercury is out of sign by only a 22' orb, it seems that John McEnroe was plagued by the attendant disruption and upheaval that can accompany the Dissociate Grand Cross. His confrontational on-court behavior frequently landed him in trouble with umpires and tennis authorities.

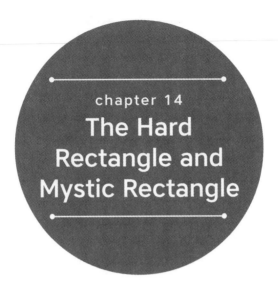

chapter 14

# The Hard Rectangle and Mystic Rectangle

A Hard Rectangle is rather rare. According to the Astro Databank, less than 1 percent of natal charts contain this aspect pattern, in which four (or more) planets form oppositions, sesquiquadrates, and semisquares. A Mystic Rectangle occurs more often, in approximately 5–6 percent of natal charts. Four (or more) planets form oppositions, trines, and sextiles in this pattern.

## The Ideal Hard Rectangle and Mystic Rectangle Patterns

The ideal Hard Rectangle is composed of two opposition aspects (figure 79), each connected by two sesquiquadrates along the length and two semisquares along the width. This results in six aspects among the four planets.

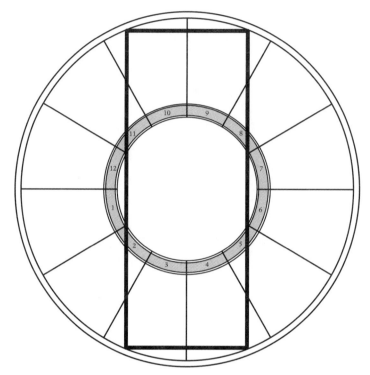

Figure 79: The Hard Rectangle

The ideal Mystic Rectangle is composed of two opposition aspects (figure 80), each connected by two trine aspects along the length of the rectangle and two sextile aspects along the width. The harmonious trine and sextile aspects can be considered release points for the tension of the oppositions. Like the Hard Rectangle, the Mystic Rectangle forms six aspects among the four planets.

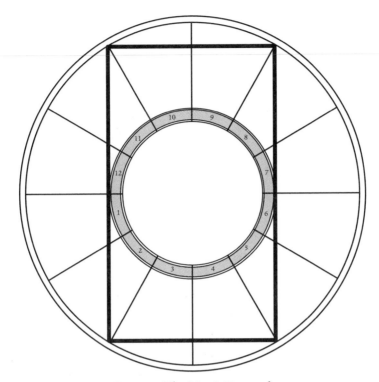

Figure 80: The Mystic Rectangle

## The Hard Rectangle and the Mystic Rectangle Pattern Temperaments

Even though all aspects in the Hard Rectangle are "hard" in nature, the oppositions receive indirect pressure from the sides to accomplish harmony and balance, according to Bil Tierney. He notes that the sesquiquadrates and semisquares "spark further antagonism and a lack of needed compromise with others, making this a very hard rectangle to control" (Tierney 2015, 95).

The trines and sextiles of the Mystic Rectangle are "soft" aspects. Since there are four soft aspects and two hard aspects in this aspect pattern, the overall effect of the Mystic Rectangle is viewed as beneficial. The two oppositions add just enough of a challenge to keep the Mystic Rectangle from being a self-contained pattern of ease, like the Grand Trine. This adds to its overall beneficial effect.

The Mystic Rectangle received its name from Dane Rudhyar. He argued that the pattern represents "practical mysticism" from its two awareness-revealing, illuminating oppositions. The two trines add creativity to the mix, and the two sextiles intelligent and innovative use of energies.

## Counseling the Individual with a Hard Rectangle or Mystic Rectangle Pattern

When two oppositions are linked by semisquares and sesquiquadrates, a dynamic potential results. The oppositions are integrated in this fashion. The well-managed Hard Rectangle gives the individual an added dollop of strength and purpose beyond what typically accompanies oppositions. Whatever is started in life should bring about very focused and concrete results, particularly when the sesquiquadrate operates as a positive aspect and the challenge of the semisquare is met.

In general, the Hard Rectangle can be an integrative force when the individual is persistent enough to carry out their vision in an uncompromising manner while taking into account the needs of their psychological and social environment at the same time. Much, of course, depends on the actual planets involved. If this type of rectangle links Mars, Uranus, Pluto, and/or the Sun, the dynamic intensity of the configuration could be particularly stressful.

Generally, the Mystic Rectangle is considered to be a mild aspect pattern. It is unlikely to generate a lot of discomfort or resistance.

Individuals tend to feel the effects of the four planets in a Mystic Rectangle as a sense of working together in a well-balanced and integrated manner. If the inner oppositions of the Mystic Rectangle can be handled well, then the pattern can provide the individual with inner harmony.

Individuals are well advised to avoid placing undue influence on any of the planets in the pattern. Otherwise the energies of the Mystic Rectangle can be thrown out of balance.

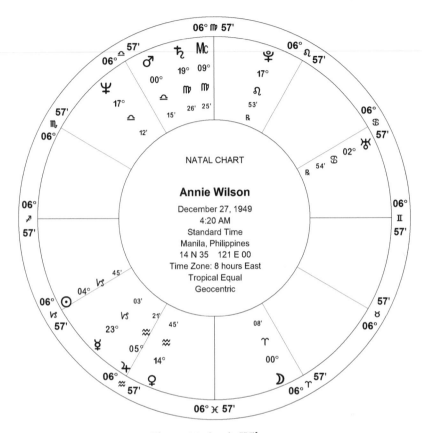

Figure 81: Annie Wilson

Annie Wilson was formerly married to Carl Wilson of the Beach Boys. The couple had two children before they divorced. Her natal chart contains a Hard Rectangle between Moon, Venus, Mars, and Pluto (figure 81).

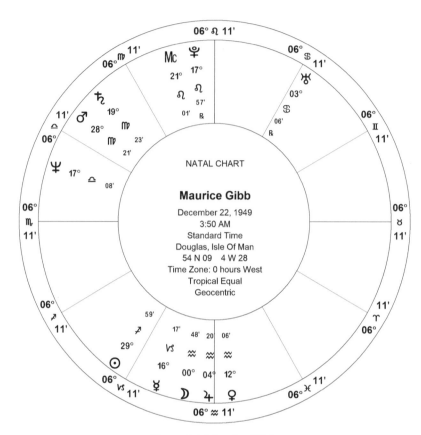

Figure 82: Maurice Gibb

Maurice Gibb and his twin brother, Robin Gibb, were members of the pop music trio the Bee Gees. Maurice achieved fame as a singer, songwriter, multi-instrumentalist, and record producer. Maurice and Robin both had a Hard Rectangle between Sun, Venus, Uranus, and Pluto (figure 82).

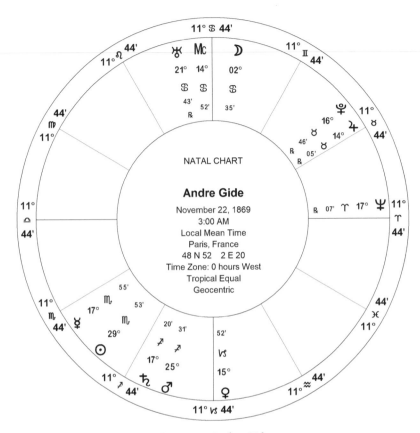

Figure 83: Andre Gide

Andre Gide was a French author and winner of the Nobel Prize in Literature (1947). The *New York Times* obituary described Andre Gide as "France's greatest contemporary man of letters" and "judged the greatest French writer of this century by the literary cognoscenti." His birth chart contains a Mystic Rectangle between Mercury, Venus, Jupiter, and Uranus (figure 83).

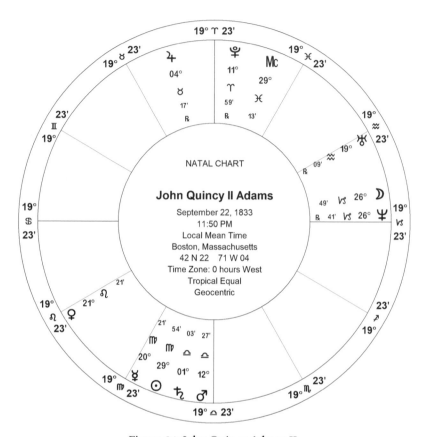

Figure 84: John Quincy Adams II

John Quincy Adams II was the grandson of the sixth US president, John Quincy Adams. Like his grandfather and great-grandfather, he was a lawyer and politician. His Mystic Rectangle contains Venus, Mars, Uranus, and Pluto (figure 84).

chapter 15

# The Grand Trine
# and the Kite

The Grand Trine is an aspect pattern where three planets form trine aspects to each other. If three lines were drawn between each planet, an equilateral triangle would result. A Grand Trine is a complete third harmonic pattern. It represents perfect equilibrium and balance that can reveal great talent, ease, or harmony. A Grand Trine is often a static, passive structure that doesn't promote the growth that results from confronting the problems of hard aspects. For this reason, the ancients used to think of the Grand Trine as evil or malefic, because these aspects can make an individual lazy and then they don't grow.

## The Ideal Grand Trine Pattern

The ideal Grand Trine has three planets in trine aspect to each other (figure 85). In addition, all three planets are in the same element (fire, earth, air, or water).

## The Grand Trine Pattern Temperament

Almost always, the Grand Trine will include the Sun or Moon. When it does include either or both, the Sun-Moon blend will be even more emphatic in the birth chart. When it does not, then the Grand Trine works in parallel with the Sun-Moon blend as a separate defensive complex of behavior.

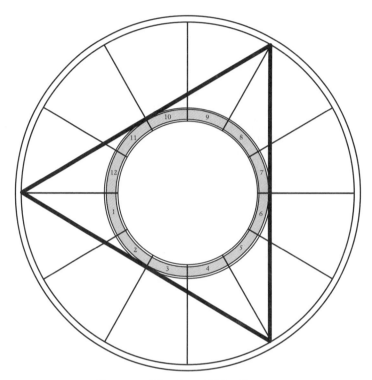

Figure 85: The Grand Trine Pattern

The Grand Trine works against the formation of relationships. It's an isolating structure. When a client isolates themselves, it becomes more difficult for them to fulfill their needs. We need others to help in need fulfillment. No individual is an island.

Noel Tyl describes the Grand Trine as a defensive structure. It's a closed circuit of protection, of self-sufficiency:

- The Fire Grand Trine is a closed circuit of motivational self-sufficiency. "You can't tell me anything I don't know."

- The Earth Grand Trine is a closed circuit of practical self-sufficiency. "I know how to do everything. I don't need your help."

- The Air Grand Trine is a closed circuit of social or intellectual self-sufficiency. "I can be alone quite nicely, thank you."

• The Water Grand Trine is a closed circuit of emotional self-sufficiency. "I just don't want to get hurt again, if you don't mind."

What is it that breaks the closed circuit in a Grand Trine? A sufficient number of oppositions and squares in the natal chart, especially when they make an aspect to one of the planets involved in the Grand Trine. In figure 86, an opposition along the Ascendant/Descendant axis helps break the closed circuit of self-sufficiency. The opposition to one angle of the Grand Trine acts like a grounding strap. It gives the energy of the Grand Trine a point of release.

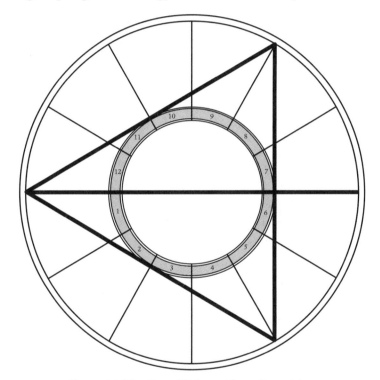

Figure 86: The Grand Trine with an Opposition

Bil Tierney correctly warns the reader that a Grand Trine is composed of three trine aspects, and the trine aspect is ease-oriented. It naturally reduces pressure, tension, and strain. It doesn't encourage the individual to struggle and further grow by accepting challenges. The Grand Trine is preoccupied with leisure and self-gratification. In Tierney's words, "The trine focuses somewhat unrealistically upon personal satisfaction at the expense of developing strength of character (which usually is attained thru stress and conflict)" (Tierney 2015, 66).

Too many trines in a natal chart suggests that the individual will project a self-indulgent temperament and avoid self-discipline. They're likely to avoid major responsibilities in life. Trines poorly handled can instill a false sense of security. As a result, a pervasive sense of passivity can set it. This can inhibit the person from attempting to surpass existing talents and skills.

The Grand Trine can amplify the inertia that the individual trines offer. Barbara Watters looks at Grand Trines in her book *The Astrologer Looks at Murder*. Many criminals, including murderers, have Grand Trines. So do many who feel defeated by the rigors of life and compensate with addictions and antisocial behavior.

## The Fire Grand Trine

The creative and inspirational power of the Grand Trine is more evident when in fire signs. Fire signs are vital, self-expressive, and spontaneous in action, seeking to manifest through direct expression of their potential. While vision is strongly emphasized, so also is egotism, selfishness, and sometimes even an unconscious assumption of special privilege. The individual will exhibit courage, adventurousness, and risk-taking. They can even be prone to excessive gambles since they believe so deeply in themselves. Impulsiveness is a common tendency, with the individual having a feeling of protection from harm and the ability to prevail against impossible odds.

## The Earth Grand Trine

The Grand Trine in earth signs is most typical of the ease we expect with the Grand Trine aspect pattern. The individual seeks to preserve the status quo of existing conditions. Neither the earth element nor the trine aspects in this pattern respond well to critical changes in life affairs. In the chart of a less ambitious individual, the Earth Grand Trine is apt to express as very self-indulgent. Handled well, this Grand Trine lends remarkable endurance and persistence, allowing the individual to steadily concentrate their attention on tangible objectives without distraction. An uncommon amount of common sense is one of the Earth Grand Trine's special assets.

### The Air Grand Trine

With the Grand Trine in air signs the individual can feel satisfied living in their head without the need to express themselves in the external world. Both the air element and the trine aspects in this pattern have the ability to conceptualize and think in abstract terms. The impractical side of this Grand Trine can be more evident when the individual is unable to ground their idealistic insights. Trines tend to be easygoing and benevolent, and individuals with an Air Grand Trine tend to be socially curious, broad-minded, and tolerant. Individuals with an Air Grand Trine take pleasure in learning new information and tend to be eternal students.

### The Water Grand Trine

The Grand Trine in water signs emphasizes the passive, receptive, and protective power of the trine. The individual seeks tranquility. Without adequate dynamic principles operating in the chart, this type of Grand Trine can result in escapist behavior. There tends to be an exaggerated need for dependency and safety from threat. This can result in overcaution and dithering. The Water Grand Trine is potentially the most problematic of the Grand Trines. There's also the potential for well-developed empathy, sympathy, and nurturance. In a less dynamic chart, there can be a tendency to feel easily defeated, dejected, and insecure.

### The Dissociate Grand Trine

Not all Grand Trines are composed of three planets from the same element. When one planet is drawn from a second element, the result is a Dissociate Grand Trine. In general, according to Tierney, the Dissociate Grand Trine has somewhat more drive and activation than the more ideal forms of the Grand Trine drawn from a single element. Flip that around and the Dissociate Grand Trine also tends to afford less protection and is less easy-flowing for the individual. The Dissociate Grand Trine is named according to the element that predominates. Actor Ed Asner, for example, has an Earth Dissociate Grand Trine with the third planet in fire.

## The Minor Grand Trine

The Minor Grand Trine combines two sextiles and a trine aspect (figure 87). Ideally, the planet forming the sextiles is at the midpoint of the two planets forming a trine. The trine adds creative potential to the Minor Grand Trine, with the added benefit of communication and self-expression from the two sextiles. The Minor Grand Trine is less static and passive, while the ideal Grand Trine is more self-contained. The Minor Grand Trine is, according to Tierney, more inclined to put its constructive energies to good use.

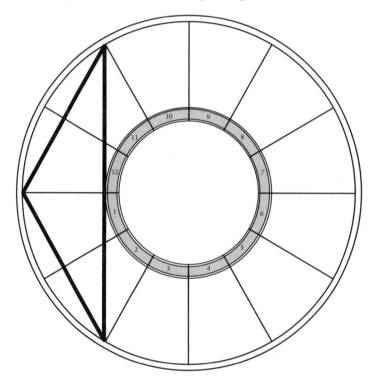

Figure 87: The Minor Grand Trine

## The Kite Pattern Temperament

The Kite is a Grand Trine bisected by an opposition from a fourth planet (figure 88). This creates a pair of sextiles to the remaining two planets, in addition to the opposition. The Kite is similar to a Grand Trine, with additional motivation and potential. For the Kite, the planet in opposition and sextile becomes the focal point. Why? Because this is the point of release for the easygoing, self-sufficient energy of the Grand Cross element. As Tierney says, this planet becomes a stimulating outlet for the creative outpouring from the Grand Trine element. The opposition forms the backbone that holds together the entire configuration. A Grand Trine alone might not provide enough challenge to develop the talents inherent in it. A Kite configuration adds tension, and the opposed planet can tell us a lot about how the individual focuses and releases this energy. The two planets in sextile to the opposition planet serve as potential areas for resolving the conflict of the opposition.

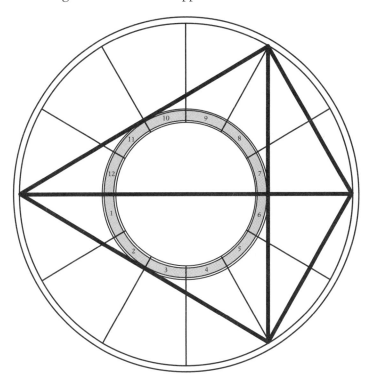

Figure 88: The Kite Pattern

# Counseling the Individual with a Grand Trine or a Kite Pattern

As Dr. Loretta Standley notes, "In order to make this Grand Trine work for you, you have to work it" (Standley 2019). The client needs to understand the need to put some work into it. Since we're talking trines instead of stress aspects, the work will be relatively easy.

Noel Tyl uses the Grand Trine as an opportunity to open a dialogue with the client. It goes something like this for a client with a Water Grand Trine: "You know, there's a very efficient defensive structure suggested in your horoscope. It protects you emotionally. It also works independent from the real you. There's a disconnection here between different developmental areas of your life. How do you see this?" (*Noel Tyl's Certification Correspondence Course for Astrologers*, lesson 2, p. 7).

How does the astrologer interpret the planets in a Grand Trine? A lot depends on the number of planets involved in the aspect pattern, and also on the nature of the individual planets.

According to Tierney, the greater the number of planets tied in to the Grand Trine, the greater the imbalance and character weakness. If by tied in he means conjunctions to planets in the trine, then I have no quarrel with the statement. But we've already discussed that adding a square or an opposition to a Grand Trine can help break the cycle of self-sufficiency that Grand Trines entail. This is an imbalance with beneficial impact, one that can restore psychological balance to the individual.

The inclination of the Grand Trine toward self-indulgence and passivity is further deepened when the Moon, Venus, Jupiter, or Neptune is involved. The same is true when Taurus, Cancer, Leo, Scorpio, or Pisces is overrepresented in the chart (these signs sharing sensuality as a common keyword).

Now flip this around. Mars, Saturn, Uranus, and Pluto are innately active and powerful, so much so that they do not permit complacency and stagnation. The signs Aries, Virgo, and Capricorn need to be constantly busy and engaged if they're to function normally. When these natural impulses are suppressed, impatience and anger can flare up.

Tierney states that the more stress aspects present in the natal chart, the greater the modification of the Grand Trine's influence. An isolated Grand

Trine is one that can keep its identity intact. Multiple Grand Trines can be even more debilitating since even more planets are involved.

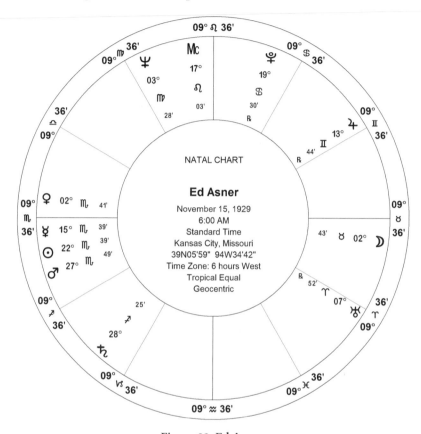

Figure 89: Ed Asner

Actor Ed Asner has a Dissociate Grand Trine with two planets in earth—the Moon in Taurus and Neptune in Virgo—and Saturn in the fire sign Sagittarius (figure 89).

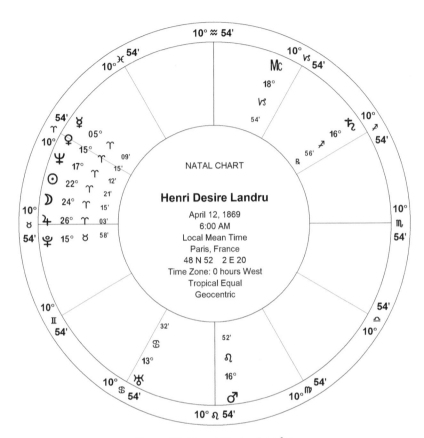

Figure 90: Henri Desire Landru

Henri Desire Landru is a famous French serial killer. A three-planet con-junction in Aries between Sun, Venus, and Neptune combines with Saturn in Sagittarius and Mars in Leo (figure 90). The Fire Grand Trine doesn't explain why Landru was a serial killer. It does help explain the luck Landru needed to avoid getting caught for so long

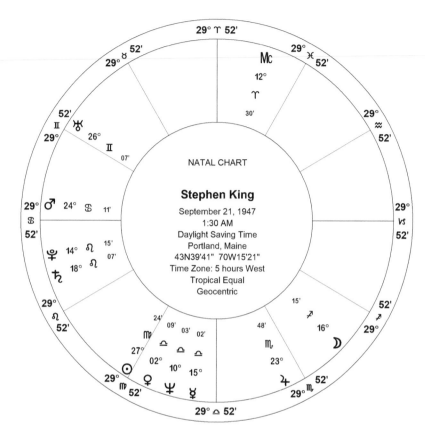

Figure 91: Stephen King

The Ascendant and Midheaven can also be part of a Grand Trine. Stephen King has a Kite pattern in his natal chart (figure 91). The Grand Trine is in fire signs: the Midheaven in Aries, the Moon in Sagittarius, and the conjunction of Saturn and Pluto in Leo. The Kite is completed by the opposition between the Midheaven and Mercury. Everything focuses on the Midheaven, the angle we associate with career and public standing.

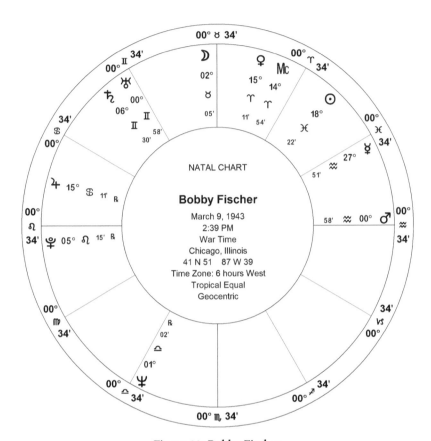

Figure 92: Bobby Fischer

Bobby Fischer's natal chart has a Kite (figure 92). The Grand Trine is in air signs, sharing Mars and Neptune. There is also a conjunction in Gemini of Saturn and Uranus. The opposition between Mars and Pluto forms the sextiles necessary to complete the Kite pattern. The Air Grand Trine lends intellect and communication, and Pluto the needed compulsion to be a World Chess Champion.

chapter 16
# The Yod and Thor's Hammer

A Yod is an astrological aspect pattern that involves any three planets or points in the horoscope that form an isosceles triangle. More specifically, a pair of quincunxes are tied together by a sextile aspect. A Yod is also called the Finger of Fate or the Finger of God. Interpretation of the Yod is subject to controversy in the astrological community.

Thor's Hammer is also an isosceles triangle aspect pattern. It's a pair of sesquiquadrate aspects tied together with a square aspect. Like the Hard Rectangle and the Grand Cross, Thor's Hammer is part of the dynamic series of aspects that are based on the eighth harmonic (45°) aspect series.

## The Ideal Yod and Thor's Hammer Patterns

The ideal Yod contains three (or more) planets (figure 93). Two quincunx aspects form the sides of the triangle. A sextile forms the base. Angles of the horoscope can form one of the points of the resulting triangle.

The ideal Thor's Hammer contains three (or more) planets (figure 94). Two sesquiquadrate aspects form the sides of the triangle. A square forms the base. Angles of the horoscope can form one of the points of the resulting triangle.

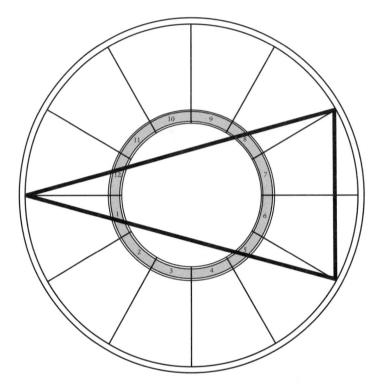

Figure 93: The Yod Pattern

## The Yod Pattern Temperament

As Karen Hamaker-Zondag notes in her book *The Yod Book*, the key to understanding the Yod is understanding the quincunx. A quincunx is formed by two planets or by a planet and the Ascendant or Midheaven separated by 150°, with a very tight orb of 2½ to 3°. What is not so obvious is that the planets/points belong to different elements, different modes, and different polarities. These differences can lead to tensions. The two signs involved in a quincunx are incompatible.

The Yod marries two quincunxes with a sextile at the base. This results in the following observations:

- A Yod links three planets that are each in a different element.

- A Yod links three planets that are each in a different mode.

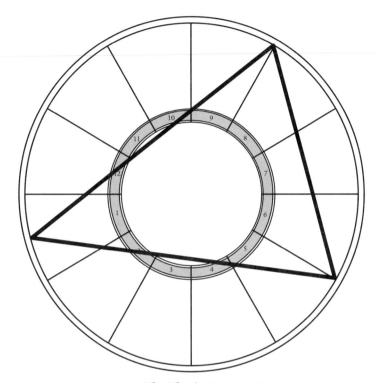

**Figure 94: The Thor's Hammer Pattern**

- The apex of a Yod belongs to a different polarity (positive or negative) than that of the points linked by the sextile at the base.
- Since three different modes are involved in a Yod, that means there will be three different motivations and three needs for coping.

Robert Jansky notes an interesting point about the Yod. Often the natal Yod doesn't manifest effects until the individual approaches forty years old, "a time when one can begin to see how prior events in the subject's life are beginning to affect the course of his destiny" (Jansky 1978, 54–55). This is the age when affairs of life associated with the house location of the apex planet appear to take on great importance in the life of the individual. The person with a Yod in their chart might spend their early years exploring different areas of experience. At the time, these might seem unrelated. Slowly, usually through hindsight, the Yod points the individual in the direction of their destiny. Jansky has colorful language describing the Yod: "like a compass needle in the wheel, pointing the way" (Jansky 1977, 55).

## Sun as Apex Planet

A Yod with the Sun as the apex planet suggests an individual whose central purpose in life likely revolves around continuous personal adjustments. Major self-corrections are typical. Bil Tierney writes, "He normally is pressured to make needed alterations in the manner with which he demonstrates his will, power, authority, and self-pride" (Tierney 2015, 153). Ego drives are often not expressed but instead internalized and bottled up.

It is common for individuals with a Sun apex to start adulthood with a low self-concept and sense of inferiority. They might feel powerless for a long time, feeling insignificant in the eyes of others. Once the Yod becomes fully activated, this can quickly change. A change in character can be evident.

The Yod can be mismanaged. When this happens, the individual can abuse personal will and authority. Tierney points to the example of the Marquis de Sade, a domineering, power-absorbed individual.

## Moon as Apex Planet

The Moon is a very personal and private apex planet. From this position in a Yod, it suggests an individual whose inner emotional development requires adjustment. There might be emotional trauma from the past. The individual can retain disorganized, distorted views from the past that need to be confronted before they can be replaced with more positive impressions and allow personal growth.

Personal maladjustments are rarely evident on the surface. The individual might even be unaware of any conflicts. The Moon can operate in a very subconscious manner.

A common experience is that the individual's reactions to the environment can be inappropriate to the circumstances that trigger them. Emotional messages from others are often misinterpreted. The individual habitually reacts in a self-defeating way until they learn to process the Yod's impulses in a more positive way.

### Mercury as Apex Planet

Activation of a Yod with Mercury as the apex planet generally requires that the individual restructure a number of mental loose ends. The individual possesses a curious mind. The problem tends to be organizing those thoughts in a productive way. There can be a tendency to combine too many concepts in a way that is haphazard. The Yod demands that the individual streamline their thought processes. Otherwise the mind continues to veer off on unnecessary tangents.

Intelligence isn't affected. It's the application of the intelligence that can be the source of trouble for the individual. Once the individual learns to harness the Yod, they can use their mental energies in a more efficient and consistent manner.

### Venus as Apex Planet

Individuals with Venus as the apex planet tend to feel out of touch with the values of their social environment until they better learn how to employ the Yod. They tend to make highly introspective judgments concerning people, which affects their relationships with others. They lack the typical Venus ability to associate with others in a comfortable, easygoing manner until they learn how to harness the Yod aspect pattern better. They instead are likely to feel socially awkward and out of place in ordinary social situations.

The individual is likely to show a heightened interest in social activities once the Yod is activated. Personal romance is also likely to improve at this time. They are better able to share themselves more thoroughly and derive great joy through contact with others.

### Mars as Apex Planet

Mars as the apex planet in a Yod suggests an individual who has difficulty initiating personal matters in a direct and open manner. They tend to assert themselves in ways that need correction and adjustment. They can be prone to plunging themselves into action without sufficient, purposeful planning. The result can be an inefficient expenditure of energy.

Adjustments are often needed with more aggressive instincts. The individual might be able to control their more aggressive impulses, but these attempts might instead result in other self-defeating behaviors until the Yod itself is mastered through the application of greater organizational intelligence.

When the Yod is ready for activation, the individual is likely to feel a need to take charge of their life and demonstrate complete self-sufficiency. Often this is the result of an acute crisis situation. A mismanaged Yod with a Mars apex can result in rash or disruptive actions.

## Jupiter as Apex Planet

When Jupiter is the apex planet in a Yod, the individual can spend many years expanding their consciousness, broadening their social vision, and enhancing their moral development in a very reflective manner. They might spend much of their youthful years feeling out of step with social laws, belief systems, and moral codes prominent in their social environment. Quincunxes to Jupiter tend to operate at a higher level and are rarely troublesome to the individual. They can, in fact, be quite beneficial. The intellectual readjustments required by quincunxes to Jupiter help the individual to keep an open mind.

Jupiter quincunxes can prove more troublesome when they are disorganizing and impractical. The individual often encounters difficulty with day-to-day matters. The individual tends to procrastinate and exhibit poor judgment, and might even over-reach.

When the Yod is ready for activation, the individual sometimes changes beliefs or ideology. They can become more aligned with their inner spirit as a result.

## Saturn as Apex Planet

Individuals with Saturn as the apex planet of a Yod, probably more than those with any other Yod configuration, give support to this aspect pattern's karmic interpretations. Tierney describes this as a "characteristic 'fated' undertone" (Tierney 2015, 162). Proper timing and sufficient inner maturity are essential to correct timing for handling this Yod.

Until the individual is ready to manage this Yod successfully, continuous adjustments will likely be required to ego-security. Self-defeating attitudes can be quite entrenched. The individual can feel like an outcast. This sense can be reinforced by harsh reactions from the social environment. Double quincunxes to Saturn tend to imbue the individual with feelings of inadequacy and insignificance. Individuals can feel painfully aware of any inadequacies. What brings the individual around in time is the corrective nature of the quincunxes and Saturn's natural tendency to overcome obstacles. A well-managed Yod with a Saturn apex prepares the individual for a meaningful life with social responsibility.

## Uranus as Apex Planet

A Yod with Uranus as the apex planet suggests the sort of individual who spends their early years feeling very different from others in their social environment. This is very much Thoreau's individual who marches to the beat of a different drummer. Learning to integrate with others in a conventional manner can be an extreme test.

Uranus represents quickened mental activity. Individuals with this Yod often possess accelerated emotional and intellectual development, which can make peer interactions difficult. This can stem from difficulty communicating on a mundane level. Often contrary and rebellious, they typically need to learn some hard life lessons before they can successfully manage the Yod aspect pattern.

Managed well, this Yod can result in the personality of a pioneer, with a higher degree of independence. When mismanaged, this Yod can result in sudden, serious repercussions in the individual's social life, the sort that can radically alter the individual's lifestyle against their will, such as sudden and lasting unemployment.

## Neptune as Apex Planet

When Neptune is the apex planet in a Yod, the individual tends to feel out of touch with the mundane realities of daily living and often longs to be somewhere—anywhere—where life is more calm, peaceful, and beautiful. Their interpretation of life is subject to distortion and delusion.

When life cannot sustain the delusion, the individual tends to become anxious or even fearful. This can result in escapist, nonproductive outlets, such as addiction to drugs or alcohol. While the imagination can be very strong, it can be a challenge to apply it in a practical and constructive way.

When this Yod becomes fully activated, the individual will typically search for some sort of emotional ideal, ultimate love, spiritual beauty, or universal truth. They can pursue this new life path with a great amount of dedication and idealism. When mismanaged, the Neptune apex Yod can result in a martyr complex.

### Pluto as Apex Planet

A Yod with Pluto as the apex planet is associated with individuals who approach early life with a great deal of emotional intensity. Typically, these feelings are buried deep down. Aware that their compulsions and obsessions are not generally shared and understood by others, the individual may be inclined to withdraw even deeper into themselves. Maladjustment (largely through antisocial behaviors) is more likely than with other Yod patterns.

The profound transformation for which Pluto is noted is typically required when this Yod is activated. This is sometimes forced upon the individual. The Yod can propel the withdrawn nature of the Pluto apex into one of organizational control. Their mental depth and penetrating social insight can find practical use. If the Yod is managed poorly, the individual could find themselves feeling further isolated and alienated, the result of self-destructive passions and futile attempts to manipulate others.

## The Thor's Hammer Pattern Temperament

Alice Portman claims that Thor's Hammer is a particularly difficult pattern. The pair of sesquiquadrate aspects tends to result in severe criticism from others. This produces considerable personal tension. To work at its best, Thor's Hammer needs at least one planet in the pattern to have an outlet (i.e., an easy flowing aspect—a trine or sextile) to another planet or aspect pattern.

Thor's Hammer is distinct from the Yod in a few important ways.

- Thor's Hammer has only hard aspects. There are no easy-flowing aspects, such as a trine or sextile.

- It is resistant to change. Due to the tight square and sesquiquadrates, the aspect pattern is "locked together" and, therefore, resistant to change.

- It is difficult to live with. Unlike the Yod, which tends to resolve with age (at least when well managed), the square and sesquiquadrates of Thor's Hammer tend to pose lifelong challenges.

# Counseling the Individual
## with a Yod or Thor's Hammer Pattern

The Yod and the Thor's Hammer aspect pattern both contain an apex planet that points to a sign and a house of the natal chart. Stock advice for this pattern has been, look at the arrow! Choose to do what the arrow is pointing to! But such advice ignores the nature of both the Yod and Thor's Hammer.

As noted earlier in this chapter, the Yod is typically resistant to change until the individual nears forty. The astrologer can gesture all they like in the direction of the Yod, but if the time isn't yet ripe, the likely result will be confusion and a lack of success. When the time is right for successfully managing the Yod, the client will scarcely require advice. If they do, that's when the advice to "follow the arrow" is most helpful.

Thor's Hammer is entirely different from the Yod. Its "hard" nature (in more ways than one) requires lifelong effort to successfully manage. "Follow the arrow" is advice easily given. It's also advice that can be difficult to follow.

Suppose, for example, that Thor's Hammer points directly at Neptune in Pisces. Neptune is the planet of illusions, dreams, addiction, etc. Jupiter is the ancient ruler of Pisces, symbolizing the fact that Pisceans tend to expand their boundaries and test their limits. They generally seek the odd, the unusual, and the exotic. Neptune is the modern ruler of Pisces. Pisceans often seem to ignore whatever limits they have to face and have an almost careless idea of duty and responsibility. What exactly is the arrow in Thor's Hammer pointing at, in this case? The astrologer might caution against a manner that's too lackadaisical and easygoing. Be more grounded. More practical. Guard against addiction.

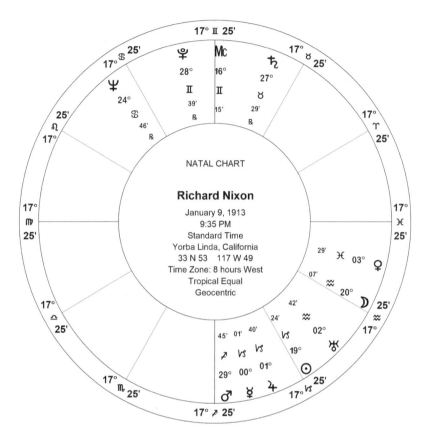

Figure 95: Richard Nixon

President Richard Nixon's chart possess a Yod with Mars as the apex planet (figure 95). Saturn and Neptune form the base of the Yod.

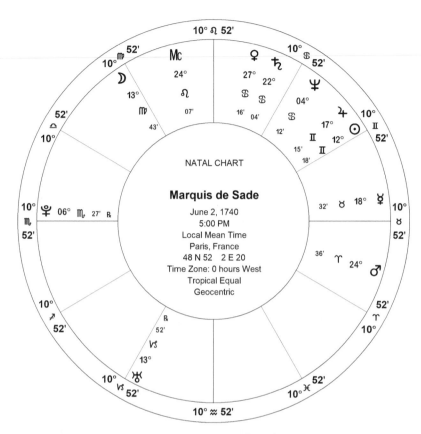

Figure 96: Marquis de Sade

The birth chart for the Marquis de Sade possesses a Yod with the Sun as the apex planet (figure 96). Pluto and Uranus form the quincunxes and are tied together by a sextile. The nature of Pluto and Uranus had much to do with Sade's ego drive and the distortions in his personality. Pluto quincunx the Sun is associated with strong power drives. Uranus quincunx the Sun lent him a sense of genius and also a hint of the madness that was likely to erupt.

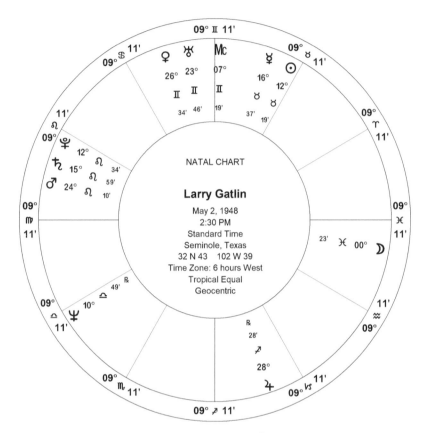

Figure 97: Larry Gatlin

Country music singer and songwriter Larry Gatlin possess a Thor's Hammer with Jupiter as apex planet and the Sun and Pluto forming the base of the aspect pattern (figure 97). Conjunctions between the Sun and Mercury and between Pluto and Saturn help provide a release from the Thor's Hammer.

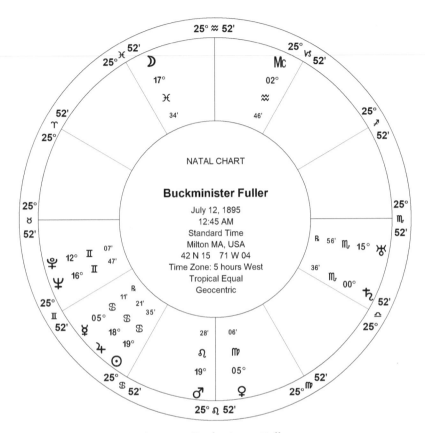

Figure 98: Buckminster Fuller

Famed architect Buckminster Fuller has a Thor's Hammer aspect pattern with Saturn as the apex planet and both Neptune and the Moon as the base (figure 98). In addition, his chart contains a Grand Trine in water between Sun-Jupiter, Uranus, and the Moon. The Moon is shared between the Thor's Hammer and the Grand Trine, providing an outlet from the hard aspects in the Thor's Hammer.

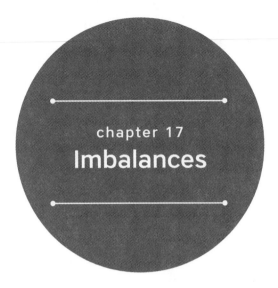

chapter 17
# Imbalances

It's relatively unusual for the planets in a chart to be evenly distributed in terms of hemisphere placement and the occupation of elements, modes, and polarities. More common is for several planets to cluster together in the same hemisphere or quadrant or among elements, modes, and polarities. When this occurs, a severe imbalance can occur, and that can cause extremism or obsession.

## Hemisphere Imbalance

Each hemisphere has its own influence on a birth chart.

Division of the circle perpendicularly produces two hemispheres, east and west. The hemisphere on the left side of the chart is the eastern hemisphere, with the extreme eastern point on the eastern horizon being the Ascendant. The opposite side of the chart contains the Descendant in the western hemisphere.

Division of the circle horizontally produces a southern hemisphere and a northern hemisphere. The upper hemisphere of the chart is the southern hemisphere, together with the *Medium Coeli* (MC), or Midheaven. The lower half of the chart is the northern hemisphere, with the *Imum Coeli* (IC).

We will consider the more traditional interpretations for the hemispheres alongside a contemporary reinterpretation by Noel Tyl. His interpretations are more psychological, and I find that they work better than the traditional inter-pretations in client consultations. How so? They open the client up more to discussion and dialogue.

The Bowl pattern can be an extreme example of hemisphere imbalance.

We're talking here about a preponderance of planets in one hemisphere, not total exclusivity.

### Northern Hemisphere Emphasis

Houses 1, 2, 3, 4, 5, 6. By tradition, an emphasis on the northern hemisphere sug-gests a very subjective view of life. Personal privacy can be a serious issue. The individual is likely to be introverted by nature. They tend to prefer to work alone.

### Southern Hemisphere Emphasis

Houses 7, 8, 9, 10, 11, 12. By tradition, an emphasis on the southern hemi-sphere suggests an objective view of life. The individual is likely extroverted by nature. There's a tendency to be ambitious and career-oriented and to want fame and recognition.

### Eastern Hemisphere Emphasis

Houses 10, 11, 12, 1, 2, 3. By tradition, an emphasis on the eastern hemisphere suggests individuals who are likely to be independent, strong-willed, and individ-ualistic. They're typically highly motivated and are often self-employed and a risk taker.

### Western Hemisphere Emphasis

Houses 4, 5, 6, 7, 8, 9. By tradition, an emphasis on the western hemisphere suggests individuals who are passive or subtle in their actions, often permitting others to take the lead. They tend to need others to motivate them before initi-ating action. They work best in a partnership or group situation.

### Quadrant Emphasis

A less common emphasis is on a particular quadrant. Each quadrant covers three houses.

Houses 1, 2, and 3 are the northeast quadrant. This is the quadrant where emergence of the self is found. These are typically self-made individuals who find outlets through self-improvement, self-development, and self-help.

Houses 4, 5, and 6 are the northwest quadrant, which suggests the individual is adaptive, creative, and practical. The self is defined through relationships with peers, lovers, and family. They tend to seek fulfillment through the development and expansion of individual talents and abilities.

Houses 7, 8, and 9 are the southwest quadrant. These individuals are typically relationship people. Actions in the life of the individual are open and exposed to others. Their activities are very much a matter of public attention and record.

Houses 10, 11, and 12 are the southeast quadrant. The individual tends to be a highly self-contained individual, very much in control of their destiny. Their sense of self might become attached to the enhancement of their reputation and participation in the right groups.

## Noel Tyl's Approach to Hemispheres

Tyl notes that the northern hemisphere is centered on the fourth-house cusp, the home environment. An emphasis here tends to call attention to early development, especially to unfinished business from early home life.

With a southern hemisphere emphasis, there is a tendency for individuals to have been pushed around, controlled, or victimized by life's experiences.

The eastern hemisphere is centered on the Ascendant. With an emphasis here, there tends to be a sense of protectionism within the identity. Life is conditioned by ego justification. A marked tendency toward defensiveness is typical.

With an emphasis on the western hemisphere, the ego is projected onto others. These individuals tend to be the sort of people who give and give and give some more. They often feel compelled to give themselves away to one degree or another.

Each of Tyl's reinterpretations offers opportunities for in depth discussion. The northern emphasis, for example, opens a discussion of early development issues. What was the early home like? How does unfinished business from the early years still affect the individual's current life? Does it affect their relationships with those near to them? With friends? With an emphasis on the southern hemisphere, the questions focus on the source of feelings of inadequacy and being taken advantage of. An emphasis on the eastern hemisphere raises questions around the topic of feeling defensive. Why do they feel they have to protect themselves all the time? What is it that they're trying to protect themselves from? When the emphasis is on the western hemisphere, the natural question to ask is why the need to give so much that they practically give themselves away? Do they get taken advantage of? What is it that they don't like about themselves that they feel compelled to hide from their own problems through giving so much?

## Element Imbalance

The four basic elements—fire, earth, air, and water—can be in a state of imbalance in a birth chart. In the typical case, the planets are scattered about roughly equally between the four elements, with two or three here, two or three there.

When the individual has five or more planets in one element, they will most often identify with that dominant element, regardless of the element of their Sun sign. When they completely lack an element (or have only one or two planets in one element), the lack of an element means the characteristics denoted by that element do not come easy to the individual. Individuals with a lack of an element usually respond by overcompensating for those missing qualities. They can end up acting as if they had that element strong in their chart.

### Dominant Fire Element

Too much fire in the chart often suggests an individual who can burn themselves out. The individual with too much fire often doesn't see this as a problem until it's too late. Too much fire can be overactive and restless. Those with fire as the dominant element in the birth chart might also be dominating, fast-paced, and inclined to invest all of themselves in their activities. They might have difficulty seeing other people as separate individuals, with their own valid needs and desires. Because these individuals are self-centered and impulsive, their relationships can suffer.

### Dominant Earth Element

When there is an overemphasis of the earth element in the birth chart, there can be an over-reliance on what is observed rather than taking in what is not so obvious. Individuals with earth as the dominant element in the birth chart will be concerned with concrete details and tangible results. They will operate most frequently in the world of their physical senses, attuned to their immediate environment, to their physical bodies, and to sensory comforts and pleasures.

### Dominant Air Element

Too much air in the birth chart suggests an overactive mind restlessly seeking knowledge and sharing their thoughts with other people. With too little earth or fire to push them forward, the individual can become a dabbler, never being able to anchor their thoughts or concentrate on any one thing. Too much air and the individual can't do anything without thinking about it first. Thus, they can experience paralysis from too much analysis.

### Dominant Water Element

The individual with too much water in the chart is typically filled with conflicting emotions and feelings. There can also be a narrowness of "vision," or an obsession with what works rather than what ideals they should strive to achieve. Individuals with water as the dominant element in the birth chart frequently lose themselves in their feelings or the feelings of others and have difficulty maintaining their separateness. Their extreme sensitivity can lead them to withdraw into themselves. Often quite psychic, they can respond with great compassion to the needs of others.

### Dominant Fire and Earth (Lava)

Maritha Pottenger wrote about combinations of elements. These occur when two elements are dominant.

The energetic drive of fire can combine with the practical achievements of earth to form a combination associated with high achievement. This can be the most productive of all the combinations. Just stay out of their way when they're on a roll. These individuals generally know what they want and how to go about getting it. You can end up flattened as they bulldoze their way to their goal. When fire is the predominant element, the individual will be inclined to live life on their own terms.

### Dominant Fire and Air (Hot Air)

Pottenger describes the fire-air combination as "life is often a party" (Pottenger 1986, 74). Sunny, optimistic, and extroverted, these individuals tend to be fun-loving and forever on the move. What they seek above all is variety and new experiences. Both charming and verbally skilled, they can make excellent salespeople and entertainers, even if they occasionally put their foot in their mouth. Quick-witted and lively, they make for interesting companions and colleagues. They refuse to endure confining or uncomfortable situations, not when they can just get up and leave.

### Dominant Fire and Water (Steam)

Fire and water are the two emotional elements. The individual with fire and water emphasized in their natal chart is likely to feel life very intensely. Fire tends to express, while water tends to suppress. The balance between those two elements will largely determine whether the individual will be the more spontaneous type or the "play it safe" variety. Wide mood swings are associated with the fire-water combination, from incredible elation and optimism to pessimism and depression. There can also be occasional emotional outbursts as the water element tries to keep the emotions in check and the fire element finally becomes too impatient and rash to hold back any longer.

### Dominant Earth and Air (Dust)

Earth and air are the two logical and rational elements. These individuals appreciate the mind. They combine the logical, analytical, and theoretical side of the mind (air) with the practical, grounded, sensible side (earth). The earth-air combination can make for great troubleshooters and problem solvers. Relatively unfeeling, they can quickly make detached observations about a situation.

### Dominant Earth and Water (Mud)

Earth and water combine the practical and the nurturing. Stated another way, they combine pragmatism and empathy. This often casts these individuals in the role of caring for others, either as mothers, fathers, or savior figures. They tend to very seriously pursue their own security needs. Both earth and water are oriented toward safety and protection, and that can give these individuals a serious or even depressive outlook.

## Dominant Air and Water (Mist)

Air-water is the more internal and cerebral of the element combinations. While fire-earth demands immediate action, air-water is quite content to just sit and think, to drift and dream and live in their own inner world. Since air and water blend both the conscious and the unconscious, these individuals can make excellent therapists and counselors. Empathy can feature in their personality. Air-water individuals are often highly imaginative and creative.

## Weak Fire

Individuals with too little fire often lack fiery energy. They can be sluggish and undermotivated. There tends to be a lack of optimism and adventure and a willingness to believe that all will work out for the best. Too little fire often suggests a lack of confidence and enthusiasm and a tendency toward depression. These individuals struggle to become self-expressive and assertive. They can alternate between withholding themselves and expressing themselves in an overly dramatic manner.

## Weak Earth

With too little earth, an individual might appear to be "spaced-out" due to a lack of being grounded in the here and now. These individuals often develop skills that have little or no practical application. With a lack of the earth element, the individual might feel out of place in this world. This can often lead to depression. They might compensate with an overemphasis on practical life affairs.

## Weak Air

A lack of air in the chart suggests that the individual has difficulty adjusting to new people and ideas. With this inability to adapt comes distrust toward others who can easily express themselves verbally or through the written word. With too little air in the chart, the individual can suffer from an inability to adjust quickly to new ideas. They can have a negative reaction to an idea they cannot process or assimilate either mentally or emotionally.

## Weak Water

The individual with too little water can be seen as uncaring and lacking empathy for others, not showing any emotion that an otherwise "normal" person might show. These individuals can have an emotional vacuum that they attempt to fill by turning to spiritual realms or universal truths. This is an attempt to find meaning in their lives. Difficulty remaining in touch with and expressing their feelings might lead these individuals to form relationships with overly emotional people.

# Mode Imbalance

As with the elements, individuals who are weak in a mode (cardinal, fixed, or mutable) are typically very aware of their lack and they strive to overcome it. They often overcompensate for the lack.

### Dominant Cardinal

Cardinal signs are energetic, dynamic, proactive, and unafraid to try new things. A preponderance of cardinal signs in a chart indicates a person who is always in "do" mode. Individuals with an extra dose of cardinality would rather be overactive than bored. Very concerned with their own activities and projects, they can focus all of their attention on their own relationships and profession. They excel at meeting challenges and resolving crises.

### Dominant Fixed

Fixed signs have persistence and perseverance. They're reliable and determined. An abundance of fixity typically results in individuals who can focus their attention laser-like on their values and goals and on the satisfaction of their desires. Slow and deliberate at the start, they tend to be powerhouses once they settle on a course of action. Persistent and strong-willed, they resist changing direction and refuse to be pushed, pulled, or pressured.

### Dominant Mutable

Mutable signs bring a nature that's flexible, changeable, adaptable, and suggestible. Excess mutability tends to bring a deep concern with personal relationships. These individuals thrive on variety and change and are excellent at multitasking. More inclined to go with the flow, they adapt readily to the people and circumstances of their lives. Too much mutability suggests a tendency to be restless and flighty. These individuals often don't know what they want or where they want to go.

### Weak Cardinal

These individuals can easily enjoy observing and simply "being" without necessarily "doing." When tempted to overcompensate, they might feel driven to prove themselves through activity, or they might instead simply substitute an emotionally charged inner life for active involvement in external activities.

### Weak Fixed

Individuals with weak fixity might have difficulty completing what they have begun. Developing structure and stability in their life can be a challenge. They can become obsessed with organizing or finishing and might test their willpower by committing themselves to overly demanding projects or goals.

### Weak Mutable

Weak mutability is associated with individuals who usually know what they want. Often unwilling to compromise, they can insist that other people be adaptable and accommodate them. Since they have difficulty bending with circumstances and making personal changes, they often attempt to force change in their external circumstances, sometimes in quite dramatic ways.

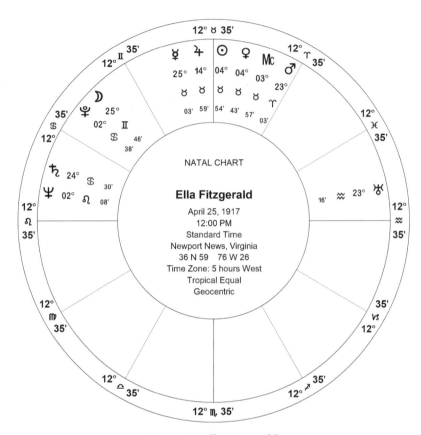

Figure 99: Ella Fitzgerald

Ella Fitzgerald was an American jazz singer, sometimes referred to as the First Lady of Song, the Queen of Jazz, and Lady Ella. Her natal chart contains a southern hemisphere emphasis with a southeast quadrant emphasis within it (figure 99). Fitzgerald was notoriously shy. In spite of that, she was ambitious and career-oriented and wanted fame and recognition. She was a civil rights activist, using her talent to break racial barriers across the nation.

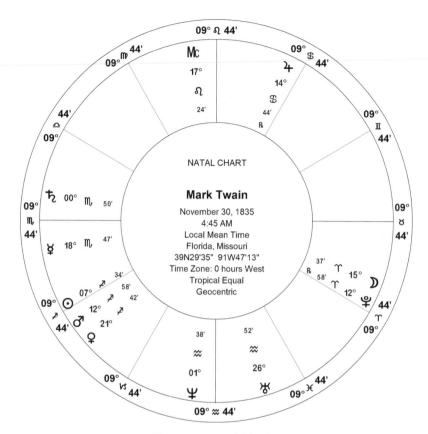

Figure 100: Mark Twain

Author, humorist, and social critic Mark Twain has a birth chart that's heavy with fire and has no earth (figure 100). A firebrand, he reveled in controversy. Twain was noted for throwing himself headlong into projects. He was fascinated with science and scientific inquiry, and many of his financial woes resulted from bad investments in new technology.

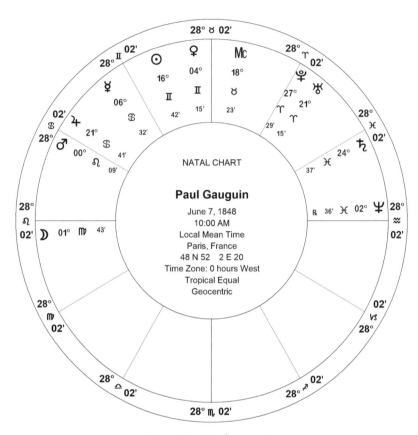

Figure 101: Paul Gauguin

Fire and water equal steam, according to Maritha Pottenger. Paul Gauguin, the post-Impressionist painter, certainly felt life very intensely (figure 101). His artwork was characterized by exaggerated body proportions, animal totems, geometric designs, and stark contrasts. His bold and colorful paintings significantly influenced modern art. Gauguin traveled the world for his art subjects.

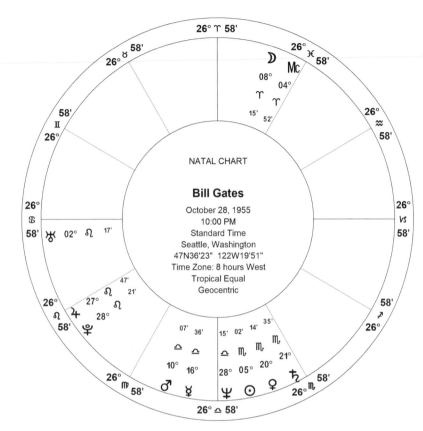

Figure 102: Bill Gates

The birth chart of Bill Gates has no air and a preponderance of planets in the northern hemisphere (figure 102). The lack of air in a chart can find its expression in the works of ultra-specialized geniuses, great thinkers, and intellectuals. Maupassant, Poe, Goethe, Hemingway, Dumas, Flaubert, Bertrand Russell, and Tolstoy are some of the examples of great geniuses compensating for a lack of air in their chart.

chapter 18
# Unaspected Planets

Innate qualities are amplified in potentially constructive ways when a planet lacks any Ptolemaic aspect (i.e., conjunction, sextile, square, trine, or opposition) with any other planet in the natal chart.

There are two theories about the unaspected planet. One line of thought is that the unaspected planet has difficulty expressing some of its qualities. It sits in the chart without any major connection to the other planets. The other line of thought is the interpretation preferred by Noel Tyl and myself. It's the preferred interpretation these days. Being unaspected can make the planet a more powerful force as it screams for attention among all of the other planetary aspects. The individual might not realize its expression in their behavior, but others recognize it unmistakably. Unaspected planets can function either as strong talents or as excessive, overcompensatory habits. Astrologers such as Dane Rudhyar believe unaspected planets actually bring more freedom to the individual and view it as a maverick, something of a wild horse in the personality, unleashing its power at any moment. Liz Greene argues that the unaspected planet is unintegrated with the rest of the natal chart, and it might act as instinctual, raw, and archaic.

Transits will make aspects to the unaspected planet at times, which can excite and stimulate it into action. The individual can have a hard time controlling its immense forces at those times.

## Interpreting Unaspected Planets

Unaspected planets lack any Ptolemaic aspect (i.e., conjunction, sextile, square, trine, or opposition) with any other planet in the natal chart. They do not connect with the rest of the psyche. Unaspected planets can indicate strong talents or excessive, overcompensatory habits. They may be interpreted as strong and dominant or excessive and vulnerable to isolation. Astrologers need to consider these potentials when they interpret unaspected planets in the natal chart.

### Unaspected Sun

With an unaspected Sun in the natal chart, both its strengths and challenges can increase. The person's charisma is strengthened, which can facilitate success. The Sun's negative features can also prevail. These include social maladjustment, paralyzed willpower, unawareness of one's rude behavior, self-centeredness, egoism, and vanity. Bil Tierney writes, "The Sun's autonomous, self-governing nature can be even more emphasized." The individual can behave like an "island unto himself" (Tierney 2015, 174).

### Unaspected Moon

An unaspected Moon in the natal chart, more than any other unaspected planet, endows the individual's changing disposition with charismatic powers. The unaspected Moon can lead the individual to express themselves without restraint or to shut themselves away in their inner world. Hypersensitivity can leave them vulnerable to fleeting impressions or to stimuli barely perceptible to other people. The Moon's main characteristics are reactivity, passivity, and emotionalism. These can be heightened during transits, progressions, and solar arcs.

### Unaspected Mercury

Mercury is seldom unaspected in a chart since it's never very far from the Sun and Venus. With an unaspected Mercury in the natal chart, the individual's nature can be quick, unstable, and changeable. The intellectualism and the nervousness that Mercury naturally bestows might blow up out of proportion. What can be beneficial about an unaspected Mercury, according to Tierney, is less of an inclination to become scattered and distracted compared with a heavily aspected Mercury.

## Unaspected Venus

Venus is seldom unaspected in a chart since it's never very far from the Sun and Mercury. With an unaspected Venus in the natal chart, there can be alternating outbursts of emotions and heightened material and sensual desires. Venus's charm and kindness are less pronounced than with a well-aspected Venus. Because of these uncontrolled characteristics, some degree of passivity can prevent the individual from achieving an active life.

## Unaspected Mars

When Mars is unaspected in the natal chart, the effects are without a doubt the most noticeable among the ten unaspected planets. Mars's very nature is synonymous with action, aggression, and anger, as well as sexuality. An unaspected Mars sometimes activates the aggressive and quick-tempered side of the individual's nature. With an unaspected Moon, Mercury, or Venus, the energy tends to be directed inward through emotions, intellect, feelings, or desires. When Mars is unaspected, there is always a concrete impact. The energy tends to be directed outward. It is usually direct, visible, and instant.

## Unaspected Jupiter

With an unaspected Jupiter in the natal chart, there can be an emphasis on philosophy and education and an international or spiritual dimension. This suggests a mind hungry for higher learning. Jupiter naturally seeks out social interaction. With an unaspected Jupiter, there can be a tendency toward solitude as well as groundless exuberance.

## Unaspected Saturn

With an unaspected Saturn in the natal chart, the individual might experience inhibition, an inferiority complex, melancholy, and failures. On the positive side, an unaspected Saturn can also suggest intensified ambition. According to psychological astrologers, an unaspected Saturn suggests a lack of support from the father figure.

## Unaspected Uranus

Most astrologers agree that when one of the trans-Saturnian planets (Uranus, Neptune, or Pluto) is unaspected in a chart, its collective nature limits its scope. With an unaspected Uranus in the natal chart, there can be periods of compulsion for freedom and independence, with a strong taste for whatever is original or even fringe. Passions can prompt the individual to rebel. These can be followed by moments without exuberance or special excitement. There can be an overwhelming urge to achieve social significance.

## Unaspected Neptune

An unaspected Neptune in the natal chart might express as heightened aesthetic sensitivity and strong ideals. It can also bring paranormal gifts and moments of mystical ecstasy. Neptune is the planet of mysticism, intuition, imagination, and faith. It is also the planet of depravity and addiction to forbidden substances. An unaspected Neptune can result in moments of doubt, confusion, and indefinable disturbances.

## Unaspected Pluto

An unaspected Pluto in the natal chart can suggest prominence, power, and influence. The individual sometimes feels very strong impulses that they cannot escape. As Tierney notes, Pluto is the planet of the isolationist. Individuals with an unaspected Pluto can be distant and remote. They can relish in standing apart from others. An unaspected Pluto is associated with periodic spurts of obsessive or compulsive behavior.

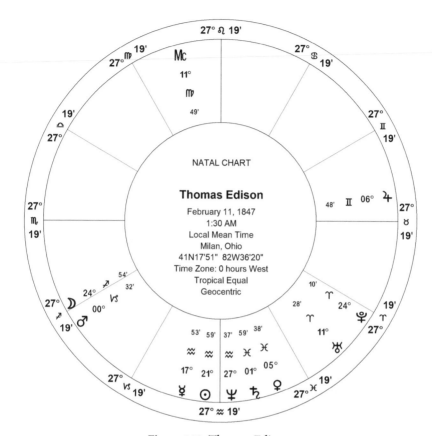

Figure 103: Thomas Edison

Thomas Edison has an unaspected Uranus, the planet of invention and scientific progress (figure 103). He's been described as America's greatest inventor. He held 1,093 US patents in his name. His patents were for devices in electric power generation, mass communication, sound recording, and motion pictures.

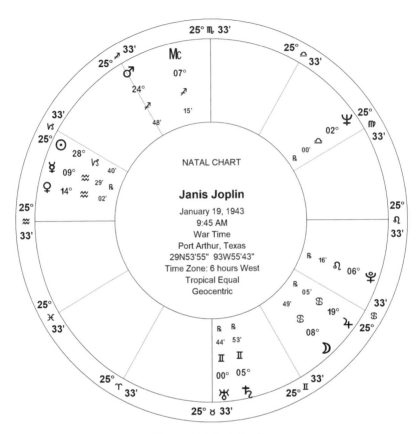

Figure 104: Janis Joplin

Non-conformist Janis Joplin has an unaspected Jupiter (figure 104). She was an American rock, soul, and blues singer and songwriter, and one of the most successful and widely known female rock stars of the 1960s. After releasing three albums, she died alone in a hotel room from a heroin overdose. She was only twenty-seven. A fourth album, *Pearl* (also her nickname), was released in January 1971, just a few months after her death. *Pearl* reached number one on the Billboard charts.

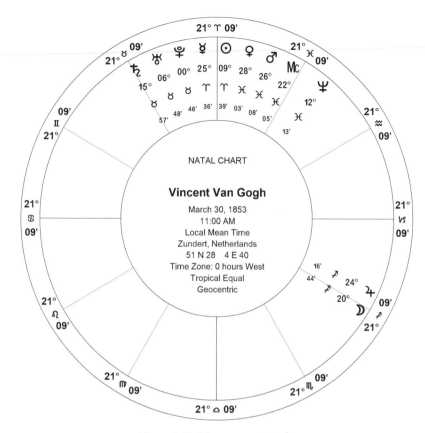

Figure 105: Vincent van Gogh

Vincent van Gogh has an unaspected Sun (figure 105). He was a Dutch Post-Impressionist painter, among the most famous and influential figures in the history of Western art. He channeled the more challenging aspects of an unaspected Sun, including social maladjustment, paralyzed willpower, and self-centeredness. Van Gogh suffered from psychotic episodes and delusions. Though he worried about his mental stability, he often neglected his physical health and drank heavily.

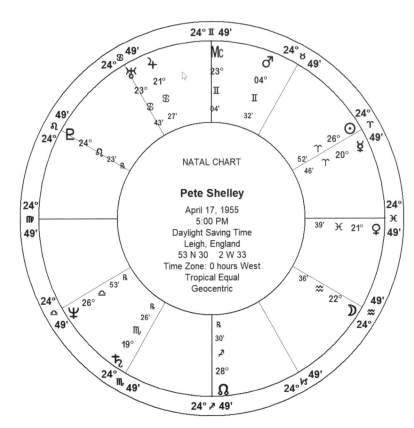

Figure 106: Pete Shelley

Punk rock singer, songwriter and guitarist Pete Shelley has an unaspected Mars. He was best known as the leader of Buzzcocks.

chapter 19
# Most Elevated Planet

The most elevated planet is the one closest to the Midheaven. It is considered strong by position and accidentally dignified. The innate qualities of the most elevated planet are amplified in potentially constructive ways. Any planet above the horizon in the horoscope reflects impulses in your life that are more visible to people around you. Those impulses are comparatively more exposed to public view.

Determining which is the most elevated planet in a chart depends on the house system selected. For example, in quadrant or time-based systems like Placidus or Koch, the Midheaven is identical to the tenth-house cusp. Any planet closest to that angle is automatically the most elevated planet. In other house systems, like Whole Sign or Equal House, the Midheaven is untethered from the tenth-house cusp, and can generally be anywhere between the eighth and the eleventh house. Usually, though, it's in the ninth or tenth house. How does one determine which is the most elevated planet in those house systems? Whichever planet is closest to the Midheaven is the most elevated planet, not the "top" of the chart as it appears visually.

The Midheaven is more than just a matter of fame or reputation. Yes, it incorporates those things, but it also represents the pinnacle of an individual's life direction, something they aspire toward. The Midheaven shows what the individual wants to be—the qualities they feel called upon to realize.

The affairs of the house ruled by the most elevated planet will be on display to the public. For example, if Mars is the most elevated planet, then the house with Aries will be prominent. Watch out when the most elevated planet rules the Sun sign or the Ascendant. That can really amp up concerns with career or the public.

## Interpreting the Most Elevated Planet

The most elevated planet in the horoscope has an exalted position and can exert a powerful influence over someone's entire life. Being near or conjunct the Midheaven, this planet is "accidentally dignified" in that its innate qualities are amplified in potentially constructive ways.

### Sun as the Most Elevated Planet

When the Sun is the most elevated planet, the individual can feel compelled to express their creativity and core ego values in a public way. The Sun positioned here typically enhances leadership, fame, and prominence. It can also reveal any mistakes or flaws in the individual's character.

### Moon as the Most Elevated Planet

When the Moon is the most elevated planet, the individual can feel compelled to project their personality or their emotions in public. With the Moon positioned here, they can feel an urge to expose their deepest and most vulnerable emotions in public.

### Mercury as the Most Elevated Planet

When Mercury is the most elevated planet, the individual can feel compelled to project their ideas or verbal skills in public. Individuals with Mercury in this position—especially when it's aspected by Neptune, Mars, Jupiter, or Saturn—need to be especially careful with any public statements since they can be misconstrued.

### Venus as the Most Elevated Planet

When Venus is the most elevated planet, the individual can feel compelled to project beauty or harmony in some way before the public. Venus positioned here and well aspected can confer charisma.

### Mars as the Most Elevated Planet

When Mars is the most elevated planet, the individual can feel compelled to project energy and strength before the public. Mars positioned here can suggest athletic or martial arts success. The forcefulness of Mars sometimes can be channeled in more creative areas such as music.

### Jupiter as the Most Elevated Planet

When Jupiter is the most elevated planet, the individual can feel compelled to exude confidence about matters relating to career. Jupiter positioned here is one of the leading astrological indicators for popularity and success.

### Saturn as the Most Elevated Planet

When Saturn is the most elevated planet, the individual can feel compelled to exude confidence about matters relating to career. Saturn positioned here, however, indicates that there will be far more work and difficulty compared with Jupiter in the same position. As Ray Grasse notes, "There's often a 'late bloomer' quality to the lives of these individuals" (Grasse 2015, 33).

### Uranus as the Most Elevated Planet

When Uranus is the most elevated planet, the individual can feel compelled to demonstrate a fiercely independent streak. There can be an urge to pursue an unconventional lifestyle. Uranus positioned here can make it difficult for the individuals to adapt to rigid routines and structured environments.

### Neptune as the Most Elevated Planet

When Neptune is the most elevated planet, the individual can feel powerful spiritual or creative impulses. They can experience confusion about their career or life's calling. When Neptune is positioned here, the individual might present an aura of glamour or illusion around their public persona.

## *Pluto as the Most Elevated Planet*

When Pluto is the most elevated planet, the individual can feel compelled to project intense primal energy related to matters of life and death, sexuality, power, and transformation. They can project a probing quality delving into life's "darker" side.

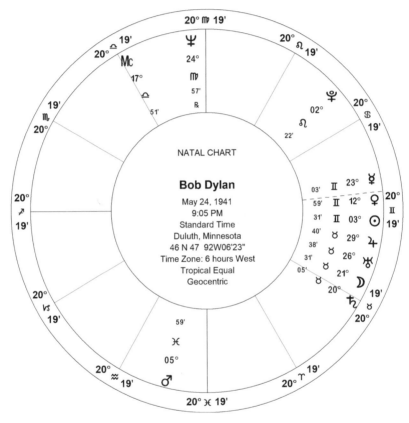

Figure 107: Bob Dylan

American singer-songwriter, author, and artist Bob Dylan has Neptune as the most elevated planet in his natal chart (figure 107). He became a reluctant "voice of a generation" with songs like "Blowin' in the Wind" and "The Times They Are a-Changin'." His songs were anthems for the civil rights movement and the anti-war movement. His lyrics incorporate a wide range of political, social, philosophical, and literary influences.

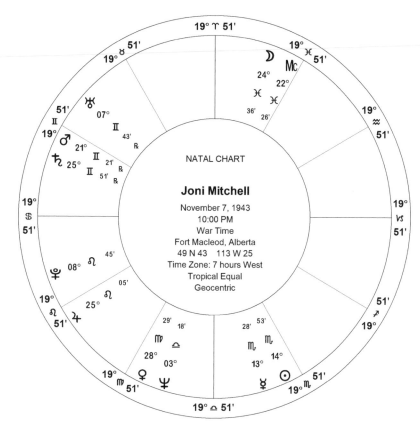

Figure 108: Joni Mitchell

Canadian singer-songwriter Joni Mitchell has the Moon as the most elevated planet (figure 108). Drawing from folk, pop, rock, and jazz, Joni Mitchell's songs often express passionate ideals for political and environmental protest.

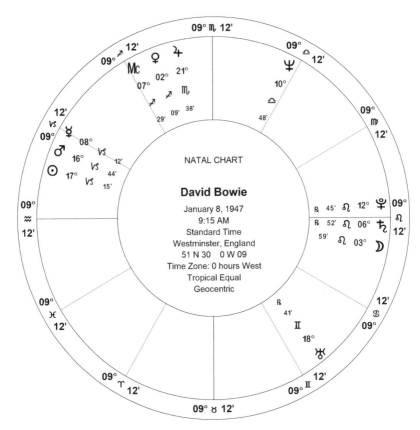

Figure 109: David Bowie

English singer, songwriter and actor David Bowie has Venus as the most elevated planet (figure 109). Often considered to be one of the most influential musicians of the twentieth century, particularly for his innovative work during the 1970s, he developed an interest in music as a child, eventually studying art, music, and design before embarking on a professional career as a musician.

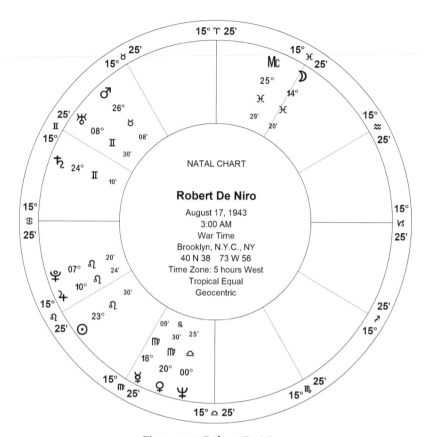

Figure 110: Robert De Niro

American actor, producer, and director Robert De Niro has the Moon as the most elevated planet (figure 110). He's not at all afraid of making controversial public statements.

## chapter 20

# Intercepted and Duplicated Signs

An intercepted sign is a zodiac sign that is completely contained within a house and does not appear on either cusp. Depending on the house system you use and how far from the equator the birth occurred, there might or might not be intercepted signs in the birth chart. At extreme latitudes, the natal charts using quadrant and time-based house systems, like Placidus and Koch, can contain multiple intercepted houses. Other house systems, like Equal House and Whole Sign, never have intercepted signs.

The Placidus natal chart for Arnold Schwarzenegger (figure 111) contains Aries intercepted in the tenth house and Libra intercepted in the fourth house. Intercepted houses always come in pairs, opposite each other.

When there is an intercepted sign, there will also be a duplicated sign. A duplicated sign appears on two consecutive house cusps. In the case of Arnold Schwarzenegger, Leo is duplicated on the second- and third-house cusps and Aquarius is duplicated on the eighth- and ninth-house cusps. Like intercepted signs, duplicate signs are always paired on opposite sides of the birth chart.

## Intercepted Signs

Joanne Wickenburg describes intercepted signs like a "room within a room." You enter the house (the area of life) in a certain way only to discover there is a whole other experience there. In the natal chart of a person, an intercepted sign shows a blockage.

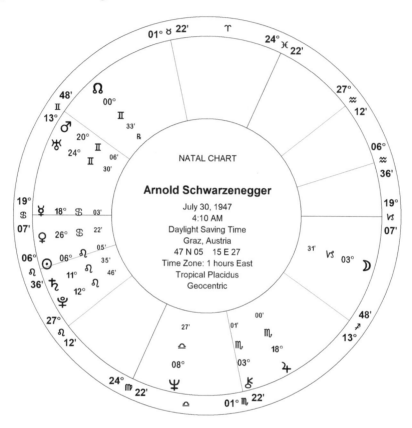

Figure 111: Arnold Schwarzenegger

Arnold Schwarzenegger has Aries intercepted in the tenth house (figure 111). That means Pisces is on the tenth-house cusp. With Pisces in the tenth, there's a talent somewhere in the natal charts of these individuals that needs to be discovered and used to spread their message to the world. Aries intercepted in the tenth means there's a deep, inherent need for the individual to focus their energy on career goals and the material future they can build. Pisces wants to merge and go with the flow. Aries wants to lead and be the boss. Pisces is a people pleaser. Aries is not. Pisces goes along with the collective will. Aries is a pioneer. The problem is that the Aries traits have difficulty manifesting in the individual's life. An interception means that the individual's early environment didn't give them the ability to deal with the traits of the intercepted sign. The qualities of intercepted signs can get repressed. Eventually, the pressure builds to the breaking point and those traits do emerge, sometimes in ways that are inappropriate.

### Intercepted Aries/Libra

Aries acts for action's sake. There's a need to prove oneself. When Aries occupies a house cusp, those impulses tend to be an obvious part of the persona. When Aries is intercepted, it's much more difficult for the individual to act. Pisces on the cusp makes it easier to daydream instead. As Wickenburg notes, the individual doesn't receive the much-needed support in early life to independently plunge into new experiences. The desire for independence is there, but it's hidden. Under the surface, the Aries traits are there: the fierce independence, the pioneering energy. At the surface level, the individual cannot find an appropriate outlet for those impulses. Acting tends to be inhibited. When they finally do act, they're likely to act rashly and be aggressive in socially inappropriate ways.

Aries is also concerned with identity development. When Aries is intercepted, the individual might have difficulty defining themselves separate from those around them. Their identity is submerged under the Pisces impulses. So on the surface, the initial impression they present is imaginative, idealistic, and passive. Under the surface, suppressed, lies the drive for independence, to be aggressive and self-proving. These individuals can be overly aggressive at times as they try to prove their independence.

When Aries is intercepted, so is Libra. Always. In the opposite house.

Bob Marks claims that it is difficult for individuals to form equal partnerships when Libra is intercepted. "For example, if the intercepted Libra is in the sixth house, that would cause problems treating co-workers as equals. If it were in the eleventh house, the problem would be with friends" (Bob Marks 2019). It is a challenge for them to develop balanced, stable relationships.

Virgo is on the house cusp when Libra is intercepted. This results in an individual who tends to be analytical and discriminating in the area of life indicated by the house containing the interception. They readily organize, analyze, and criticize in matters related to that department of life. At the same time, the individual will likely feel reluctant to share the results of their analysis. Their early environment didn't encourage the sharing of knowledge. They might have been actively discouraged from sharing their opinions.

According to Wickenburg, "Aries, in polarity with Libra, provides the initiative to act after balancing the pros and cons of any given situation" (Wickenburg 2011, 23). This polarity doesn't function as it might when Aries and Libra are intercepted. The individual instead vacillates, unable to make independent decisions. They look to others for leadership rather than initiating projects and sharing responsibilities.

### Intercepted Taurus/Scorpio

Taurus tends to be preoccupied with practical, determined, stable approaches. While Aries has no problem initiating projects, these individuals do tend to have difficulty with follow-through. It's just the opposite with Taurus. They are not self-initiating like Aries, but once they get started, they can see an endeavor through to the end. They're motivated by tangible, concrete results.

When Taurus is intercepted, establishing self-worth can be a challenge. The environment doesn't offer the opportunities to build self-worth. That can translate into relationship difficulties.

Scorpio expresses the reactions of others toward the assets and accomplishments acquired by Taurus. Here the individual experiences the reactions of others to their acquisition and (mis)use of resources. This important feedback from others tends to be disregarded when Scorpio is intercepted.

Scorpio's house describes the department of life where the individual wants to merge resources (material, emotional, spiritual). When Scorpio is intercepted, this sharing with others can be a serious issue. There can be a reluctance to share resources with another. The individual needs to learn the life lesson of contribution to joint enterprises.

Taurus is in polarity with Scorpio. Taurus is associated with what a person values, as well as a tendency to accumulate what they value. Scorpio is the sign of shared values, but it is also the sign of renewal and disposal. When possessions and values are no longer useful, Scorpio either fixes or gets rid of them. When these signs are intercepted, the polarity is broken. In the house with Taurus intercepted, the individual might constantly accumulate things and seldom dispose of anything. As Bob Marks writes, "If Taurus is intercepted in the fifth house (hobbies, sports, games, children, and, of course, romance) it could indicate someone who is always starting hobbies or taking up a new sport which they quickly drop. Their closet is full of all the equipment they bought, which they cannot bring themselves to throw away" (Bob Marks 2019).

If Taurus is intercepted in the fifth house, then Scorpio is intercepted in the eleventh. When a friendship experiences strain, any unpleasantness wouldn't be openly confronted. Libra on the house cusp avoids conflict. The Scorpio capacity to confront people and—if need be—to end the friendship is suppressed. Again, we look to early childhood experiences for an explanation, and in this case the answer might be a parent's insistence that the individual always be nice to friends no matter what. Ignoring relationship problems doesn't make them go away. The pressure builds. Then, instead of a minor problem being easily resolved, there's a powerful confrontation.

### Intercepted Gemini/Sagittarius

Gemini and Sagittarius are the communication signs. Gemini is the sign we associate with curiosity and is noted for its deep concern with communication, information, and mental stimulation. Gemini makes associations and distinctions. These individuals need the freedom to pursue self-understanding.

Gemini seeks information related to concrete facts. Sagittarius, opposite Gemini in the zodiac, values information in order to derive theories, principles, and abstractions. It is the sign of generalities. Sagittarius views life from a broader frame of reference than does Gemini. It allows these individuals to make value judgments based on the information gathered by Gemini.

Interception breaks this balance between data gathering and the synthesis and analysis needed to generate useful information from that data. In the house with Gemini intercepted, all sorts of useless information will be gathered. The intercepted Sagittarius can't discriminate between facts that are significant and those that are not.

When the Gemini/Sagittarius polarity is intercepted, there are no house cusps to project their ideas out into the world. That doesn't mean the individual is unable to speak, but it does suggest problems with communicating ideals. Frustration with communication and feedback is common. Wickenburg describes it like this: "When Sagittarius does not function with Gemini, the power contained in the spoken word eludes you. When the environment furnishes you with information, the data presented to you does not 'speak' to you in a way that has meaning" (Wickenburg 2011, 28).

Intercepted Gemini has Taurus on the cusp. That lends a tendency for the individual to be closed-minded. Information needs to be practical and tangible or the individual is likely to disregard it. They might have a problem communicating reasons to back up what they say. Their claims can sound dogmatic. As a result, others will tend to ignore their views.

When Sagittarius is intercepted, Scorpio is on the cusp. As Bob Marks says, "Scorpio likes to get into things in depth" (Bob Marks 2019). This sign is intense and deep. When Sagittarius is on a house cusp, it shows the department of life where an individual is likely to form philosophical principles. When Sagittarius is intercepted, the individual still has strong principles but has difficulty expressing them. Sagittarius is a sign of expansion. This need to expand tends to go unfulfilled when Sagittarius is intercepted. These individuals are likely to be reticent and reluctant to voice their opinions since Scorpio is prone to keeping secrets.

### Intercepted Cancer/Capricorn

Cancer rules our emotions, our home, and our history. It's where our personal security needs are greatest. As Wickenburg says, "Here, you need to be nurtured, you need to belong" (Wickenburg 2011, 29). Once the individual establishes sufficient personal security, they can play the role of nurturer as well as be nurtured.

Until some degree of personal security has been established, the intercepted Cancer individual tends to feel vulnerable and defensive. They fear losing those individuals and things to which they have formed strong personal attachments.

Capricorn also tends to be preoccupied with security needs. Instead of individual security relating largely to home and family, the security focus for Capricorn is on social status. The place the individual occupies in the social structure is critical to their feelings of self-worth. It's where they tend to feel territorial.

The Cancer/Capricorn polarity contrasts personal, emotional security versus career ambitions. Cancer helps the individual develop the necessary emotional strength that can support the needed social status to defend their place in the social hierarchy. When this polarity is intercepted, it doesn't function as it otherwise might. The individual can be preoccupied with personal security to the detriment of reaching their social potential.

When Cancer is intercepted, the individual can either overreact to emotional stimuli or suppress their emotions. Gemini is on the house cusp, and Gemini is largely a mental sign. It encourages a cerebral reaction. The emotions of Cancer, locked away without a house cusp for their expression, tend to get suppressed until they reach the point of a major blow-up. As a consequence, emotional needs and emotional vulnerability tend to go unnoticed, further contributing to emotional outbursts that others consider excessive and inappropriate.

Sagittarius is on the cusp of the house in which Capricorn is intercepted. The individual's innate Capricorn ability to organize and control is blocked. What does tend to emerge is a tendency to micromanage: a control freak. When the boat rocks, they need to clamp down—hard!

The early environment for the individual likely didn't provide the emotional support and nurturance needed to develop feelings of deep-seated security. They were likely forced to suppress their serious, ambitious side. The individual needs to learn to let go.

### Intercepted Leo/Aquarius

Bob Marks nails it when he writes, "Leo is where we want to be on stage. Aquarius is where we want to rebel and be original and 'different.'" (Bob Marks 2019). These two impulses—Aquarius, an air sign, and Leo, a fire sign—combine to give Leo an awareness of others.

The house where Leo resides is where the individual feels compelled to make a personal difference. They need to stamp their identity on the affairs of that house. Individuals with Leo feel a need to prove themselves. Leo is ruled by the Sun, and that's where a person expresses their inner sense of importance. It's where the individual feels the need to be appreciated.

Aquarius is the sign we associate with rebellion. Its house is where the individual feels compelled to break free from social conventions and express their true individuality.

The Leo/Aquarius polarity gives originality to Leo's need for self-expression and purpose to Aquarius's need for rebellion. When that polarity is intercepted, frustration is felt when attempting to integrate them in the individual's personality. They find it difficult to get noticed and appreciated. The drive to be original is suppressed.

When Leo is intercepted, Cancer is on the house cusp. People view the individual as emotional and nurturing. They come seeking support from the individual. What they don't offer is a stage and applause. This can lead these individuals to demand attention in socially inappropriate ways. Or, as an alternative, the Leo individual may suppress their creativity.

When Aquarius is intercepted, Capricorn is on the house cusp. The need for independence and individuality is locked up inside the practical, status-conscious exterior of Capricorn. Opposites converge. The individual's impulse to be different is suppressed. They learn early in life that their desire to be different and explore socially unacceptable things and ideas is not going to be tolerated. They cover those impulses with a Capricorn veneer. That way, they appear to be "normal."

The life lesson when the Leo/Aquarius polarity is intercepted is to learn how to break free from this rigid social conditioning. This is tricky, because the individual wants to be part of the social structure (Capricorn) and wants social approval and applause (Leo), yet at the same time they need to rebel to discover who they really are (Aquarius).

## Intercepted Virgo/Pisces

Virgo is the sign of mental analysis, synthesis, and discrimination. It takes the data from Gemini and organizes, processes, and refines it into practical information. The individual learns to criticize and ask questions. Virgo recognizes imperfections. It's also capable of developing techniques for correcting those deficiencies.

Virgo deals with material reality, the here and now. Pisces, by contrast, is concerned with the ideal. It deals with acceptance, dreams, faith, and imagination rather than the concrete. Pisces gives the individual the ability to visualize: to see what's possible and act upon that impulse. Virgo sees all the details, all the tiny parts. Pisces bestows the ability to see the abstract whole. According to Bob Marks, "The dreams and ideals of Pisces can never be reached, but striving for them is what keeps us all going!" (Bob Marks 2019).

When Pisces is intercepted, the individual can have difficulty distinguishing between what's real and fantasy. At the same time, Virgo is also intercepted.

The individual lacks Virgo's discrimination. They can have great visions of what they would like to do, but without the help of Virgo, they don't know how to put their dreams into practice. The house with the Pisces interception shows where the individual can be easily deceived, by themselves as well as others.

Virgo is intercepted in the opposite house. These individuals can become too critical and judgmental. The loss of Virgo's objectivity means the individual can accept their own inadequacies in their ability to analyze, organize, and discriminate. Perfecting those skills is an important life lesson when Virgo is intercepted.

Pisces rules both faith and fear. When Pisces is intercepted, the individual can become obsessed with unrealistic fears.

Leo occupies the house cusp when Virgo is intercepted. Others tend to see the individual as confident, proud, and generous, but the individual doesn't have the same perception. They can be filled with self-doubt, self-criticism, and self-deprecation. They lack the Pisces faith in themselves. Without a door (a cusp) to express their Virgo impulses, the individual can become hypercritical in reaction. The opposite is possible as well. The individual can be reluctant to apply a critical mind where one is needed.

Aquarius occupies the house cusp when Pisces is intercepted. Others view the individual as progressive, humanitarian, and quite possibly eccentric. They fail to recognize the individual's ideals and emotional sensitivity. Others find it difficult to understand those things that deeply inspire the individual.

## Duplicated Signs

Whenever there's a set of intercepted signs in a natal chart, there's also a set of duplicated signs. Two adjacent houses have the same sign on their cusps. Like intercepted signs, duplicated signs come in opposing sets.

Wickenburg claims, "The potential represented by the sign on these two sequential house cusps is so strong and highly developed that it carries the power to dominate the environment defined by the intercepted house" (Wickenburg 2011, 41). Unlike intercepted signs, which reflect repressed and pent-up impulses, duplicated signs represent departments of life where you can control the environment.

Each sign of the zodiac contains exactly 30°. Intercepted and duplicate signs don't alter this fact. When the same sign is found on two adjacent house cusps, the house with the lesser degree is smaller than 30°. That sign, according to Wickenburg, is intercepting the house.

When signs are intercepted, their expression can be a problem. The qualities they represent tend to be repressed. When houses are duplicated, the opposite holds true. The same qualities are developed to such an extent that they can become dominant. Those qualities get expressed in the house with the larger degree of the sign. Looking back at Arnold Schwarzenegger's natal chart (figure 111), the second and third houses have Leo on the cusp. Likewise, the eighth and ninth houses have Aquarius on their cusps.

### Intercepted First House

The same sign is found on the first- and second-house cusps, the houses of identity and self-worth. The individual's personality tends to be extremely powerful. People notice them. The challenge is for the individual to focus on matters other than their own persona (first house). Those qualities are already well developed. They need to demonstrate they can produce concrete results by using their personal charisma (first house). They need to concern themselves less with appearances (first house) and more with value and substance (second house).

### Intercepted Second House

The same sign is found on the second- and third-house cusps, the houses of self-worth and communication. Rather than simply acquiring objects and other forms of wealth (second house), the individual is pressed to use their resources to acquire knowledge and information (third house). Self-worth (second house) is connected strongly to intellectual pursuits (third house). Knowledge (third house) in turn can produce the needed resources for productive living (second house).

### Intercepted Third House

The same sign is found on the third- and fourth-house cusps, the houses of communication and emotional security. The individual possesses information (third house) to secure their life, establish a foundation, and interact within their community (fourth house). Security (fourth house) is built from knowledge (third house). The life challenge of this individual is to direct that knowledge (third house) into emotionally satisfying channels (fourth house).

### Intercepted Fourth House
The same sign is found on the fourth- and fifth-house cusps, the houses of emotional security and creativity. The challenge is to use experience accumulated from the past (fourth house) as a source of creative inspiration (fifth house). Security and emotional needs (fourth house) affect their creative, procreative, and recreational interests (fifth house). The life challenge for this individual is to inject emotional intelligence into all fifth-house activities.

### Intercepted Fifth House
The same sign is found on the fifth- and sixth-house cusps, the houses of creativity and work. These individuals have well-defined creative talents. The sign of the two houses determines the departments of life where the talents are expressed. These individuals are generally fortunate to have a job (sixth house) that they love. They're likely to work (sixth house) in a field that leverages their creative talents (fifth house). Due to their playful nature (fifth house), they might not take their job (sixth house) seriously enough and encounter difficulties with supervisors.

### Intercepted Sixth House
The same sign is found on the sixth- and seventh-house cusps, the houses of work and relationships. These individuals need to work closely (sixth house) with colleagues (seventh house). They handle routine responsibilities well (sixth house). They are likely to think of coworkers (seventh house) almost as a surrogate family. Since the seventh house is also the house of marriage, it's possible that these individuals work together with their spouse. Their life challenge is to use their work skills in harmony with others, learn to delegate, and share credit for a job well done.

### Intercepted Seventh House
The same sign is found on the seventh- and eighth-house cusps, the houses of relationships and shared resources. This is where we find people-pleaser

types. Bob Marks claims that the partner (seventh house) is viewed as an asset (eighth house). I find Wickenburg's interpretation more appropriate. She notes, "Growth comes not from the process of forming relationships (seventh house), but as a result of maintaining them (eighth house)" (Wickenburg 2011, 46). These individuals know how to interact well with others. This can give them a great deal of influence.

### Intercepted Eighth House

The same sign is found on the eighth- and ninth-house cusps, the houses of shared resources and the higher mind. The departments of the eighth house include shared resources, death, regeneration, open enemies, taxes, etc. These individuals often have a penetrating psychological outlook on philosophy and religion (ninth house). Bob Marks focuses on the ninth house. He says that "values of the groups you belong to also have to be taught" (Bob Marks 2019). Important life lessons concerning the eighth house also need to be learned, especially the skill to experience regeneration, which stable, long-term relationships require.

### Intercepted Ninth House

The same sign is found on the ninth- and tenth-house cusps, the houses of the higher mind and social status. Here the individual develops a core set of principles (ninth house). These become key to career decisions and affect public reputation (tenth house). These individuals tend to be comfortable with people who have different ideas and are from different cultures (ninth house). This is an ideal combination for a teacher, writer, or consultant.

### Intercepted Tenth House

The same sign is found on the tenth- and eleventh-house cusps, the houses of social status and community. Bob Marks claims that for individuals with an intercepted tenth house, people (eleventh) are more important to them than career (tenth). This identifies the tenth house too much with career. According to Wickenburg, what matters when the tenth house is intercepted is the "ability to be noticed, to acquire recognition, and to gain professional status" (Wickenburg 2011, 47). These are all personal drives. The eleventh house adds the dimension of group needs and goals. The important life lesson for these individuals is how to blend personal activities with group goals and contribute to social development.

### Intercepted Eleventh House

The same sign is found on the eleventh- and twelfth-house cusps, the houses of community and hidden self. These individuals have an innate ability to play an influential role in social groups (eleventh house). They can easily work with people (eleventh house) to advance social reform and humanitarian goals (twelfth house). Their life challenge is to take on leadership in a group (eleventh house) and to pursue individual aggrandizement but also serve the larger community. These individuals tend to be sensitive to people who have suffered in some way and are in need of healing (twelfth house).

### Intercepted Twelfth House

The same sign is found on the twelfth- and first-house cusps, the houses of the hidden self and identity. The twelfth house is concerned with everything hidden and mysterious. As Wickenburg notes, "The twelfth house deals with inner life" (Wickenburg 2011, 49). The life lesson for these individuals is to learn to live out (first house) their inner beliefs and principles (twelfth house).

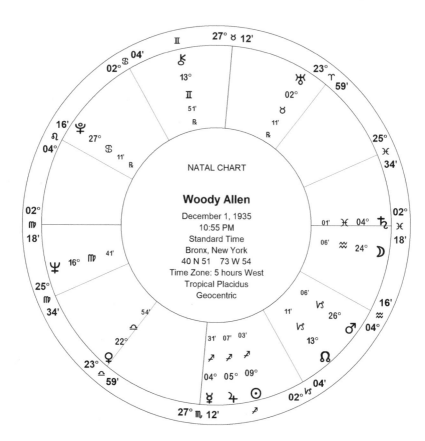

Figure 112: Woody Allen

Woody Allen has an intercepted Gemini/Sagittarius polarity (figure 112). His first and seventh houses are intercepted. As a stand-up comedian in the 1960s, he helped turn stand-up into biting cultural satire. The subjects of his jokes were rarely topical, political, or socially relevant. He felt people were taking themselves too seriously, which became the subject of much of his satire. Even Allen's comedies have serious, philosophical subtexts.

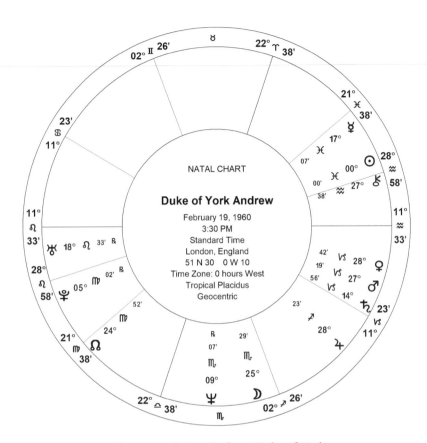

Figure 113: Prince Andrew, Duke of York

Prince Andrew, Duke of York, is the third child of Queen Elizabeth II and Prince Philip, Duke of Edinburgh. He has an intercepted Taurus/Scorpio polarity, with the first and seventh houses intercepted (figure 113). He's been party to several controversies and scandals, including allegations of sexual abuse by himself and by close associates.

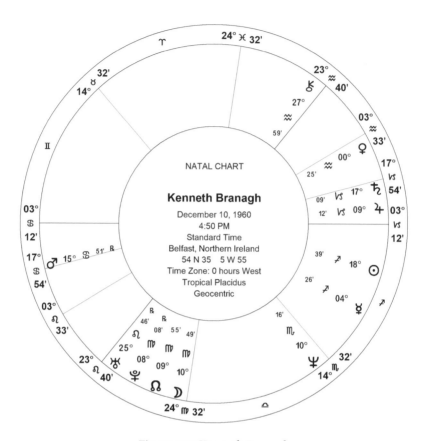

Figure 114: Kenneth Branagh

Kenneth Branagh is a greatly respected British actor, director, producer, and screenwriter. Born in Belfast, at 54 North 35 latitude, his chart features double intercepted signs (figure 114). Both the Aries/Libra polarity and the Gemini/Sagittarius polarity are intercepted. This also results in the first, third, seventh, and ninth houses being intercepted.

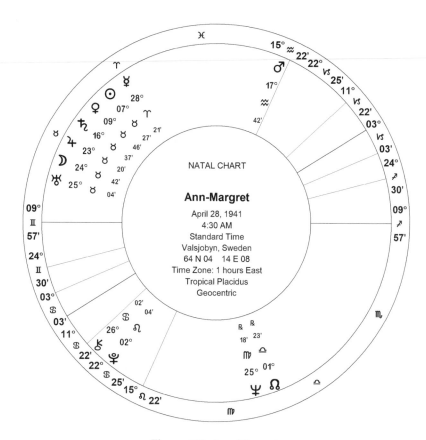

Figure 115: Ann-Margret

At extreme north and south latitudes, the quadrant and time-based house
systems can break down completely. Born in Sweden, high above the Arctic
Circle, singer and actress Ann-Margret's chart contains triple intercepted signs
(figure 115). Pisces, Aries, and Taurus are all intercepted in a twelfth house that
spans more than the width of a trine aspect. Opposite is Virgo, Libra, and Scorpio in the sixth house. Interpretation gets messy with intercepted first, third,
fourth, seventh, ninth, and tenth houses.

## chapter 21

# Retrograde Planets

Due to the concentric orbits of the planets around the Sun, it sometimes appears from our vantage point on Earth that a planet is moving backward in the zodiac. This is a condition called "retrograde."

A retrograde planet is at its closest to Earth, is at its brightest in the sky, is stronger than usual, and is powerful in its effects.

When a planet is retrograde, its energies are turned inward. It becomes more subjective. Its energies are slower to manifest in the external world. Partly this is because the individual with retrograde planets tends to think more deeply about the energies involved. Many notable individuals have retrograde planets. In the Astro Databank, 62.5 percent of the charts have one or more retrograde planets, as shown in the following table.

| Retrograde Planet in Natal Chart | Percentage |
| --- | --- |
| Mercury | 17.86 |
| Venus | 7.14 |
| Mars | 8.93 |
| Jupiter | 27.78 |

*(continued)*

| Retrograde Planet in Natal Chart | Percentage |
|---|---|
| Saturn | 31.25 |
| Uranus | 27.78 |
| Neptune | 25.00 |
| Pluto | 19.23 |

## Interpreting Retrograde Planets

You will have retrograde planets in your birth chart if one or more of your planets was traveling backward in the skies at the moment you were born. What effect does this have? Having planets retrograde at birth provides an individual with an extra challenge. Their energy and meaning is generally expressed on an inner level. The urges and needs of a retrograde planet tend to be held back or blocked in the individual's life.

### Retrograde Mercury

Mercury involves mental processes and communication, exploring ideas, seeking knowledge, writing, public speaking, making contacts, short trips, and commerce. Natal Mercury retrograde turns the mind inward, with a tendency to ruminate over prior events and lessons. It is good for abstract knowledge and for writing, but not so good for public speaking or dialogue with others. The rational mind is usually quite perceptive. When an individual has Mercury retrograde and doesn't allow sufficient time to process each piece of data, they could have problems communicating in a way that others comprehend. Due to withholding communication under Mercury retrograde, the intelligence is less obvious to others. These individuals absorb the essence rather than the details.

### Retrograde Venus

Natal Venus retrograde can cause difficulty achieving fulfillment or finding the right romantic partner. The individual might be more in love with their ideas about love than with any real person. Strong personal aesthetics and unconventional creative expression often make these people artists. Idealism or an unconventional attitude regarding love suggests problems finding satisfaction in relationships. These individuals might feel they lack emotional fulfillment and tend to interpret life's events through the lens of "how much am I loved?" Emotionally based relationships can be difficult because these individuals tend to internalize and exaggerate hurts. When Venus is retrograde, they can be unable to fully appreciate their own self-worth until they compare their life in relation to others.

## Retrograde Mars

When Mars is retrograde in the natal chart, it operates with great intensity. Retrograde Mars causes difficulty for an individual in asserting themselves because they're afraid of the consequences of releasing their anger. They might tend to overthink before they act. An individual with retrograde Mars might find that they're waging an internal battle. The planet of energy and action is held back. This results in delayed or deferred action until forced by an external stimulus. The aggressive energy of Mars is experienced inwardly. This results in a buildup of pressure, which can suddenly explode. There can be great determination to get the seemingly impossible done, which yields the potential for great accomplishments. These individuals tend to expend a lot of energy ruminating over past experiences.

## Retrograde Jupiter

Jupiter begins the process of socialization, and retrograde Jupiter in the natal chart can cause these individuals to encounter one impediment after another in their search for understanding and positive experiences, especially in early life. Positive abilities, talents, and skills tend to be developed later in life. Higher education is prone to be delayed. One of the beneficial aspects of this placement is that the individual is more likely to be introspective, which assists in the development of higher spiritual ideals. Jupiter retrograde turns its energy of expansion inward. Much inner growth takes place, often through philosophical or spiritually oriented studies. These individuals tend to procrastinate and to plan, then replan, to the point of failing to get anywhere. The material acquisition bestowed by the planet of prosperity is not realized as much or is delayed until later in life.

## Retrograde Saturn

Retrograde Saturn individuals tend to be extremely introspective, conservative, frugal, and serious. The energy of the planet of structure, when experienced inwardly, leads to strong resilience, endurance, and steadfastness, and also a chronic adherence to preformed attitudes. The individual becomes less adaptable and less flexible, and therefore suffers when the external situation requires change. When Saturn is retrograde in the natal chart, it can be difficult for the individual to determine where they fit in the social structure. Until they willingly accept self-discipline, they will experience Saturn as feelings of limitation, deprivation, delay, and disappointment. Noel Tyl introduces another interpretation for Saturn retrograde. For Tyl, it suggests "a grand conditioning of life circumstances and patterning of behavior centered upon a legacy of inferiority feelings taken on in early homelife related to an absent, passive, or tyrannical father, or to a breakup of the family structure altogether" (Tyl 2012, 19).

## Retrograde Uranus

Uranus retrograde in the natal chart creates difficulty in being aware of and expressing inner individuality. The planet of freedom and rebellion, turned inward, gives a need to rebel against oneself. This can lead to extreme individualism and even self-destructive behavior. These individuals must be original, must explore the new, must share their ideas with others. They are free spirits. They are likely to experience wide fluctuations in circumstances and tend to push things to extremes. Rather than tear down what exists, retrograde Uranus renovates what already exists.

## Retrograde Neptune

Neptune retrograde in the natal chart gives the desire to unveil mysteries and to expose religious shams. When Neptune is retrograde, the individual finds it a challenge to use available knowledge to uncover life's mysteries. The planet of dreams and illusions, expressed inwardly, makes the individual inclined to retreat into a subjective world of fantasies. If affected by challenging aspects, retrograde Neptune can make the individual overly suspicious, even doubting themselves, creating paralyzing paranoia. Substance abuse can be triggered by a need to escape, and these individuals can fall prey to their own illusions if they don't accept people as they are.

## Retrograde Pluto

While individuals wrestle with inner conflicts when Pluto is retrograde in their natal chart, outside forces are likely to upset their life. Pluto is an impersonal (generational) planet. As a consequence, most people are not fully aware of its full effect on their lives. When driven inward by retrograde motion, Pluto's quality of destruction and regeneration can produce real spiritual progress if it is in a good position in the chart. In other cases, Pluto's power plays can lead to the reverse, making the individual into the ultimate outcast. Part of the individual's life lesson is to refuse to get locked in a battle of egos.

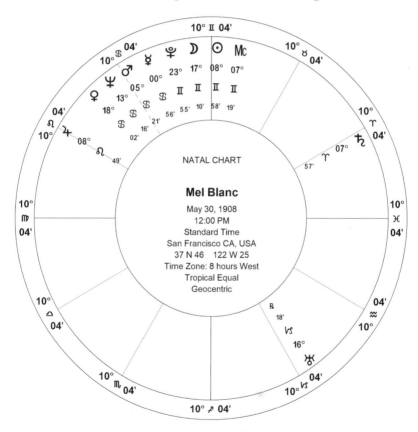

Figure 116: Mel Blanc

Mel Blanc was an American voice actor, comedian, singer, and radio personality. He is best known for his animation work as the voices of Bugs Bunny, Daffy Duck, Porky Pig, and many of the other characters from Looney Tunes and Merrie Melodies. Mel Blanc has one retrograde planet. Appropriately, it's Uranus in the fifth house, the house of play and creativity (figure 116).

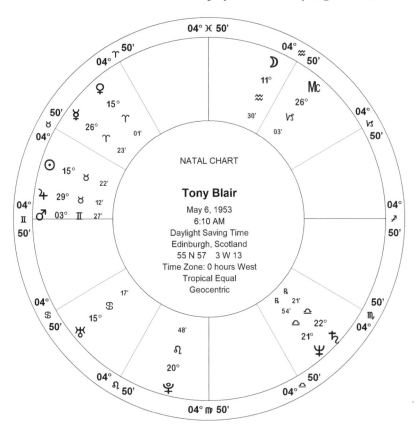

Figure 117: Tony Blair

Former British prime minister and statesman Tony Blair has two retrograde planets, both in the fifth house: Saturn and Neptune (figure 117). Under Blair's leadership, the party used the phrase "New Labour" to distance it from previous Labour policies and the traditional conception of socialism. Critics of Blair denounced him for bringing the Labour Party toward the perceived center ground of British politics, abandoning "genuine" socialism and being too amenable to capitalism.

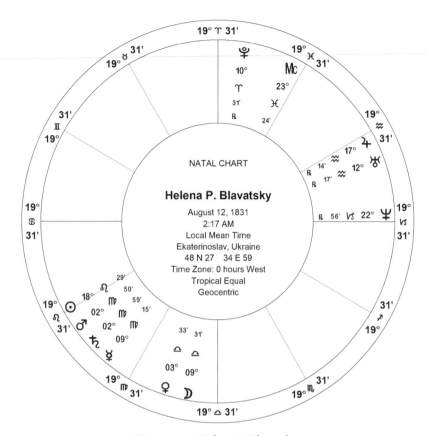

Figure 118: Helena P. Blavatsky

Helena P. Blavatsky was a Russian occultist, philosopher, and author who cofounded the Theosophical Society in 1875. She gained an international following as the leading theoretician of Theosophy. Her natal chart contains four retrograde planets: Jupiter, Uranus, and Neptune in the seventh house and Pluto in the ninth house (figure 118).

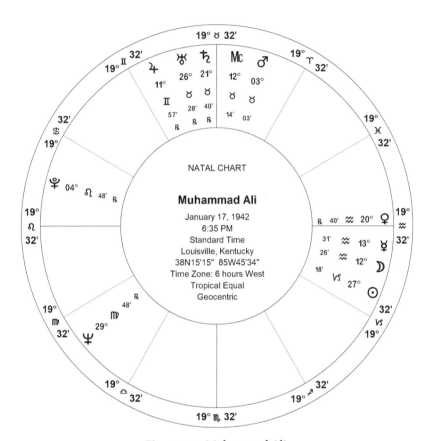

Figure 119: Muhammad Ali

The natal chart for boxer Muhammad Ali contains six retrograde planets: Neptune in the second, Venus in the seventh, Jupiter, Saturn, and Uranus in the tenth, and Pluto in the twelfth (figure 119). Given that the Sun and Moon cannot go retrograde, that leaves Mercury and Mars as the only two planets in his chart that aren't retrograde (among the eight possibilities).

chapter 22
# Leading Planets

The Sun rises in the east, culminates overhead, and sets in the west. A planet is leading in the natal chart when it is the last planet to rise before the Sun. To find the leading planet in your natal chart, look for the Sun and then find the first planet clockwise from the Sun. That will be the leading planet.

There is some controversy over the inclusion of Mercury and Venus as the leading planet, since both Mercury and Venus never get far away from the Sun. Mercury is always within 28° of the Sun and Venus within 47° of the Sun. I'm including delineations for Mercury and Venus here, but feel free to skip over them.

Other names for the leading planet include oriental planet, eastern planet, vespertine planet, scout planet, guiding planet, and skill symbol.

Michael Meyer says the leading planet is a "practical channel through which solar will and vitality is expressed." He continues by saying, "It represents both your inner guiding principle and your innate skills and special faculties, and how both might be best realized, enhanced and applied" (Meyer 2019). Stated differently, the leading planet shows how to best handle the demands and opportunities of daily life in a meaningful and productive way. Planets—when leading—are given added significance, especially within a vocational analysis. The leading planet usually describes the individual's approach to life.

There can be more than one leading planet. This occurs when a conjunction of planets is the last planet to rise before the Sun.

Determining the leading planet when the birth time is unknown can be a challenge. If you want to use the leading planet in this situation it is best to cast a noon natal chart. That way, your error in birth time is at most twelve hours. Remember, the Sun moves approximately 1° each day. So too do Mercury and Venus. The Moon is especially troublesome. It moves approximately 12–13° per day, and as little as 11° and as much as 15°. To be safe, consult an ephemeris to determine the Moon's speed and the speed of the Sun, Mercury, and Venus.

## Interpreting the Leading Planet

The leading planet is an important one to study. It is almost like a harbinger for the Sun, which has much to say about it's meaning.

### Leading Moon

Each month the Moon will assume the place of the leading planet. The Moon's length of time as the leading planet varies from a few hours to a few days, depending on the placement of the other planets. When the Moon is leading, it's usually in the waxing half of its cycle and most often balsamic, according to Alison Price.

When the Moon is leading, the individual tends to develop a reputation for practicality. They're predictable. They can keep matters running smoothly. The leading Moon placement suggests that the individual prefers a workplace where they can feel secure and at home.

### Leading Mercury

When Mercury is leading, the individual tends to have their life well planned along an easily predicted path. These individuals need to be careful. They tend to think and talk too quickly. They can have a habit of dismissing as irrelevant much of the information and experience that comes their way. Those with leading Mercury are often good conversationalists. As Michael Meyer notes, individuals can easily fall into an "all talk and no action" syndrome.

People with Mercury leading often have two careers running. They tend to be especially good in the areas of communication and information sharing. A quick study, they can easily master new systems and technology. Natural multitaskers, these people can juggle several tasks at once.

## Leading Venus

When Venus is leading, the individual tends to be very concerned with how others value them. They can feel compelled to leave a mark on everything they do. They tend to feel alienated when others fail to recognize and praise their contributions.

These individuals need be especially careful about their career choice. High expectations and sensitivity to criticism suggest that careers that require creativity, judgment, or evaluation are probably best for long-term happiness.

## Leading Mars

Mars is leading only every other year. It takes two and a half years for Mars to go around the Sun. The Sun overtakes it every other year. So in some years Mars is not leading at all.

When Mars is leading, the individual tends to have a memorable personality. They can be aggressive and confrontational. They are generally direct and to the point. They can, through sheer force of will, accomplish whatever goals they set for themselves. Endurance, productivity, drive, and self-promotion can help ensure success. They need to dial back a tendency toward domination and ruthlessness, lest they create enemies by their insensitive conduct.

These individuals often find success and happiness in the fields of sales, promotion, and athletics.

## Leading Jupiter

Alison Price claims that Jupiter is leading 5 percent of the time. When it's leading, it's most likely in direct motion.

When Jupiter is leading, the individual tends to have an ability to get things done. They have a good social sense and possess a natural skill for handling people and social activities. Because of their varied and many simultaneous interests, they can become spread too thin at times. They can be a Jack of all trades and master of none.

The individual with Jupiter leading often does well in the area of promotions and as a technical evangelist. They can be an excellent fit to a company's growth area.

### Leading Saturn

Saturn is leading 5 percent of the time, according to Price.

When Saturn is leading, the individual tends toward caution. Planners to the nth degree, they prefer to master their emotions first. There tends to be a lot of concern regarding their public status. Individuals with Saturn leading have patience for the long game, so they will bide their time. They often exhibit an even greater capacity for work, self-discipline and overcoming obstacles than those with Mars leading. They can best achieve their highly focused goals through sheer perseverance and a profound understanding of the nature of people and things.

Vocational markers for leading Saturn lean heavily in many cases toward management. The can give and follow instructions.

### Leading Uranus

This is surely the most eccentric leading planet a person can have. Life is exciting for these individuals. They want to revolutionize—or at least update and improve—their social environment. Individuals with Uranus leading often encounter resistance from conservative people when seeking ingenious new solutions. It's best to cultivate people skills, stability, perseverance, and patience.

People with Uranus leading do well in innovative fields and cutting-edge careers. Repetitive tasks will become irksome and tax their patience. They're even likely to create a new niche for themselves that was not there before.

### Leading Neptune

When Neptune is leading, the individual is inclined to see the mystical or transcendental side of things. People with Neptune leading bring vision to their vocation. They're highly imaginative, with a sharp intuition. They can easily picture things, but they need time and space to absorb them. Leading Neptune people can certainly get things done, but they need more than most to feel deeply motivated about what they're working toward. They need the respect of their coworkers.

With leading Neptune, the individual is likely to have a compassionate nature and a special skill for understanding the difficulties of others and sympathizing with them. When confronted with difficult situations, they try to see all sides of the issue, then work out a harmonious solution that includes everyone.

Although Neptune is the planet most connected with music, it does not figure largely as the leading planet in the natal charts of famous and successful musicians and composers. Leading Mars, Mercury, Jupiter, and Saturn are more likely, with their skills for self-promotion, communication, socializing, goal setting, determination, and perseverance.

Acting as a counselor can be a good career choice for these individuals, as leading Neptune tends to bestow a holistic understanding of people, situations, and life.

## Leading Pluto

When Pluto is leading, the individual tends to have a skill for reinventing themselves. They can cast off a past period in their life as if it never existed.

Their special skill lies in their penetrating insight, which enables them to develop new systems. It gives them the power to give old ideas and concepts new meaning. People with Pluto leading tend to be very intense. They can possess a high degree of personal force and will. When faced with obstacles, their first response is probably to steamroll the opposition, forcing others to conform. This can make them feared as much as loved. They should learn to listen to the views of others and take all possibilities into account before they pursue a course of action.

Leading Pluto inclines the person to be good at ferreting out problems with systems. They can discover where a company is ineffective and hemorrhaging resources and stop waste.

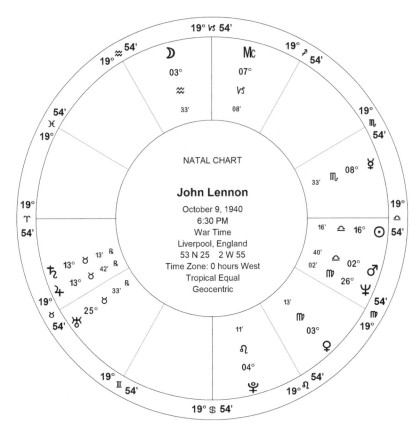

Figure 120: John Lennon

John Lennon was born with leading Mars, close to Neptune and forming a close trine to the Moon in Aquarius (figure 120). Force of personality, promotional ability, and a sense of coming social trends allowed him and the Beatles to rise from humble English origins to become the most famous band of their time.

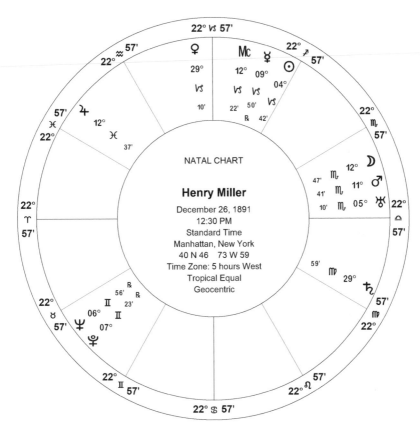

Figure 121: Henry Miller

Controversial novelist Henry Miller has both Moon and Mars as leading planets (figure 121). Their conjunction is very tight (an orb of 1°7'). Miller was known for breaking free from existing literary forms and developing a new type of semiautobiographical novel that included stream of consciousness, profane language, and sex. He was an American expatriate in Paris at the height of his career. He spent much of his later years living a simple life in a cabin on the remote Big Sur coast of California.

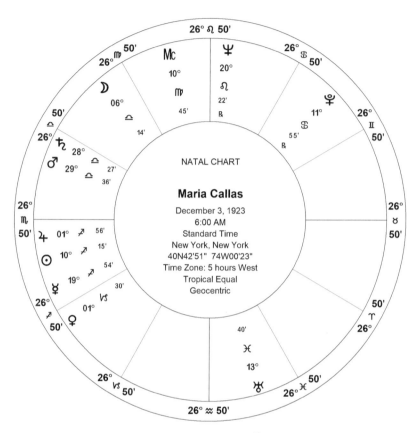

Figure 122: Maria Callas

Maria Callas was one of the most renowned and influential opera singers of the twentieth century. She has leading Jupiter in the first house (figure 122). Critics praised her wide-ranging voice and dramatic interpretations. She endured struggles and scandal over the course of her career, including her temperamental behavior, her rivalry with other singers, and her love affair with Greek shipping tycoon Aristotle Onassis.

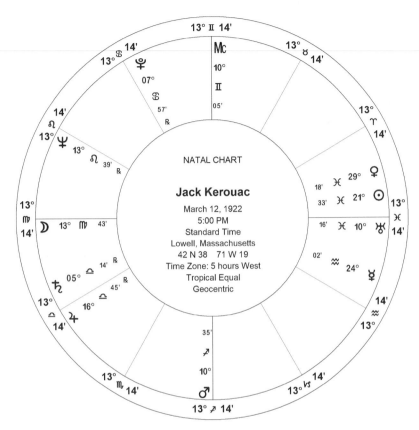

Figure 123: Jack Kerouac

The natal horoscope Jack Kerouac, Beat writer and author of *The Dharma Bums* and *On the Road*, features leading Uranus (figure 123). Uranus is near the Descendant and opposite the Moon, which is near the Ascendant. Both Uranus and the Moon square Mars at the IC. The result is a well-defined Angular Grand Cross aspect pattern. Kerouac's chart emphasizes the need for chart synthesis. Don't stop at just one feature that stands out, like the leading planet.

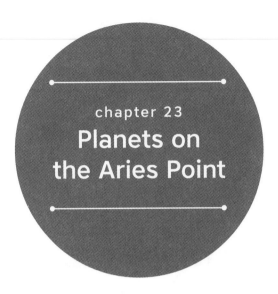

chapter 23
# Planets on the Aries Point

The Aries Point (AP) is an indicator of our potential for public presentation. It's our claim to fame, what we'll be remembered for. Most of what has been written on the AP comes from my mentor Noel Tyl and from his student Don McBroom.

The AP is more than a single point. There are four of them around the horoscope (figure 124). Zero degrees of any cardinal sign is an AP. That's 00 Aries, Cancer, Libra, or Capricorn. We typically apply a 2° orb. The result is that 4½ percent of the zodiac is covered by an AP.

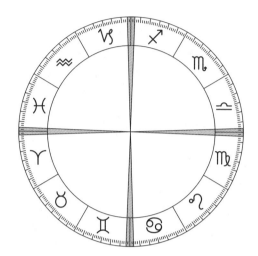

Figure 124: The Aries Point

When we include the orbs, an AP can be found in the following regions:

• 28 Pisces to 02 Aries

• 28 Gemini to 02 Cancer

• 28 Virgo to 02 Libra

• 28 Sagittarius to 02 Capricorn

What we look for is a planet or horoscope angle (in particular the Ascendant or Midheaven) in conjunction or square to the AP.

## How Common Are Planets on the Aries Point?

Having a planet on the AP is a relatively uncommon. According to the Astro Databank, 4.51 percent of all natal charts have a planet, the Ascendant, or the Midheaven on an AP. A breakdown by planet and point is given in the following table.

| Planet on AP in Natal Chart | Percentage |
| --- | --- |
| Sun | 3.44 |
| Moon | 3.30 |
| Mercury | 3.23 |

*(continued)*

| Planet on AP in Natal Chart | Percentage |
|---|---|
| Venus | 3.39 |
| Mars | 3.46 |
| Jupiter | 3.66 |
| Saturn | 3.24 |
| Uranus | 3.36 |
| Neptune | 3.96 |
| Pluto | 4.15 |
| Ascendant | 3.88 |
| Midheaven | 3.40 |

## Interpreting the Aries Point

Don McBroom's interpretation guidelines for planets and horoscope angles conjunct, square, or in opposition to the AP include the following.

### Sun on the Aries Point

Potential for public projection to become well known; energy expended for ego recognition of the significance of one's actions.

### Moon on the Aries Point

Potential for the desire to connect emotionally with the public; to nurture, protect, or provoke an emotional response.

### Mercury on the Aries Point

Potential for public projection by communication, writing, intellectual talents, or travel.

### Venus on the Aries Point

Potential for public projection and recognition of anything pleasing to the senses—art, music, physical beauty.

### Mars on the Aries Point

Potential for public projection of aggression, courage, ruggedness, impulsive behavior, sexuality, or athleticism.

### Jupiter on the Aries Point

Potential for public projection of success, wealth, optimism, enthusiasm, religion, higher mind, or position of respect—OR—excess, careless risk-taking, or overspending.

### Saturn on the Aries Point

Aspiration to be perceived by the public as conservative, restrained, disciplined, rigid, self-sufficient, and ambitious.

### Uranus on the Aries Point

Potential to seek public notice by being inventive, innovative, rebellious, socially reforming, or eccentric.

### Neptune on the Aries Point

Potential to seek public attention through ideals—as a visionary, spiritual leader, or dreamer—or gaining a reputation for confused, dishonest, or concealed behavior.

### Pluto on the Aries Point

Potential for public power as a pioneer, a reformer for evolutionary change—or involvement in hidden or subversive behavior.

### Node on the Aries Point

Potential for public identification or involvement with large social groups; an easy connection with groups.

### Ascendant on the Aries Point

Potential to easily align with public popularity; personality traits conducive to commanding public notice.

### Midheaven on the Aries Point

Potential to easily align career to attract public attention and exposure.

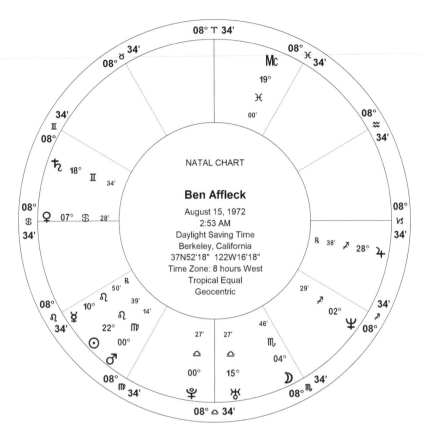

Figure 125: Ben Affleck

Actor Ben Affleck (figure 125) has Pluto on the Libra AP (00 Libra 27). He's noted for his humanitarian and other social causes. For example, after travelling in the region of eastern Congo between 2007 and early 2010, Affleck and Whitney Williams cofounded the nonprofit organization Eastern Congo Initiative in 2010. Ben Affleck is also a supporter of the A-T Children's Project, which focuses attention on the rare disease ataxia-telangiectasia.

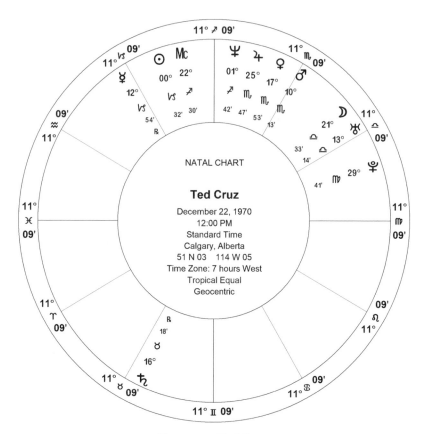

Figure 126: Ted Cruz

Ted Cruz (figure 126), US senator from Texas, has his Sun on the Capricorn AP (00 Capricorn 32). This is ideal for an elected official, since it represents a potential for public projection to become well known.

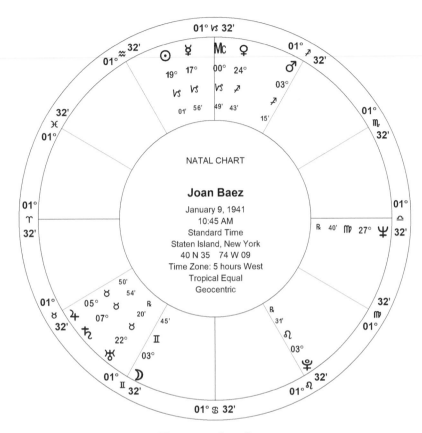

Figure 127: Joan Baez

It's important to remember that not only can planets be located on an AP, but so can the Ascendant or Midheaven. Singer Joan Baez (figure 127), a popular performing artist and social activist, has her Midheaven on the Capricorn AP (00 Capricorn 49). There is an easy alignment between her career and her ability to attract public attention and exposure for social causes like support for civil rights, opposition to the Vietnam War, and environmental activism.

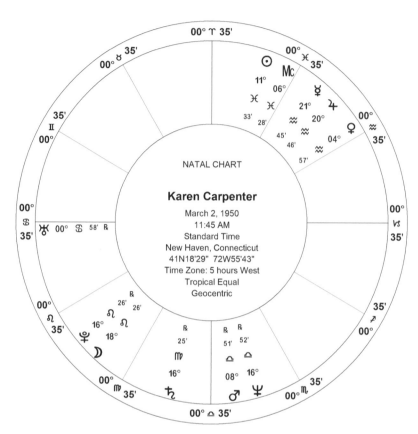

Figure 128: Karen Carpenter

The natal chart for singer and drummer Karen Carpenter is interesting for its double AP (figure 128). Both the Ascendant and Uranus are on the Cancer AP (00 Cancer 35 for the Ascendant and 00 Cancer 58 for Uranus). Painfully shy (she preferred to hide behind her drum set rather than stand out front to sing), Karen's Ascendant on the AP helped her easily align with public popularity. Her Uranus AP made itself felt through her activism as an outspoken advocate for eating disorders, urging people to learn about them and encouraging people to seek treatment.

chapter 24
# Tying It All Together

This book was written to help you prioritize the right information from the chart and make correct inferences. Now that you've read through the entire book, you should have a sense for how the pieces fit together.

Most people who study and practice astrology today have no problem learning the building blocks of the science. Where they struggle enormously is to put those elements into practice, to create a coherent picture of the person described by the natal chart.

Many novice astrologers feel they must cover everything in a chart during a consultation. That's why they can spend hours in preparation. There is simply no way that a sixty- to ninety-minute consultation can cover everything in a natal chart. We have to choose. We need to use discretion. If you cover the topics in this book during a consultation, you'll have a lot to discuss.

We have focused on the bigger bells: what can be seen at a brief glance at the birth chart. We haven't covered everything that a full and robust consultation might include. No planets in signs and houses. No planetary aspects. No rulership networks and mutual receptions. No forecast techniques. Each of these is a book-length topic of its own. Just as you will have to pick and choose what's relevant to cover during a consultation, I had to make choices about what to cover in this book.

Cover the topics in this book with your clients and you will be surprised how true they ring to your client's ears.

To quote Tracy Marks: "Some of us might approach a chart by interpreting it house by house, beginning with the first house and moving counterclockwise around the wheel. Others might begin with the Sun and consider every planet in turn—Moon, Mercury, Venus, etc. Still others might attempt to transform chaos into order by considering each area of life important to the client—love, work, home and family, etc., and interpreting all the planets, signs and houses associated with it" (Tracy Marks 2008, loc. 93, Kindle).

My hope is that you will begin with the topics in this book. After covering them, you might then prefer to move on and interpret a chart house by house, planet by planet, or by each area of life. I hope you won't. I hope instead that the topics in this book will lead you into the heart of the natal chart, and from that point you can further synthesize what really matters in the chart.

Again, to quote Tracy Marks: "If we want our clients to emerge with clearer mental pictures of themselves, including the understanding of their predominant strengths and talents, and the weaknesses and conflicts which can become strengths and talents once they develop the desire and resolution to transform them, we must aim for quality and depth of insight in our readings rather than quantity and breadth of scope" (Tracy Marks 2008, loc. 102, Kindle).

If we want to give coherent readings, we must determine what is most important in the chart and what is least important. Together, we have focused here on what is truly important.

## Creating Your Own Shorthand

Time is critical during a consultation. We have sixty to ninety minutes to discuss a lot of information with the client. While we can determine everything in this book with a glance at the chart, it's helpful to make notes during our preparation.

My mentor Noel Tyl encouraged his students to develop their own shorthand. I encourage readers to do the same.

Dustin Hoffman's natal chart appears in figure 129. Normally I would handwrite my shorthand, but I'll spare the reader having to decipher my handwriting. My notes are printed.

I don't like the aspect lines that most astrology programs print by default. They make a muddle that's hard to disentangle. I instead draw in the important patterns. In the case of Dustin Hoffman, that's a pair of Grand Trines and a pair of T-Squares. Those four aspect patterns alone will merit several minutes of discussion with the client.

In addition to drawing the aspect patterns, I also make shorthand notes to jog my memory:

EGT = Earth Grand Trine

FGT(D) = Fire Grand Trine (Dissociate)

T2C = T-Square Cardinal

T2F = T-Square Fixed

I note the Sun, Moon, and Ascendant signs so I don't have to search for them during our discussion. Pluto is the leading planet (LP). Mars is the most elevated planet (MEP). Jupiter and Saturn are retrograde ($R_x$). When there's an unaspected planet, I draw an oval around it.

I also include shorthand for important aspects, especially hard aspects, like squares (not shown)—anything that will trigger my memory during the consultation.

I write all over the natal chart during my preparation. It's only paper. I give my clients a clean copy, with no shorthand.

## Parting Comments

We've covered a lot of ground together. In closing, the best advice I can share is this: start with the chart features that are most extreme, most powerful, most outstanding, and then allow the rest of the chart interpretation to take shape around them.

Good luck!

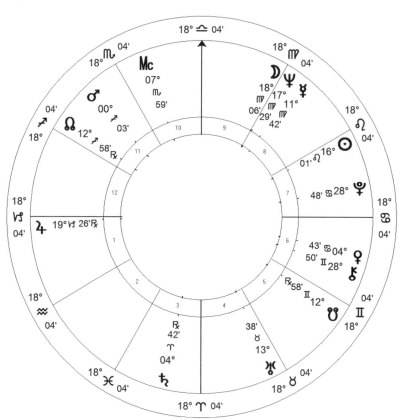

Figure 129: Dustin Hoffman—Astrological Shorthand

**Dustin Hoffman**
August 8, 1937
5:07 p.m. +8:00
Los Angeles, CA
34°N03'08" 118°W14'34"
Geocentric
Tropical
Equal
True Node
Rating: AA

# Bibliography

Carter, Lance. *Planetary Patterns and High Focus Planets in Spherical Astrology.* Saratoga, CA: LightCorps, 2010.

Clement, Stephanie. *Aspect Patterns: What They Reveal and How They Are Triggered.* Woodbury, MN: Llewellyn Publications, 2007.

Clifford, Frank C. *Getting to the Heart of Your Chart: Playing Astrological Detective.* London: LSA/Flare Publications, 2012.

———. *The Solar Arc Handbook.* London: LSA/Flare Publications, 2018.

Cunningham, Donna. *The Stellium Handbook: Parts 1 and 2.* Moon Maven, 2013.

Grasse, Ray. *Under a Sacred Sky: Essays on the Practice and Philosophy of Astrology.* Bournemouth, England: Wessex Astrologer, 2015.

Greene, Liz. *Barriers and Boundaries: The Horoscope and the Defences of the Personality.* London: CPA Press, 2014.

Hamaker-Zondag, Karen. *The Yod Book: Including a Complete Discussion of Unaspected Planets.* York Beach, ME: Samuel Weiser, 2000.

Jansky, Robert C. *Interpreting the Aspects.* Van Nuys, CA: Astro-Analytics, 1978.

———. *Planetary Patterns.* 1973. Reprint, Van Nuys, CA: Astro-Analytics, 1977.

———. *Selected Topics in Astrology.* Van Nuys, CA: Astro-Analytics, 1974.

Jones, Marc Edmund. *The Guide to Horoscope Interpretation.* Quest Books, 1981.

Marks, Bob. "Intercepted Signs." Accessed November 19, 2019. https://www.bobmarksastrologer.com/Intercepted_signs.htm.

Marks, Tracy. *The Art of Chart Interpretation: A Step-By-Step Method for Analyzing, Synthesizing & Understanding the Birth Chart.* Lake Worth, FL: Ibis Press, 2008.

———. *Planetary Aspects: An Astrological Guide to Managing Your T-Square.* Lake Worth, FL: Ibis Press, 2014. Originally published in 1979 as *How to Handle Your T-Square.*

McBroom, Don. *Midpoints: Identify & Integrate Midpoints into Horoscope Synthesis.* Woodbury, MN: Llewellyn Publications, 2007.

Meyer, Michael. "Your Guiding Planet: Discover Your Innate Skills and Inner Faculties." Accessed November 19, 2019. https://www.khaldea.com/planets/oriental_intro.shtml.

Portman, Alice. "Thor's Hammer." Accessed November 19, 2019. https://aliceportman.com/thors-hammer.

Pottenger, Maritha. *Complete Horoscope Interpretation: Putting Together Your Planetary Profile.* San Diego, CA: ACS Publications, 1986.

Price, Alison. "How to Find the Leading Planet." Accessed November 19, 2019. https://www.starzology.com/how-to-find-the-oriental-planet/.

Rudhyar, Dane. *The Astrology of Personality: A Reformulation of Astrological Concepts and Ideals in Terms of Contemporary Psychology and Philosophy.* New York: Lucis Publishing, 1936.

Standley, Loretta. "What Is a Grant Trine?" Accessed November 19, 2019. https://www.drstandley.com/astrologycharts_grandtrine.shtml.

Tierney, Bil. *Dynamics of Aspect Analysis: New Perceptions in Astrology.* Sebastopol, CA: CRCS Publications, 1983. Originally published in 1980 as *Perceptions in Astrology.*

Tyl, Noel. Noel Tyl Master's Degree Certification Course in Astrology. https://www.noeltyl.com/masters.html.

———. *Synthesis & Counseling in Astrology: The Professional Manual.* 1994. Reprint, Woodbury, MN: Llewellyn Publications, 2012.

Watters, Barbara. *The Astrologer Looks at Murder.* Washington, DC: Valhalla Paperbacks, 1969.

Wickenburg, Joanne. *A Journey Through the Birth Chart: Using Astrology on Your Life Path.* Tempe, AZ: American Federation of Astrologers, 1998.

———. *Your Hidden Powers: Intercepted Signs and Retrograde Planets.* Tempe, AZ: American Federation of Astrologers, 2011.

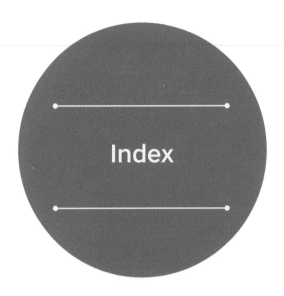

Index

## C

## D

## F

## G

## H

## I

## J

## To Write to the Author

If you wish to contact the author or would like more information about this book, please write to the author in care of Llewellyn Worldwide Ltd. and we will forward your request. Both the author and the publisher appreciate hearing from you and learning of your enjoyment of this book and how it has helped you. Llewellyn Worldwide Ltd. cannot guarantee that every letter written to the author can be answered, but all will be forwarded. Please write to:

Glenn Mitchell
℅ Llewellyn Worldwide
2143 Wooddale Drive
Woodbury, MN 55125-2989
Please enclose a self-addressed stamped envelope for reply,
or $1.00 to cover costs. If outside the U.S.A., enclose
an international postal reply coupon.

Many of Llewellyn's authors have websites with additional information and resources. For more information, please visit our website at http://www.llewellyn.com.